IMAGES
*of America*

# DUNELLEN

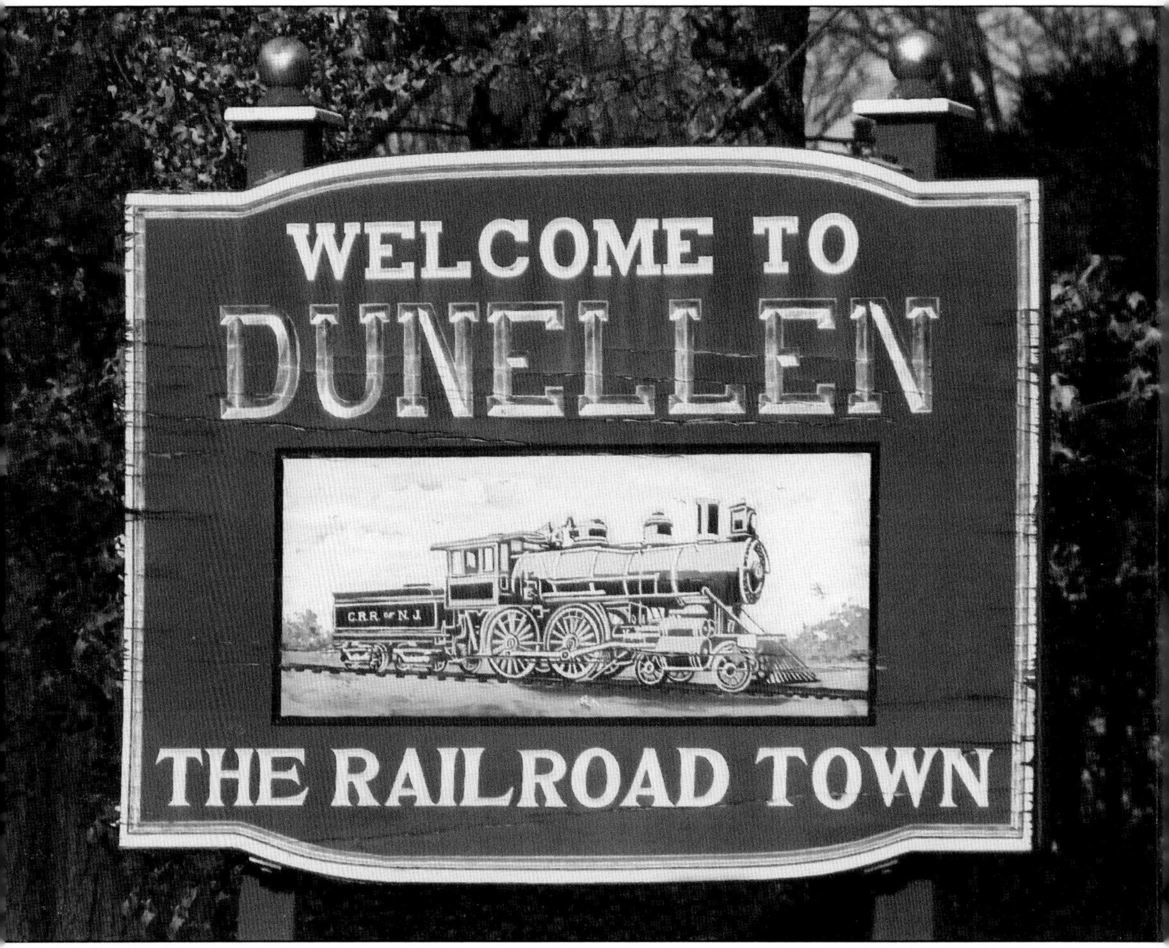


"Welcome to Dunellen the Railroad Town," announces the sign pictured above. Dunellen is the only town with that name in the United States. In fact, it is the only town by this name in the entire world. There is, however, a section of the town of Craignure, Isle of Mull, Scotland, that bears this name. Piscataway, New Jersey, has a Dunellen Avenue, and Jonesboro, Georgia, has a Dunellen Lane. The late Leona Helmsley's Greenwich, Connecticut, estate is named Dunnellen Hall, but it is spelled with double *n*'s in the first syllable. (Courtesy of Liz Marren-Licht.)

**On the Cover:** This photograph taken in 1951 at Dunellen shows the crew of Jersey Central Lines engine No. 777 and two conductors. Dunellen resident Jack Cooper, the engineer, is sitting on the front. (Courtesy of Loretta Pasko.)

IMAGES
*of America*

# DUNELLEN

John Triolo and Liz Marren-Licht

ARCADIA
PUBLISHING

ISBN 978-0-7385-9161-2

Published by Arcadia Publishing
Charleston, South Carolina

Printed in the United States of America

Library of Congress Control Number: 2011941040

For all general information, please contact Arcadia Publishing:
Telephone 843-853-2070
Fax 843-853-0044
E-mail sales@arcadiapublishing.com
For customer service and orders:
Toll-Free 1-888-313-2665

Visit us on the Internet at www.arcadiapublishing.com

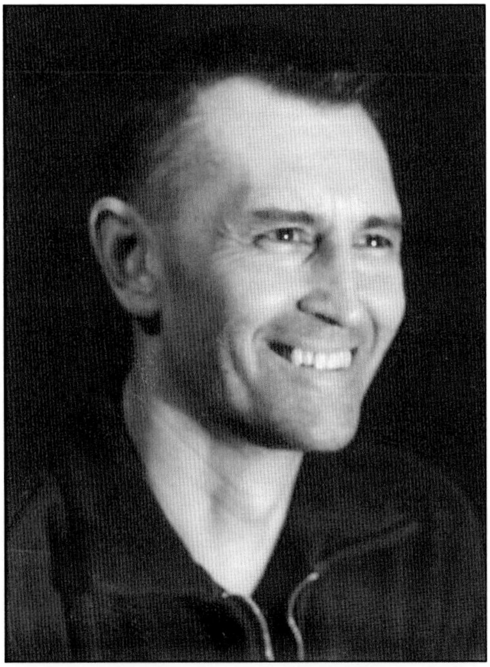

Wesley H. Ott, 1915–2002

*This book is dedicated to Wesley Ott, the unofficial historian of Dunellen. No one will ever know the countless hours and expense that Mr. Ott devoted to his research about Dunellen, all before the Internet.*

# CONTENTS

# ACKNOWLEDGMENTS

The authors wish to express their sincere gratitude to everyone who contributed to this project. Special thanks go to Sylvia Ott, who gave us access to her late husband's photograph and document collections. Without them, this book would not have been possible.

We also give thanks to Lawrence Anzavino, Charlie Batcha, Chuck Bender, Mike Byrnes, George Deene, Dunellen Historical Society, Dunellen Public Library, Dunellen Rescue Squad, Ron Eskesen, Richard Gianchiglia, Fred Heilich III, John P. Faber School, Patricia "Heidi" Leuschner, Nancy Magee, Jeff Marren, Joan Marren, Middlesex County Tax Board, Loretta Pasko, Matt Phillips, Al Refino, William Robins, Bob Salvin, Roberta Scott, John Snyder, John Yavorski, and Mrs. Zalenty for photographs, information, and help with this book. Dave Ulmes, of Color Lab, Middlesex, New Jersey, provided digitization of vintage maps.

Special thanks to Joy Harmon, Anthony Pino, and Sylvia Switzer for contributing the Schuyler family collection.

Unless otherwise noted, all images appear courtesy of Sylvia Ott, photographs from the Wesley Ott Collection.

# INTRODUCTION

Foremost, this cross section of the history of Dunellen from 1656 to the mid-20th century would have been impossible to complete without the information from two excellent sources: the Federal Writers Project's *The Story of Dunellen 1887–1937* and Wesley Ott's *The History of Dunellen, New Jersey, 1887–1987.*

Although there is no evidence of permanent Native American villages in Dunellen, the Lenape, or Delaware, inhibited the region. A 1656 Dutch map showing New Jersey as Nova Caesarea lists numerous tribes in the area, and a 1915 *New Jersey Geological Survey* shows artifacts of temporary camps along the south side of the Green Brook. The Dunellen area was verdant farmland settled by early colonialists, such as David Coriell in 1682, Reune Runyon in 1736, Cornelius Boice in 1768, and Peter Marcellas and Zachariah Pound in 1780.

A 1777 map drawn by Gen. George Washington's cartographer, Robert Erskine, shows a house on the northeast corner of New Market Road and Grove Street and lists the homeowner as D. Reynolds. It is said that during the American Revolution, General Washington used this house as a temporary headquarters when his army was at their Middlebrook encampment. And a 1778 British army map by royal engineer I. Hills shows the Royal army's line of march (under the command of his excellency Gen. Sir Henry Clinton) traveling from New Brunswick across the Raritan River at Bound Brook and following the Green Brook right through the farmland that is now Dunellen.

During those early days, communication among the settlers was by boat on the Raritan River or by stagecoach along the Old York Road from Philadelphia to New York City. That changed between 1839 and 1842 when the Elizabethtown & Somerville Railroad laid its tracks to Plainfield, bisecting Dunellen.

The train station in present-day Dunellen was at the time known as New Market. Also known as Quibbletown, New Market was part of Piscataway Township, which was incorporated in 1798. With the train service, residents began sending and receiving their mail by rail. Charles Pope had a store at the depot and was the postmaster. Slowly, businesses developed around the station, and by 1860, the area had a general store, blacksmith shop, carriage and wheelwright establishment, slaughterhouse, tannery, and a small hat factory. Everything changed in 1866 when John Taylor Johnston, president of the Central Railroad of New Jersey, conceived the idea of establishing towns along his rail line to be bedroom communities to New York City.

The Central New Jersey Land Improvement Company was incorporated on April 9, 1867, and purchased 300 acres north of the tracks from seven farmers. After this area was mapped with street layouts, a copy showing the new town was filed with the county clerk in New Brunswick. George M. Angleman cut and graded the streets and changed the farmland into building lots. Some of the first purchases were made on May 11, 1868, by John Runyon and his brother Augustus S. Runyon. For $500, John purchased the northeast corner of Washington Avenue and Front Street, and his brother bought the lot at 226 Front Street for $400.

Joseph Maier Sr. moved from Martinsville, purchased two lots at 370 North Avenue in 1868, and constructed a small building in which he had a saloon and a shoe store. In 1870, Maier added an extension at the back of the building to serve as accommodations for travelers. He erected another two-story building that was occupied by a saloon on the first floor and a hall for parties on the second. His buildings were known as the Park Hotel, which sat directly across the street from the present-day police headquarters and borough hall.

William Richardson built a house on the southeast corner of Washington Avenue and Front Street in 1869. The original Richardson house, greatly altered, is now the Dunellen Hotel. Steven Afflek erected a house on the northwest corner, and Henry van Middlesworth built on the southwest corner. The borough began to establish as more buildings were added to North Avenue: Charles Pope's grocery in 1868, J.Y. Wilson's hardware shop, James Phillips's shoe shop, Dr. Peter Brakeley's drugstore, and Isaac Dunn's feed store. While these buildings would burn down in the disastrous fire of 1875, the owners were resolute and would rebuild with brick. By 1891, North Avenue was filled with both businesses and residences.

All the territory acquired by the Central New Jersey Land Improvement Company lay on the north and west of the railroad tracks. The south side of the tracks remained mostly farms and was still known as North New Market, part of Piscataway Township. But in 1882, a movement started to unite the property north and south of the railroad under a borough commission. After an application was granted, an election was held on March 20, 1886, and a majority voted for the borough commission, uniting both sides of the town for a total area of 650 acres. Because of a delay in filing, the borough was not officially incorporated until October 28, 1887. This filing failure moved Dunellen's birthday from March 1886 to October 28, 1887. The troublesome situation was finally resolved on April 15, 1914, by the state legislature, which passed an act certifying Dunellen as completely independent.

One of the oldest schoolhouses in Piscataway Township is visible on Robert Erskine's 1777 map for General Washington as a log cabin school where the Whittier School building now stands. The log cabin was replaced by a one-room school in 1838, and a second room was added 1841. When Whittier School was built in 1875, it was a brick structure; a two-room addition was made in 1901 and another in 1909. A renovation was done in 1920, and this is how the building remains.

Lincoln School was built on the corner of Lincoln and Dunellen Avenues in 1888 and remodeled in 1914. Beneath the recent renovations of Dunellen High School on that same corner lies hidden the original Lincoln School. St. John's Parochial School was completed in 1924 on First Street between Lincoln and Washington Avenues. Roosevelt Junior High School was opened in September 1935; an addition was built in 1936, and it became a six-year high school. John P. Faber Elementary School was opened on High Street in 1960.

The first parks were in front of the railroad station and on the triangle at North and Madison Avenues. Washington Park was land pre-allocated by the Central New Jersey Land Improvement Company. There are now five parks in town, including Columbia Park, which is the home sports fields for the Dunellen Destroyers.

Though now long forgotten, there were once more than 30 fraternal organizations in Dunellen: the Oriole Club, B.G. Club, Junior Mechanics of America, Dunellen Dramatic Society, the Gun Club of Dunellen, Dunellen Lawn Bowling Club, and numerous Slovak, German, and Polish clubs.

Dunellen was once home for many industries, including the Aluminum Press Company, Rojette Brickyard, R. Hoe, Art Color Printing Company, Buffalo Tank, Levgar Steel Company, Dunellen Cement Block Company, Dunellen Lumber and Coal, Morecraft Coal Company, Van Blaircom Curtain Factory, and many more. As the industries disappeared, Dunellen has come full circle as the bedroom community envisioned by John Taylor Johnson in 1866.

We hope this book piques your interest to learn more of the history of our little town of Dunellen.

# One

# Early History

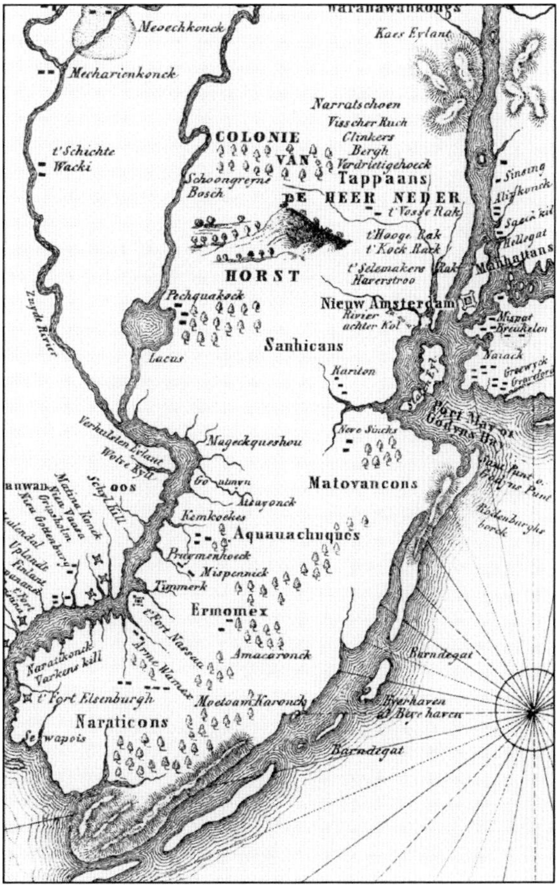


This 1656 Dutch map of New Jersey by A. Vanderdouck was created to show the Indian tribes of the region. All were part of the Lenape Nation. Lenape translates to "original people." European settlers called them the Delaware tribe. The clan that inhabited the area around Dunellen was the Munsee. The area that would become Dunellen was originally part of Piscataway Township, which was founded in 1666.

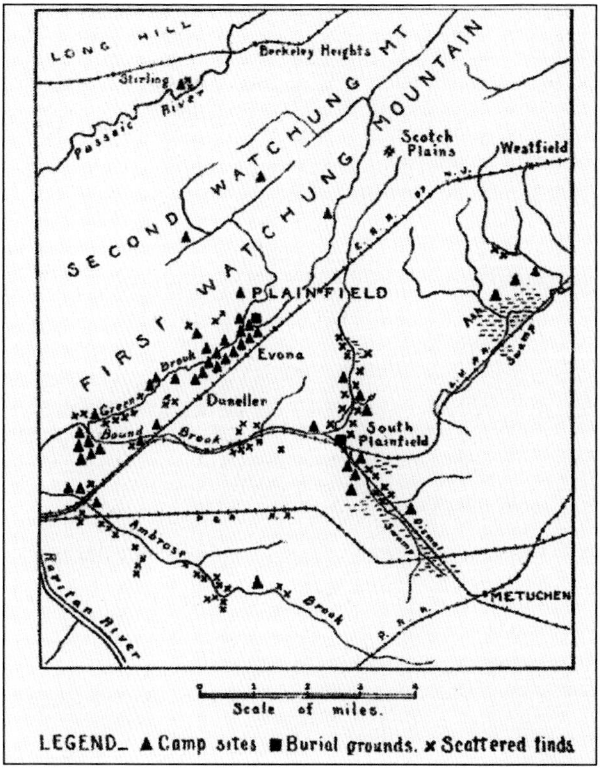


Here is a map that was published in the 1915 *Geological Survey of New Jersey*. Many of the triangles represent Indian campsites found on the south side of the Green Brook in Dunellen. The main cluster stretches from Plainfield, Evona, and Dunellen to present-day Middlesex. Evona was a village adjoining Dunellen with a population of 107 in 1882. It later became part of Plainfield. (Courtesy of John Triolo.)

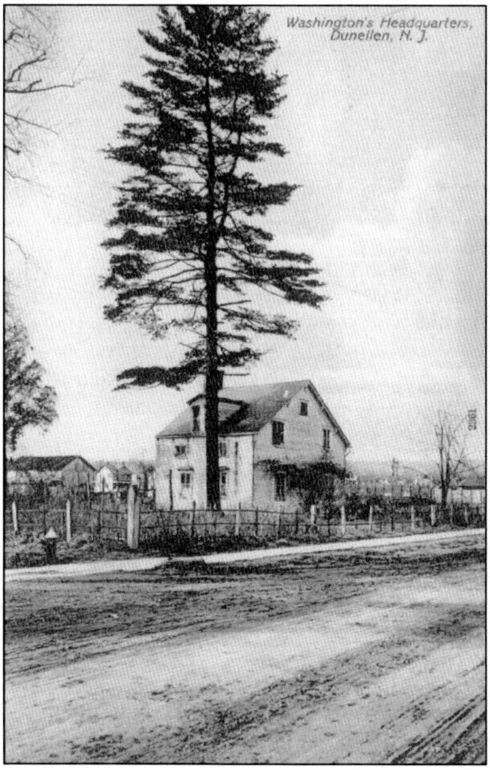


This c. 1907 picture claims historical fame as Washington's headquarters. This house stood on the northwest corner of New Market Road and Grove Street. A 1777 map drawn by Robert Erskine for George Washington shows a house owned by D. Reynolds. It is said that Washington used it as his headquarters from time to time while his troops were encamped at Middlebrook. The house was torn down in 1922. Botwin's Market later stood there for over 30 years until it was destroyed by fire in 1964. Apartments are on the property today. (Courtesy of John Triolo.)

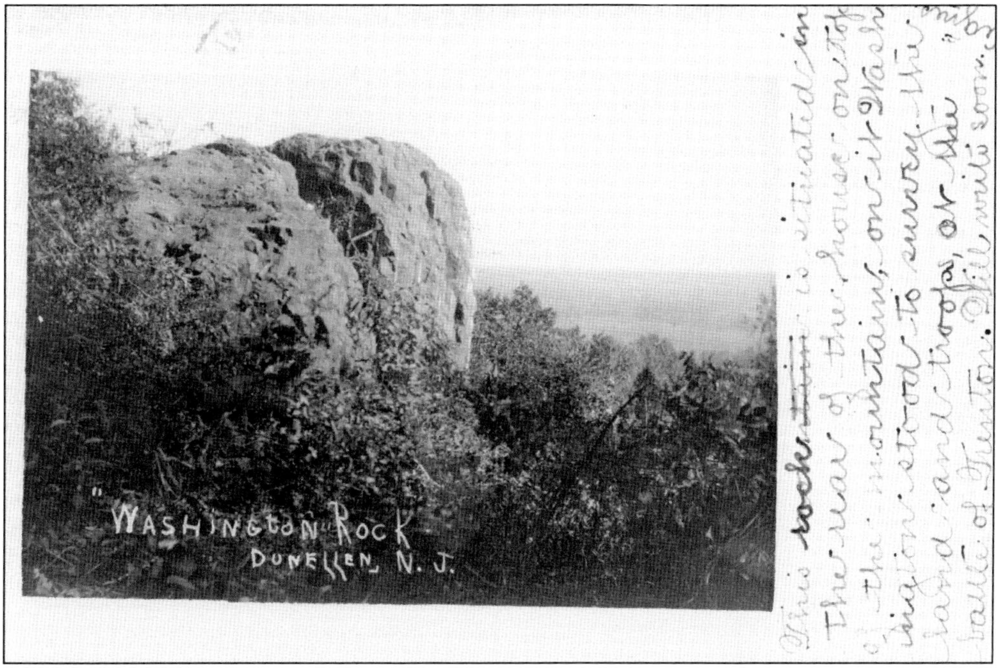


Although Washington Rock is located in Somerset County, it has always been a historic site identified with Dunellen. In 1777, General Washington and 7,300 men from Continental army were encamped at Middlebrook. Washington was shown this vantage point to watch the movements of the British troops in the surrounding countryside. On the 75th anniversary of Independence Day in 1851, a total of 2,500 people visited Washington Rock. In 1872, a 75-man crew constructed a road 25 feet wide and almost a mile long up the mountain to the rock from what is today's Washington Avenue. It took them just 18 days, all done by hand with teams of horses. Daily stagecoaches took tourists from the Dunellen railroad station to Washington Rock.

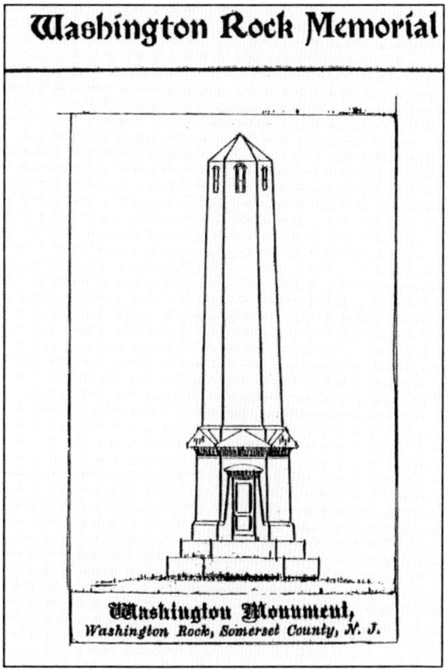


The original design of the Washington Rock monument was an obelisk. Nathan Hayser of Plainfield formed the Washington Monument and Historical Association in 1867. On July 4 of that year, the cornerstone of a monument was laid, but the project languished until 1912 when the Daughters of the American Revolution (DAR) erected the present monument, which consists of a stonework base and flagpole.

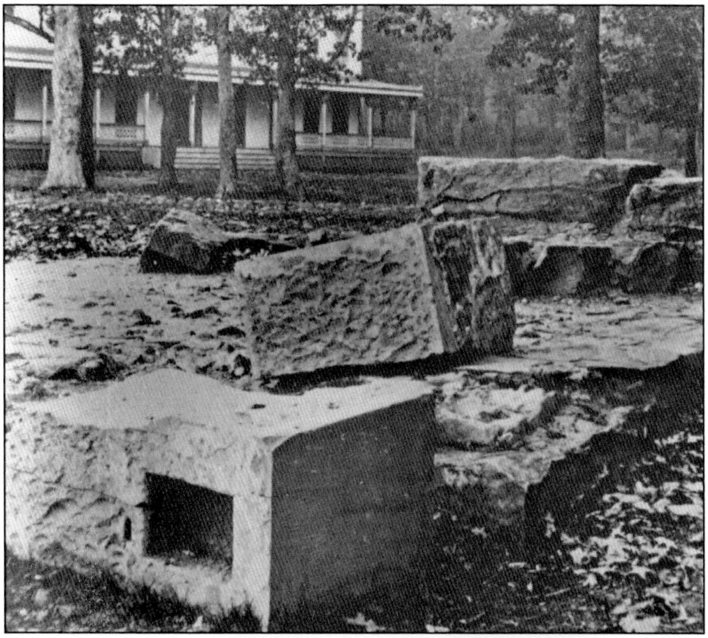

This 1880 photograph shows the remnants of the Washington Rock monument that was started in 1867. In the background is the Washington Rock House, which was built in 1852. This hotel was operated from 1876 until 1885 by Stephen Staats. During that period, the picnic grove was enlarged to 12 acres, the plaza and an observation partition were constructed, and swings, croquet grounds, a dancing pavilion, and a roller-skating rink were added.

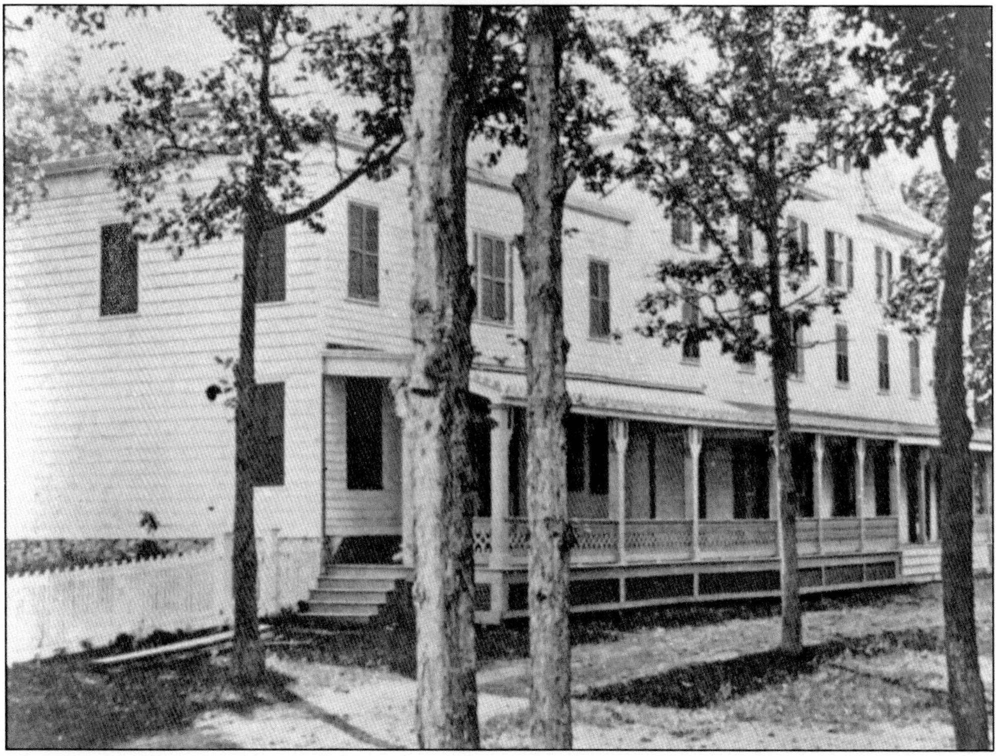

Thomas A. Edison and his wife hosted a party at the Washington Rock House for professional men from France and Italy in 1882. The party was catered by Delmonico's of New York City. On May 27, 1883, a fire that started in the bar and billiard room totally destroyed the building. The spectacular fire was seen for miles around. In 1913, the state legislature passed an act providing for the property to become a 34-acre state park.

# CENTRAL RAILROAD OF NEW JERSEY.

## TIME TABLE. H

**To take effect on MONDAY, NOVEMBER 22nd, 1854.**

**TRAINS GOING WEST.**
NEW YORK TO PHILLIPSBURG.

| STATION. | Passenger Train. No. 1. | Pass. & Fr't Train. No. 3. | Passenger Train. No. 5. | No. 7. | Freight Train. No. 9. |
|---|---|---|---|---|---|
| New York, | 8.00 A. M. | 1.00 M. | 4.00 P. M. | 5.00 P. M. | ------ |
| Elizabethport, | 8.55 " | 1.55 P. M. | 4.55 " | 5.50 " | 4.30 A. M. |
| Elizabethtown, | 9.07 " | 2.05 " | 5.05 " | 6.00 " | 4.45 " |
| Craneville, | 9.18 " | 2.23 " | 5.15 " | 6.10 " | 5.05 " |
| Westfield, | 9.25 " | 2.30 " | 5.25 " | 6.15 " | 5.20 " |
| Scotch Plains, | 9.32 " | 2.38 " | 5.33 " | 6.20 " | 5.35 " |
| Plainfield, | 9.45 " | 2.50 " | 5.45 " | 6.35 " | 6.10 " |
| New Market, | 9.50 " | 2.56 " | 5.50 " | 6.40 " | 6.55 " |
| Bound Brook, | 10.00 " | 3.07 " | 6.00 " | 6.50 " | 7.20 " |
| Somerville, | 10.12 " | 3.18 " | 6.15 " | 7.05 " | 8.00 " |
| Raritan, | 10.15 " | 3.23 " | 6.20 " | ------ | 8.10 " |
| North Branch. | 10.22 " | 3.30 " | 6.30 " | ------ | 8.30 " |
| White House, | 10.37 " | 3.45 " | 6.40 " | ------ | 8.53 " |
| Lebanon, | 10.47 " | 4.05 " | 6.50 " | ------ | 9.12 " |
| Clinton, | 11.00 " | 4.10 " | 6.58 " | ------ | 9.30 " |
| Clarksville, | 11.15 " | 4.30 " | 7.15 " | ------ | 9.55 " |
| N. Hampton, | 11.20 " | 4.35 " | 7.20 | ------ | 10.15 " |
| Asbury, | 11.27 " | 4.43 " | 7.25 " | ------ | 10.30 " |
| Bethlehem, | 11.32 " | 4.50 " | 7.30 " | ------ | 10.40 " |
| Bloomsbury, | 11.40 " | 4.57 " | 7.38 " | ------ | 10.55 " |
| Springtown, | 11.45 " | 5.05 " | 7.45 " | ------ | 11.20 " |
| Phillipbsurg, | 12.00 M. | 5.20 " | 8.00 " | ------ | 11.40 " |

**TRAINS GOING EAST.**
PHILLIPSBURG TO NEW YORK.

| STATION. | Passenger Train. No. 2. | Passenger Train. | Pass. & Fr't Train. No. 6. | No. 8. | No. 10. |
|---|---|---|---|---|---|
| Phillipsburg, | ------ | 6.15 A. M. | 9.20 A. M. | 3.00 P. M. | 1.45 P. M. |
| Springtown, | ------ | 6.25 " | 9.35 " | 3.10 " | 2.10 " |
| Bloomsbury, | ------ | 6.30 " | 9.45 " | 3.15 " | 2.30 " |
| Bethlehem, | ------ | 6.37 " | 9.52 " | 3.21 " | 2.45 " |
| Asbury, | ------ | 6.45 " | 10.00 " | 3.27 " | 3.00 " |
| N. Hampton, | ------ | 6.55 " | 10.15 " | 3.35 " | 3.25 " |
| Clarksville, | ------ | 7.00 " | 10.20 " | *3.40 " | *3.40 " |
| Clinton, | ------ | 7.20 " | 10.40 " | 4.00 " | 4.10 " |
| Lebanon, | ------ | 7.25 " | 10.47 " | 4.05 " | 4.23 " |
| White House, | ------ | 7.35 " | 11.05 " | 4.15 " | 4.50 " |
| North Branch, | ------ | 7.45 " | 11.15 " | 4.25 " | 5.20 " |
| Raritan, | ------ | 7.55 " | 11.24 " | 4.32 " | 5.50 " |
| Somerville, | 6.35 A. M. | 8.00 " | 11.37 " | 4.35 " | 6.15 " |
| Bound Brook, | 6.45 " | 8.10 " | 11.48 " | 4.45 " | 6.50 " |
| New Market, | 6.55 " | 8.20 " | 12.00 M. | 4.55 " | 7.10 " |
| Plainfield, | 7.05 " | 8.28 " | 12.12 P. M. | 5.07 " | 7.35 " |
| Scotch Plains, | 7.18 " | 8.38 " | 12.25 " | 5.15 " | 8.00 " |
| Westfield, | 7.25 " | 8.45 " | 12.35 " | 5.25 " | 8.25 " |
| Craneville, | 7.30 " | 8.50 " | 12.40 " | 5.35 " | 8.35 " |
| Elizabethtown, | 7.45 " | 9.07 " | 1.00 " | 5.45 " | 9.10 " |
| Elizabethport, | 8.00 " | 9.45 " | 1.15 " | 6.00 " | ------ |
| New York, | 9.00 " | 10.45 " | 2.10 " | ------ | ------ |

**ELIZABETHPORT AND NEW YORK FERRY BOATS**

WILL RUN AS FOLLOWS:

**Leave Elizabethport at 8 & 9.45 A. M., and 1.15 & 3.30 P. M.**
**" New York at 8 & 10.40 A. M., and 1 & 4 P. M.**

Printed at the office of the Elizabeth Gazetteer, Elizabethtown, N. J.

The Elizabethtown & Somerville Railroad laid tracks to Plainfield in 1839, then to Dunellen, and arrived at Somerville in 1842. It later became the Central Railroad of New Jersey. Shown here is an 1854 timetable. It lists the station in present-day Dunellen as "New Market." New Market, or Quibbletown, was part of Piscataway at that time. The mail arrived at the station where a post office and a store were operated by Charles Pope.

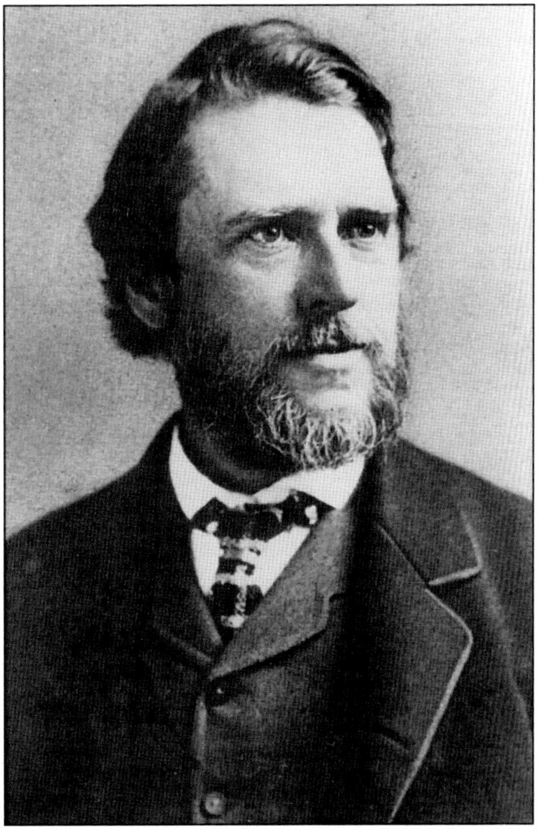

In 1866, John Taylor Johnston, president of the Central Railroad of New Jersey, conceived the idea of establishing towns along the railroad line, and the Central New Jersey Land Improvement Company was founded in 1867. Dunellen was comprised of about 300 acres. Johnston often named his real estate ventures after family and friends. "Ellen" Betts was a family friend, and it is said that he added prefix "Dun." Johnston often traveled to England, and there is a Dunellen section in Craignure, Scotland. The word *dun* in England meant "fort on a hill or roundhouse."

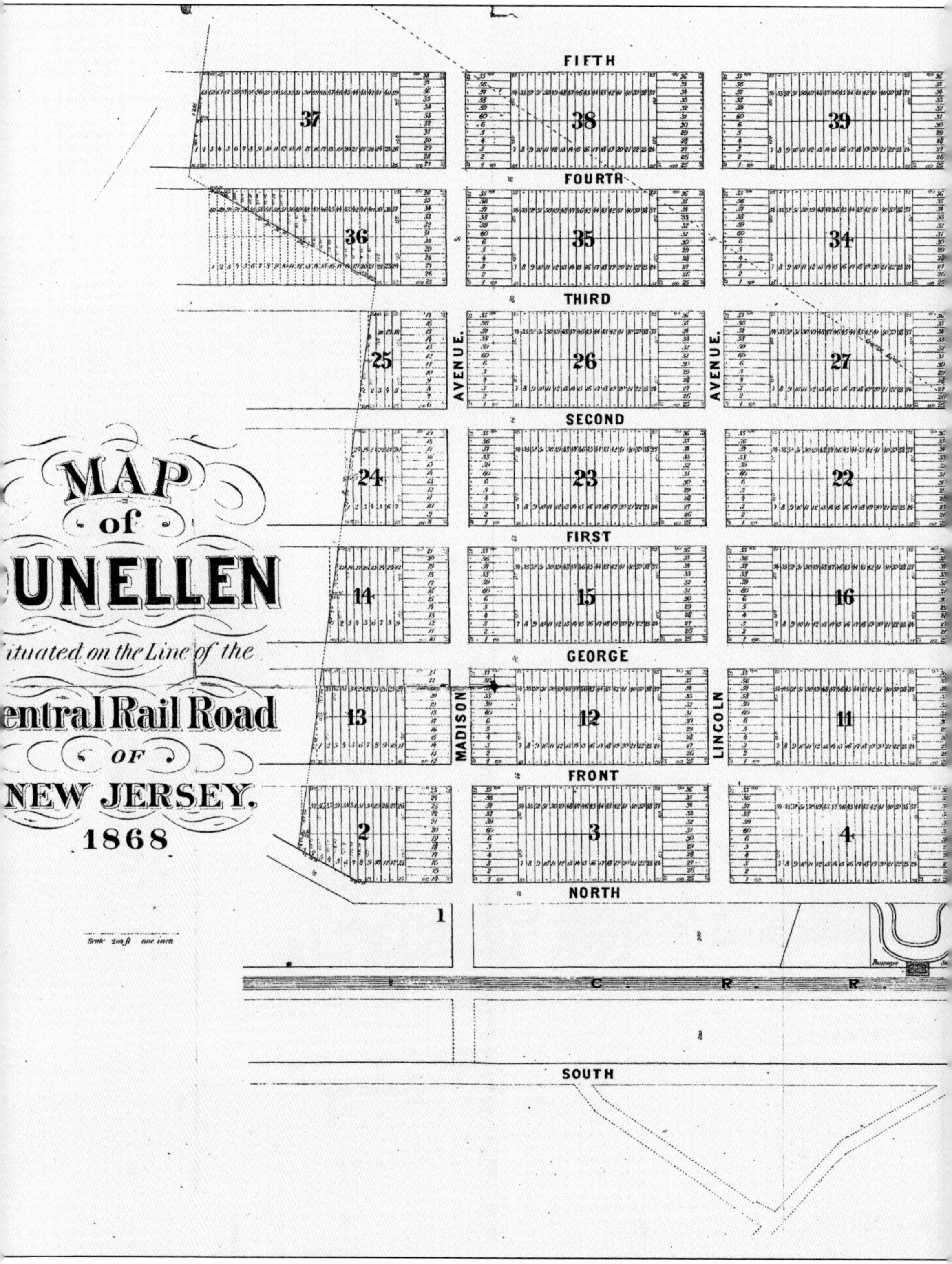
MAP
of
UNELLEN
ituated on the Line of the
entral Rail Road
OF
NEW JERSEY.
1868
FIFTH
FOURTH
THIRD
SECOND
FIRST
GEORGE
FRONT
NORTH
SOUTH
AVENUE.
AVENUE.
MADISON
LINCOLN
C. R. R.
37
38
39
36
35
34
25
26
27
24
23
22
14
15
16
13
12
11
2
3
4
1

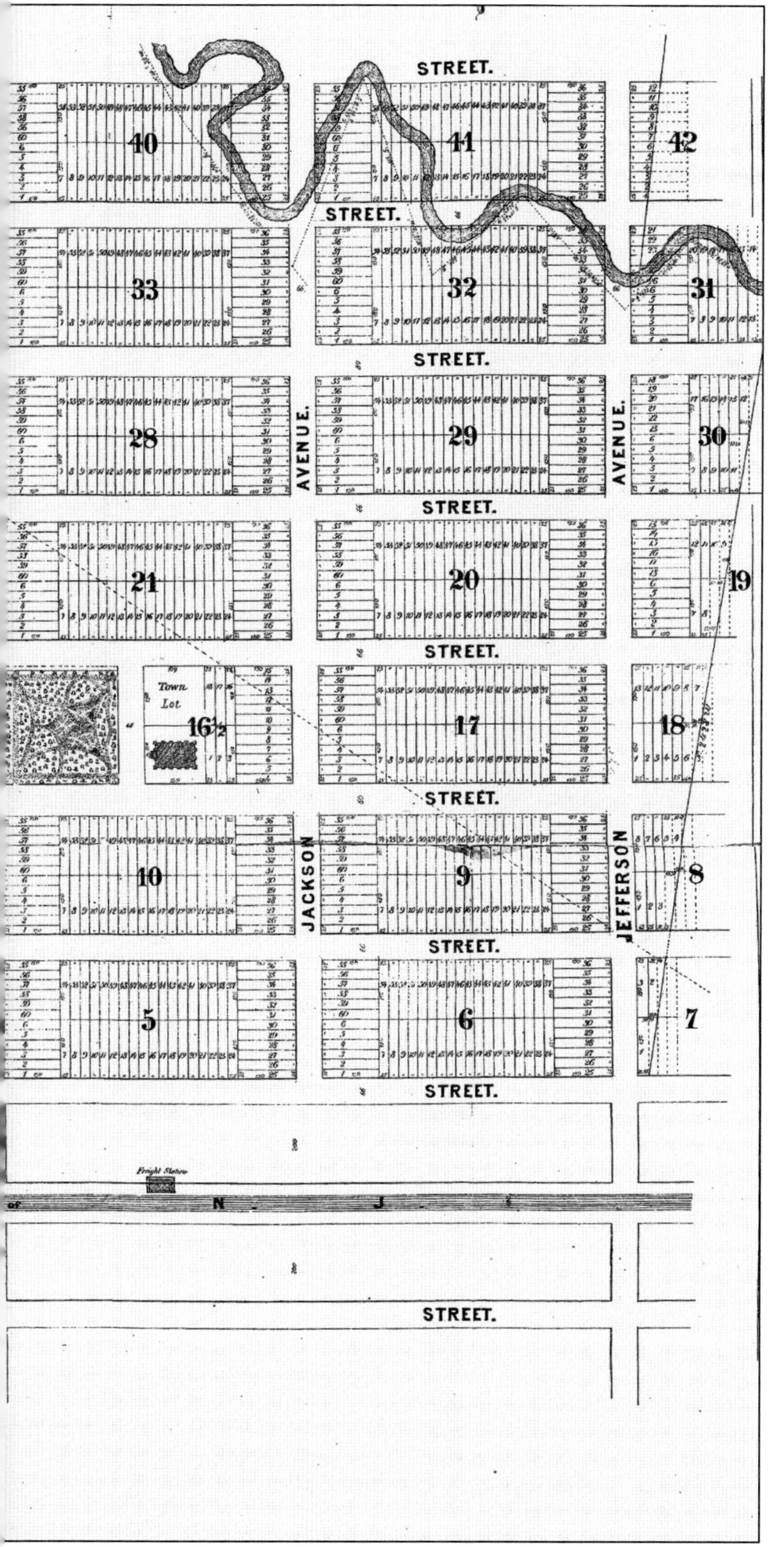


This 1868 map of Dunellen shows streets, blocks, and lots laid out by the Central Jersey Land Improvement Company. In the upper-right corner, lots were placed across the Green Brook and also into what is now Plainfield. On paper, Dunellen was in Middlesex, Somerset, and Union Counties in 1868. Mountain View Terrace was called Fifth Street. Dunellen Avenue was called George Street and later named Church Street. The Presbyterian church is on this map, although the older Methodist Episcopal church on New Market Road is not.

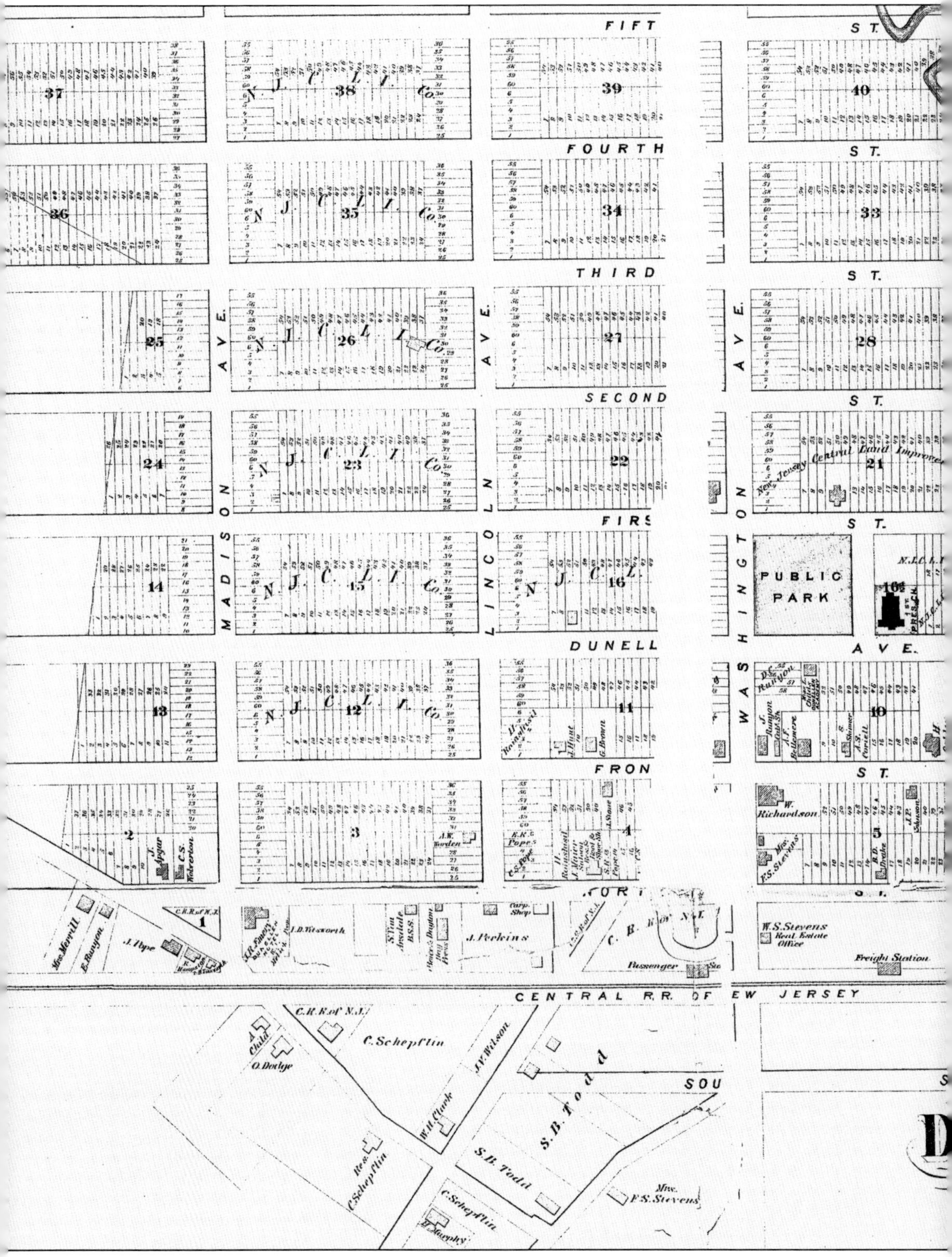
FIFTH ST.
FOURTH ST.
THIRD ST.
SECOND ST.
FIRST ST.
DUNELL AVE.
FRONT ST.
MADISON AVE.
LINCOLN AVE.
WASHINGTON AVE.
N. J. C. L. I. Co.
PUBLIC PARK
New Jersey Central Land Improve
CENTRAL R.R. OF NEW JERSEY
Passenger Sta.
Freight Station
W.S. Stevens Real Estate Office
J. Perkins
C. Schepflin
S.B. Todd
Mrs. F.S. Stevens
W. Richardson
J. Apgar
C.S. Walrerton
Mrs. Merrill
E. Runyon
J.D. Titsworth
O. Dodge
W.H. Clark
J.V. Wilson
1st. PRES. CH.

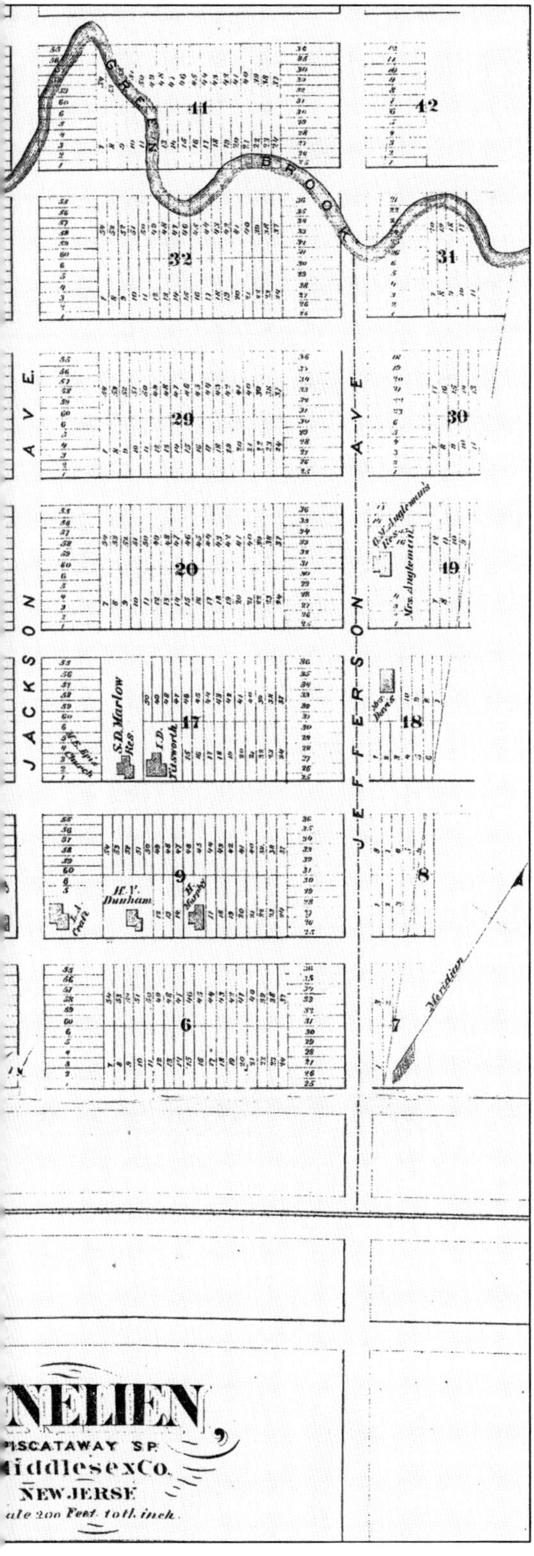


This c. 1871 map shows how the town had developed in just a few years. There were over 50 dwellings and businesses. Some of the businesses included a hotel, livery and hay press, carpenter shop, realtor, saloon and restaurant, boot and shoe shop, a private school called Miss Childs Academy, and an undertaker. The map also shows five building lots reserved for the Methodist Episcopal church at its present location. (Courtesy of John Triolo.)

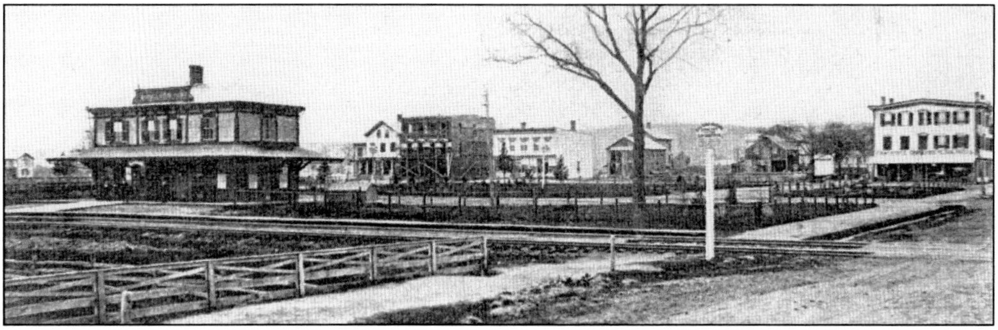

This is a view of North Avenue from South Washington Avenue in 1873. The new railroad station on the left labeled "Dunellen" was erected in 1870. In July 1875, the three large buildings across from the train station were destroyed by fire. A fire committee was appointed five days later. The following month, the Defender Fire Company No. 1 was formed. It was a bucket brigade, as no other fire apparatus was available.

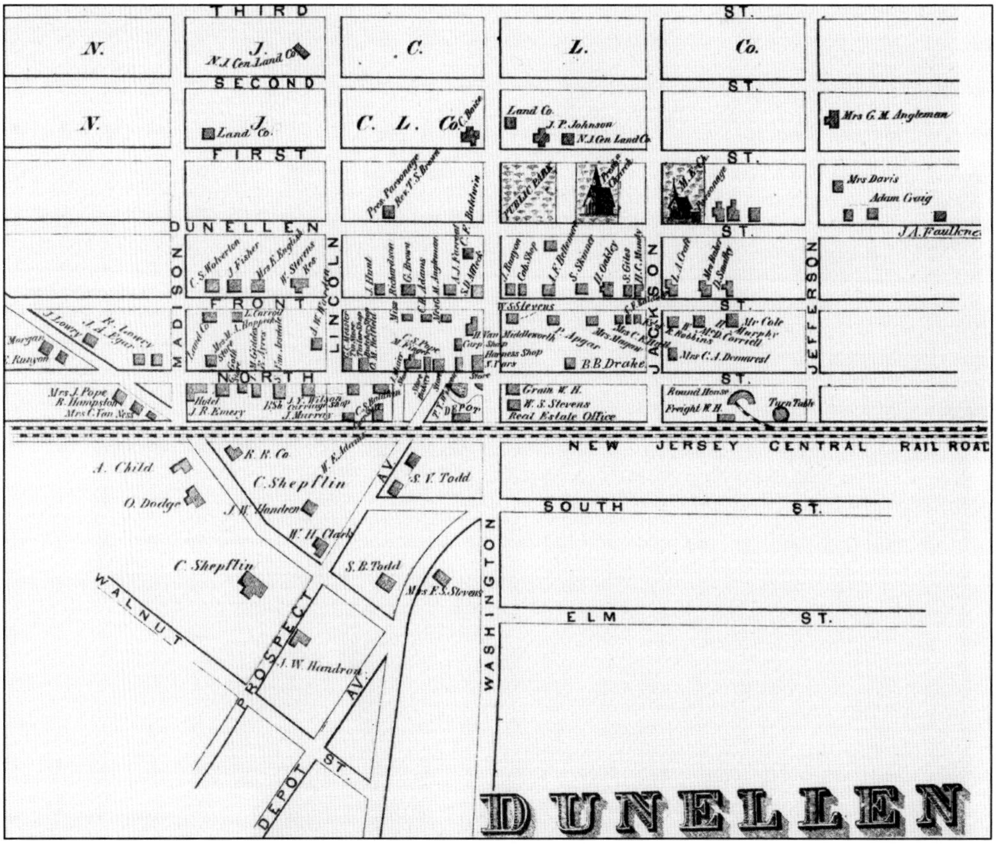


By 1876, the number of residences and businesses had increased. In 1882, voters passed the Act for the Formation of Borough Commissioners, but with limited powers, and left it under the jurisdiction of Piscataway. In 1886, they applied to the county to withdraw from Piscataway and form Dunellen Borough. On March 23, 1886, elections were held and it was voted to incorporate. The election was not certified nor was a certificate of incorporation filled with the county clerk until October 28, 1887. Because of this oversight, the birthday of the borough of Dunellen was October 28, 1887, instead of March 23, 1886.

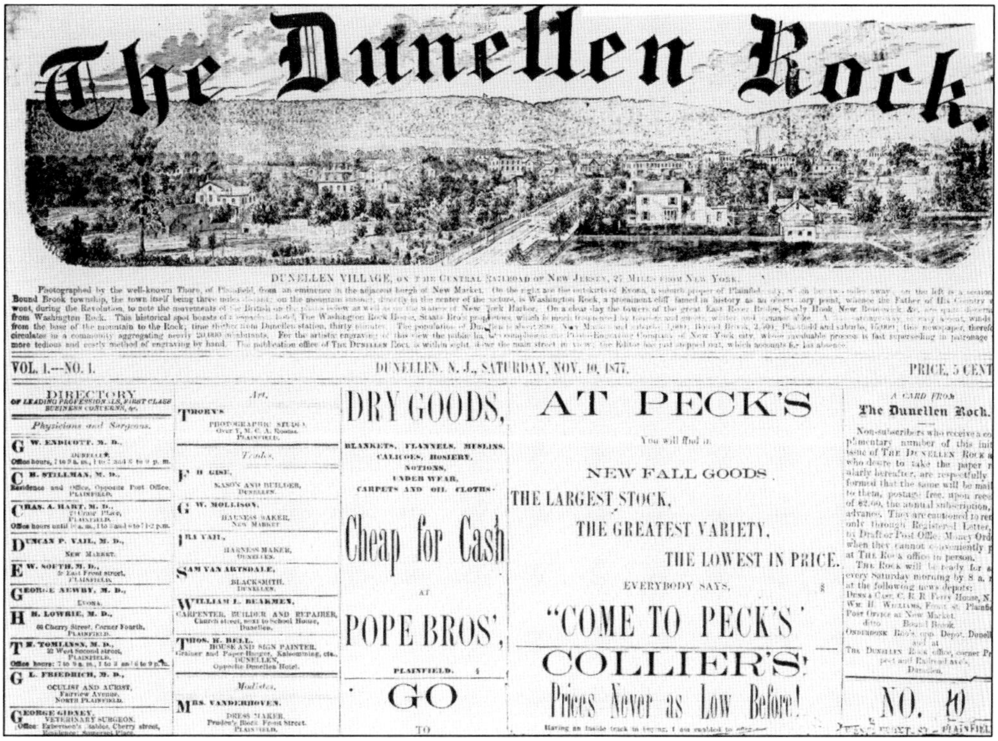

# The Dunellen Rock.

DUNELLEN VILLAGE, ON THE CENTRAL RAILROAD OF NEW JERSEY, 27 MILES FROM NEW YORK.

VOL. 1.---NO. 1. DUNELLEN, N. J., SATURDAY, NOV. 10, 1877. PRICE, 5 CENT

DIRECTORY OF LEADING PROFESSIONALS, FIRST CLASS BUSINESS CONCERNS, &c.

*Physicians and Surgeons.*

G. W. ENDICOTT, M. D., DUNELLEN. Office hours, 7 to 9 a. m., 1 to 2 and 6 to 9 p. m.

C. H. STILLMAN, M. D., Residence and Office, Opposite Post Office, PLAINFIELD.

CHAS. A. HART, M. D., 2 Craig Place, PLAINFIELD.

DUNCAN P. VAIL, M. D., NEW MARKET.

E. W. SOUTH, M. D., East Front street, PLAINFIELD.

GEORGE NEWBY, M. D., EVONA.

H. H. LOWRIE, M. D., 66 Cherry Street, Corner Fourth, PLAINFIELD.

T. H. TOMLINSON, M. D., 22 West Second street, PLAINFIELD.

G. L. FRIEDRICH, M. D., OCULIST AND AURIST, Fairview Avenue, NORTH PLAINFIELD.

GEORGE GIDNEY, VETERINARY SURGEON.

*Art.*

THORN'S PHOTOGRAPHIC STUDIO, Over Y. M. C. A. Rooms, PLAINFIELD.

*Trades.*

F. D. GISE, MASON AND BUILDER, DUNELLEN.

G. W. MOLLISON, HARNESS MAKER, NEW MARKET.

IRA VAIL, HARNESS MAKER, DUNELLEN.

SAM VAN ARTSDALE, BLACKSMITH, DUNELLEN.

WILLIAM L. BEAKMEN, CARPENTER, BUILDER AND REPAIRER, Church street, next to School House, Dunellen.

THOS. H. BELL, HOUSE AND SIGN PAINTER, Grainer and Paper-Hanger, Kalsomining, etc., DUNELLEN, Opposite Dunellen Hotel.

*Modistes.*

MRS. VANDERHOVEN, DRESS MAKER, Pruden's Block, Front Street, PLAINFIELD.

DRY GOODS,

BLANKETS, FLANNELS, MUSLINS, CALICOES, HOSIERY, NOTIONS, UNDER WEAR, CARPETS AND OIL CLOTHS.

Cheap for Cash

AT

POPE BROS',

PLAINFIELD.

GO

TO

AT PECK'S

You will find a

NEW FALL GOODS,

THE LARGEST STOCK,

THE GREATEST VARIETY,

THE LOWEST IN PRICE.

EVERYBODY SAYS,

"COME TO PECK'S"

COLLIER'S!

Prices Never as Low Before!

A CARD FROM The Dunellen Rock.

NO. 10

The *Dunellen Rock* newspaper was founded in 1877 and lasted for two years. In the weekly edition pictured, the article under the banner gave some local statistics. It states that at the right of the picture is the village of Evona, which directly adjoined Dunellen to the east. Dunellen's population was 600, Bound Brook was 2,500, and Plainfield about 8,000. The Dunellen depot was only a half-hour wagon journey from Washington Rock, and it was 26 miles to New York City by train. The *Rock*'s type was hand set, and the office was at 12 Prospect Avenue.

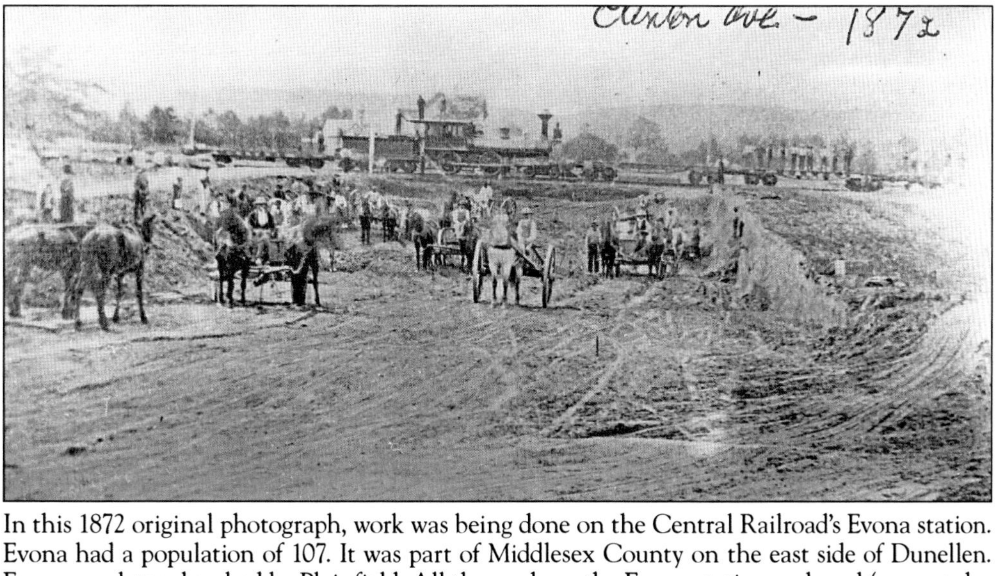


In this 1872 original photograph, work was being done on the Central Railroad's Evona station. Evona had a population of 107. It was part of Middlesex County on the east side of Dunellen. Evona was later absorbed by Plainfield. All the work on the Evona station and road (present-day Clinton Avenue) was done by hand and teams of horses. (Courtesy of Loretta Pasko.)

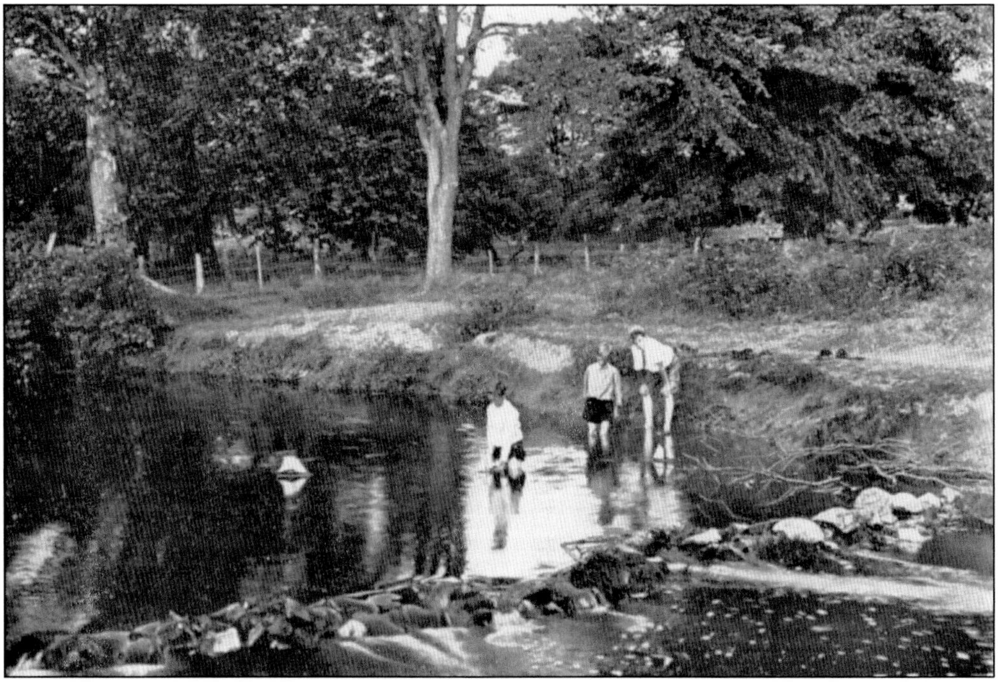

This Dunellen Board of Trade image shows three boys and their toy sailboat in the Green Brook. In the late 19th century, Dunellen was promoted as a health resort and vacation destination featuring fresh air and pure water. In 1911, they wrote in their promotion booklet, "Healthfulness was a characteristic of the borough. Malaria is almost unknown. The same may be said of mosquitoes. During the past ten years not one case of typhoid fever exists in the borough."

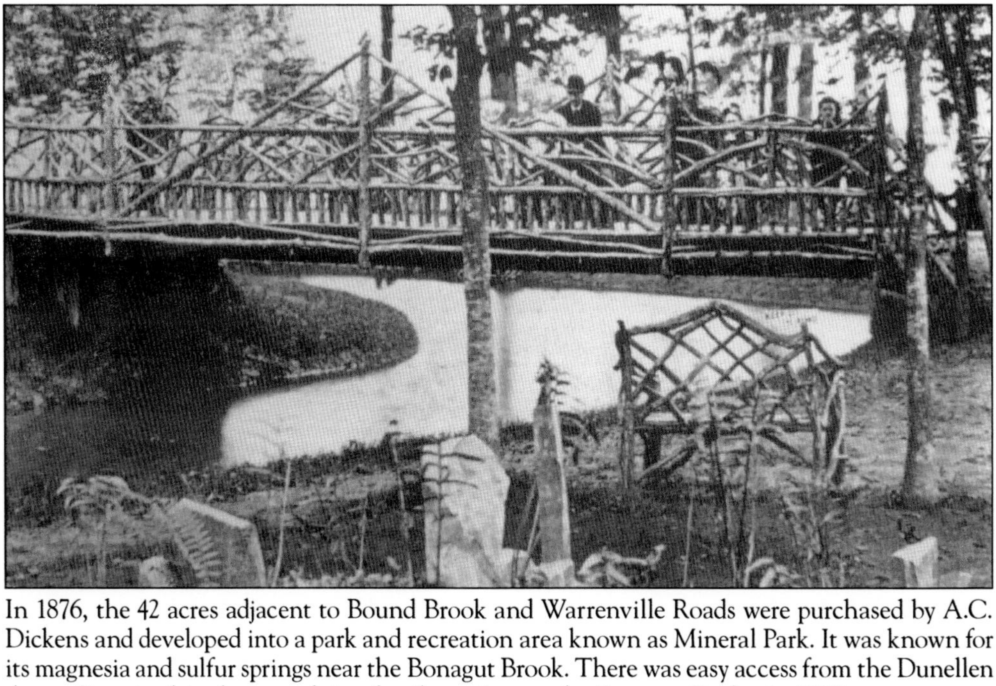

In 1876, the 42 acres adjacent to Bound Brook and Warrenville Roads were purchased by A.C. Dickens and developed into a park and recreation area known as Mineral Park. It was known for its magnesia and sulfur springs near the Bonagut Brook. There was easy access from the Dunellen depot. Seen in this photograph is a family resting on the Prospect Bridge in 1880.

# *Two*

# Railroad Town

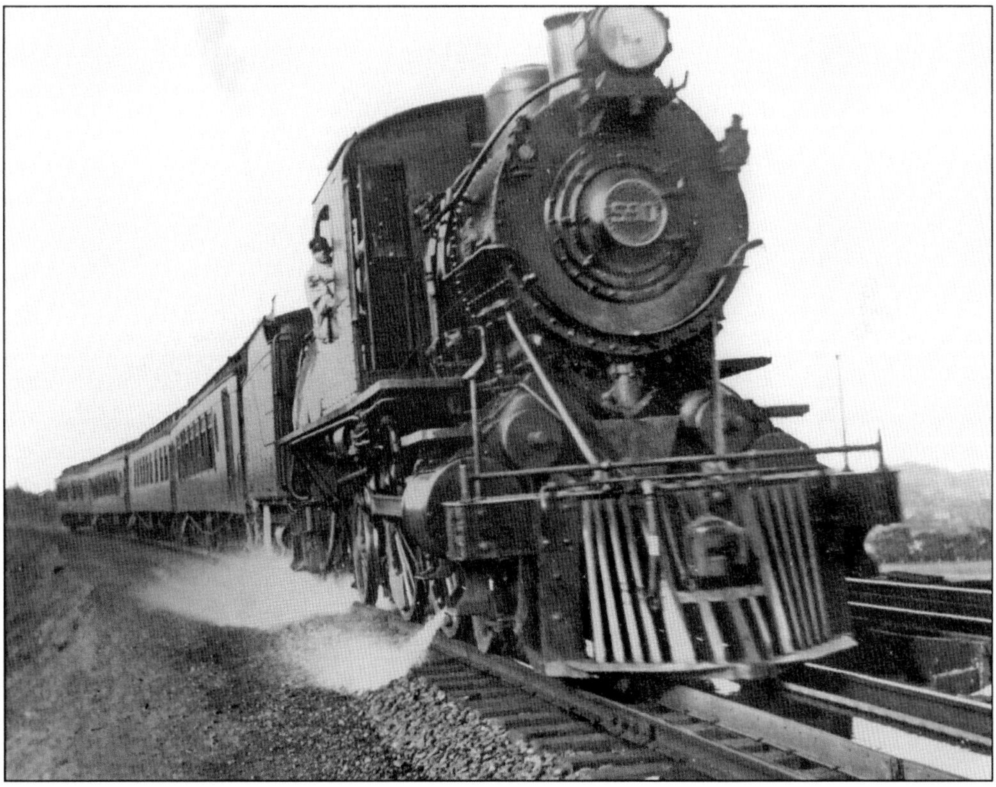

Here comes engine No. 590 with its passenger train approaching Dunellen from the west in 1908. Before 1870, Dunellen only had a freight station. In 1875, a large construction force built the roundhouse, turntable, and car yard and moved the freight station east. The roundhouse and turntable was located on the rail line between Jackson and Jefferson Avenues.

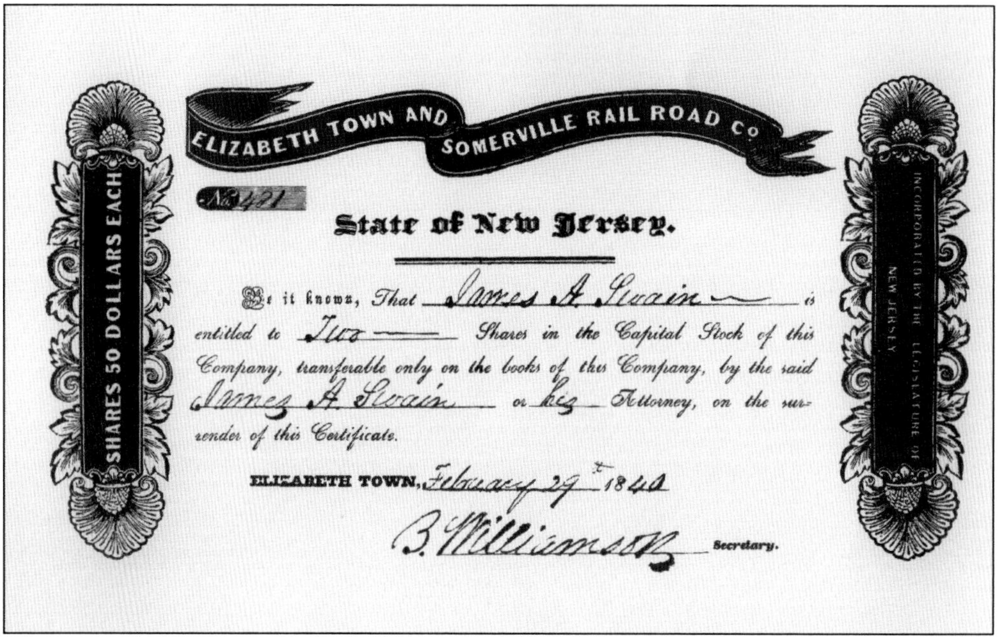

ELIZABETH TOWN AND SOMERVILLE RAIL ROAD Co

SHARES 50 DOLLARS EACH

INCORPORATED BY THE LEGISLATURE OF NEW JERSEY

State of New Jersey.

Be it known, That James A. Swain is entitled to Two Shares in the Capital Stock of this Company, transferable only on the books of this Company, by the said James A. Swain or his Attorney, on the surrender of this Certificate.

ELIZABETH TOWN, February 29th 1840

B. Williamson Secretary.

Here is an example of a stock certificate for the Elizabeth & Somerville Railroad Company chartered by the of New Jersey State Legislature in 1831. It was the predecessor of the New Jersey Central Railroad. The stock certificate was issued for two shares of stock at $50 each on February 29, 1840. To put that in perspective, it would be $2,100 in today's dollars, for both shares.

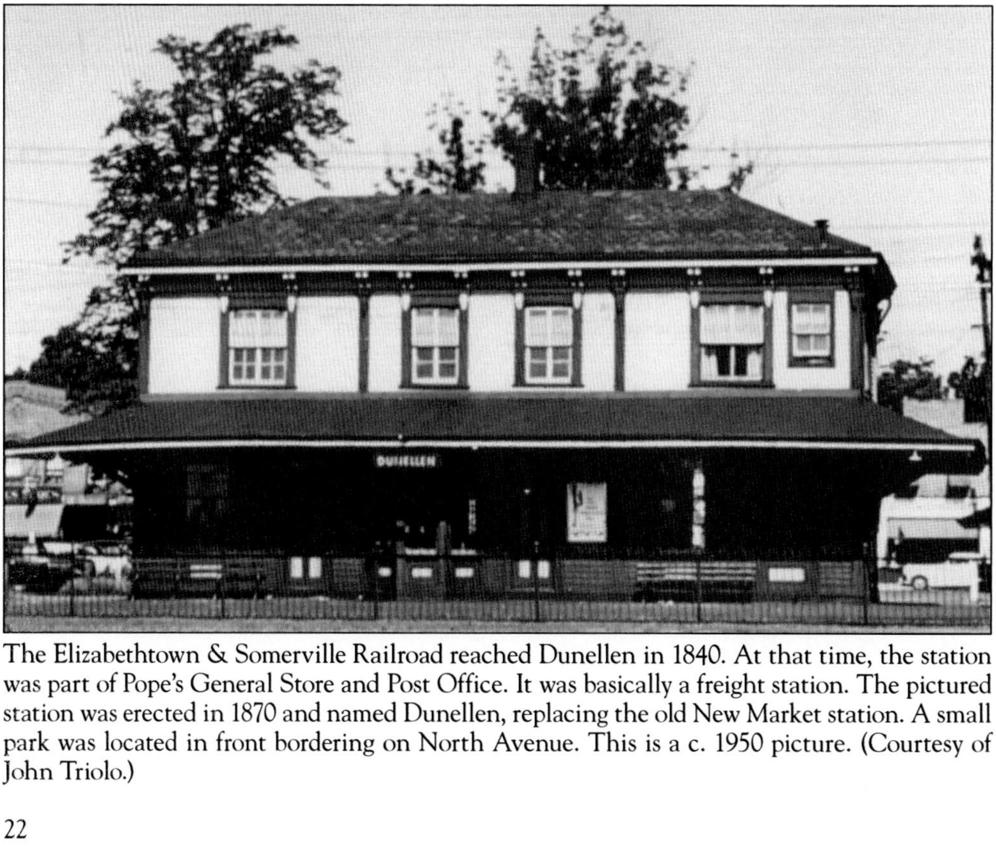


The Elizabethtown & Somerville Railroad reached Dunellen in 1840. At that time, the station was part of Pope's General Store and Post Office. It was basically a freight station. The pictured station was erected in 1870 and named Dunellen, replacing the old New Market station. A small park was located in front bordering on North Avenue. This is a c. 1950 picture. (Courtesy of John Triolo.)

Pictured here is Dunellen's passenger station in 1910 with a Camelback engine and three passenger cars approaching from the west. In 1912, a small waiting room and shelter was constructed on the eastbound side. A steel fence was also installed to separate the eastbound and westbound tracks. By 1915, over 219,000 passengers used the Dunellen station, and 174 people living in Dunellen worked for the railroad, of which 67 worked at the Dunellen railroad yards and depots.

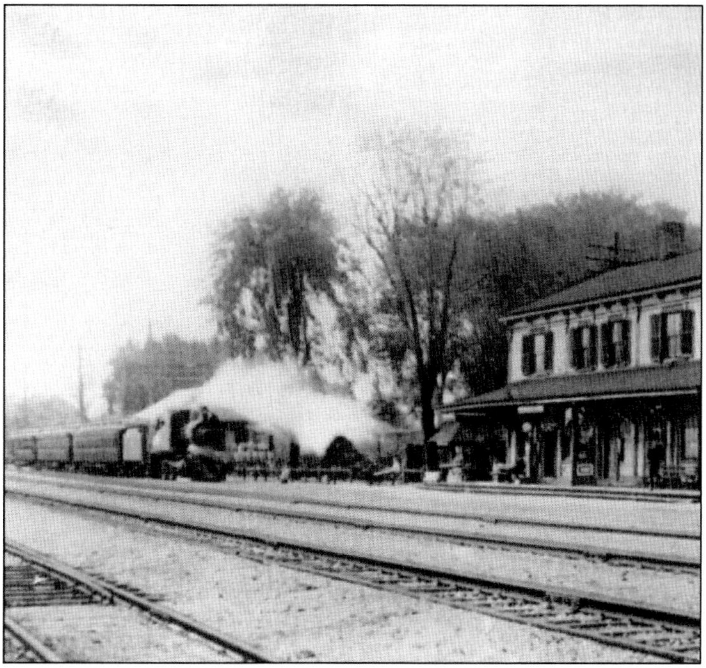

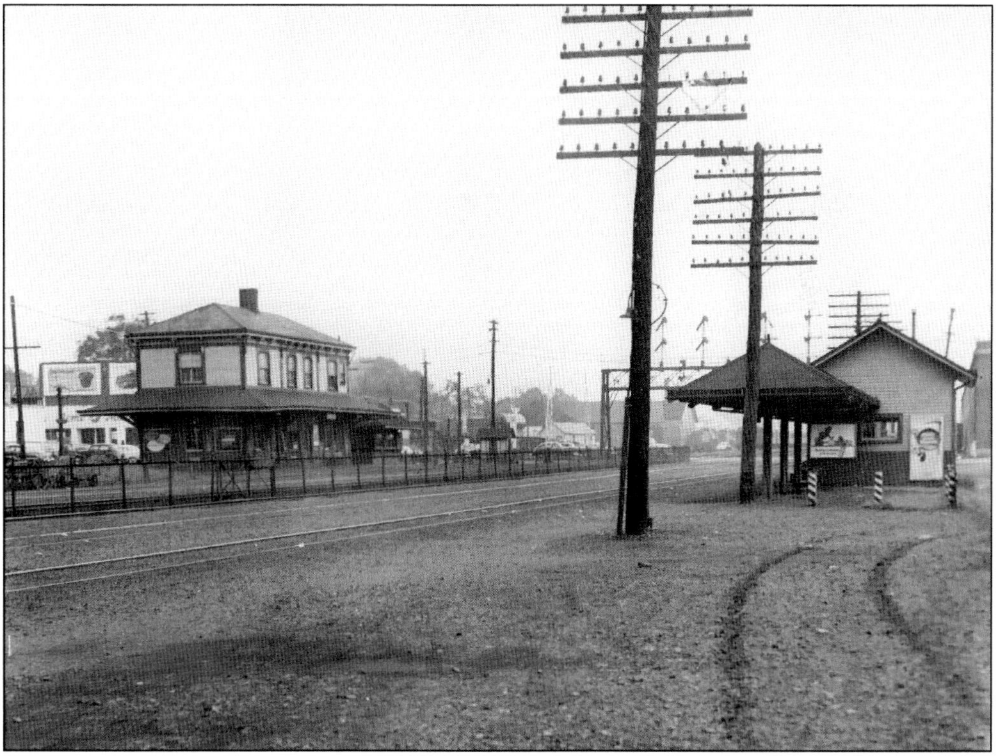

This is a view of the passenger station in 1951. At that time, all the crossings were at ground level. Commuter parking lots adjoined Washington Avenue. In 1944, the New Jersey Central Railroad became Jersey Central Lines and adopted the Statue of Liberty logo. Steam locomotives were still in use. (Courtesy of Charlie Batcha.)

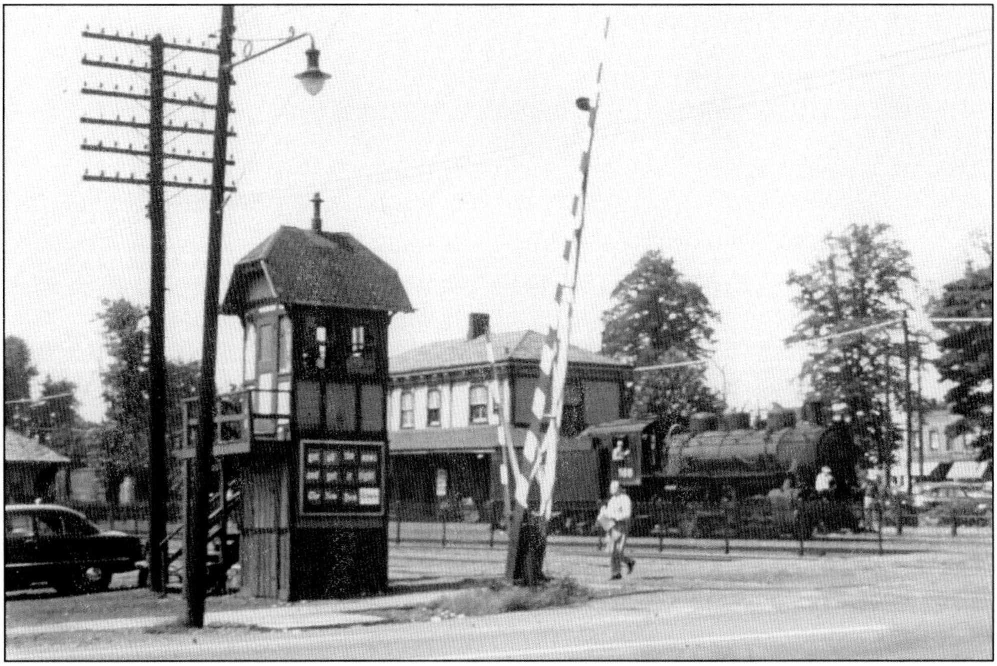

Pictured is the Washington Avenue railroad crossing in 1951. A switching engine waits for the signal to drop before sounding its whistle alerting the gate tender to lower the pedestrian gates. The engine could then proceed to the yards across the roadway to make up a train. The gate tender's shanty was lowered to street level by 1953. Gates were lowered and raised by hand until 1905, and compressed air was used thereafter.

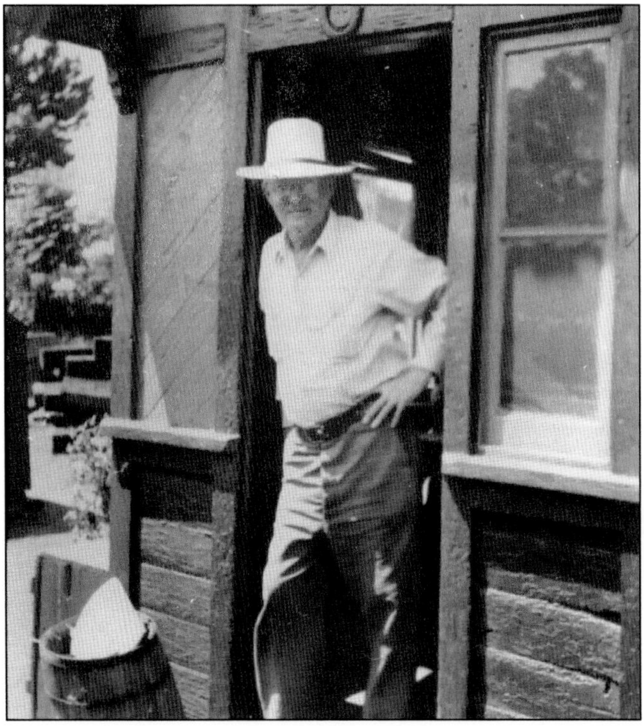

This unidentified crossing gateman is shown at the Grove Street crossing in 1940. Crossing gates were located on Washington and Prospect Avenues and Grove and Pulaski Streets. Prior to the tracks being elevated to their present level, Grove Street and South Avenue were rerouted in 1949. There were numerous fatal accidents over the years. The death of high school boy William Pangborn in 1948 shocked the community, and work was started on elevating the tracks.

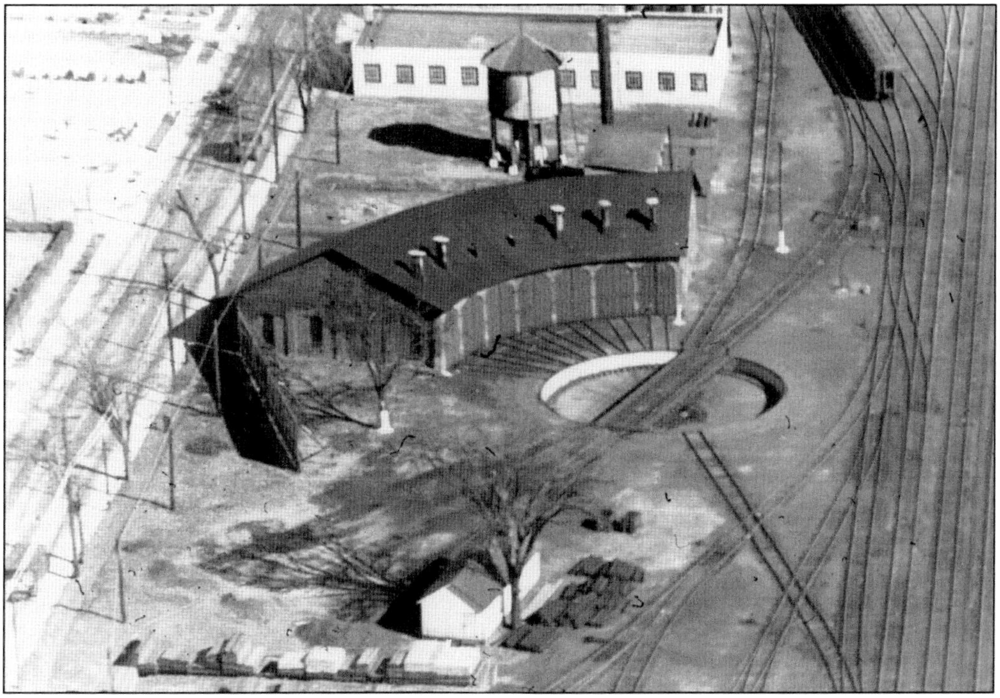

This is the Dunellen roundhouse and turntable in 1932. Roundhouses were used to do maintenance on the engines used in the yards. The 1875 Dunellen roundhouse had four stalls but increased to seven by 1904. The turntable was used to switch out engines and cars, and it was powered by two Babcock steam boilers added in 1913 and enclosed by a brick structure behind the roundhouse.

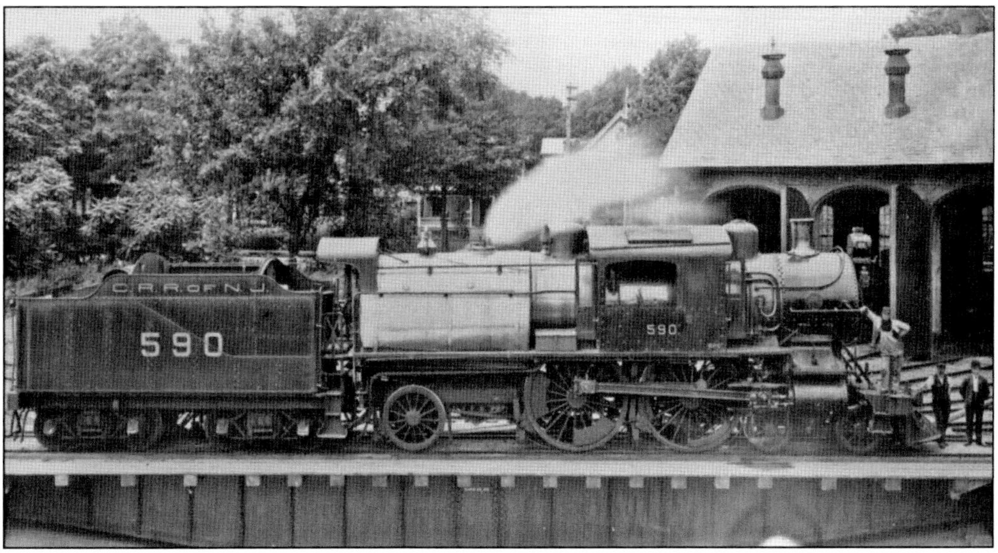


Camelback engine No. 590 appears on the turntable at Dunellen c. 1908. These Brooks 4-4-2 engines required a three-man crew to operate them: the engineer on the left, a fireman on the right, and a stoker to supply coal to the firebox. In the engine pictured above, with everyone in their proper places, no one could see what the other was doing. In this photograph, the crew of three is shown at the front of the engine. The man in the middle is Fred "Dutch" Heilich, the engineer and a Dunellen resident. (Courtesy of Fred Heilich III.)

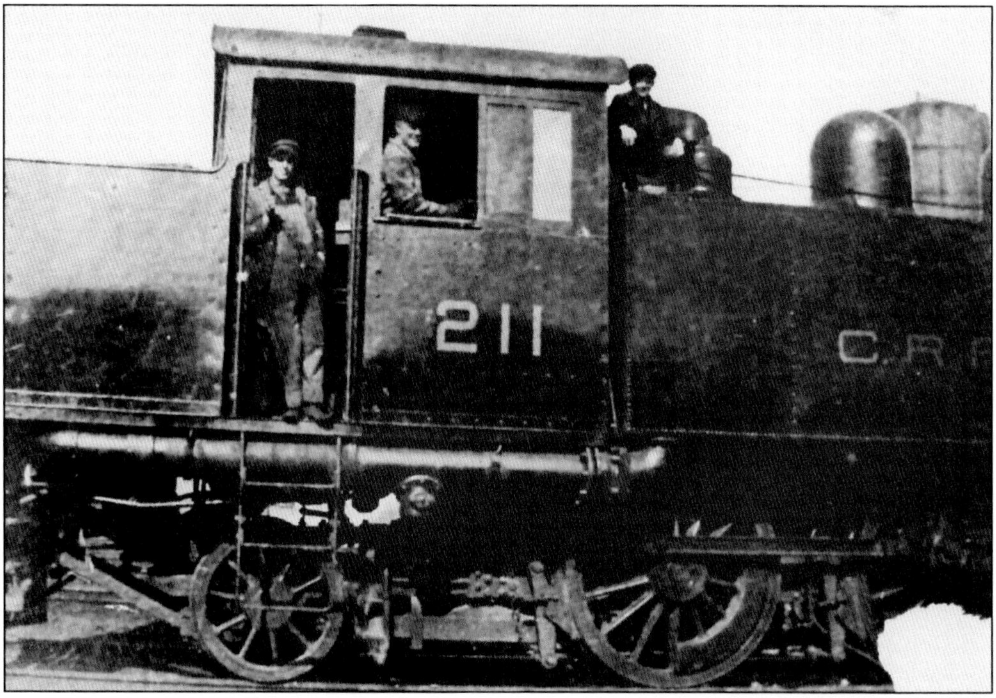


Central Railroad of New Jersey engine No. 211 appears at Dunellen. In this November 9, 1919, photograph, lifelong resident and fireman Jack Cooper is seen standing in the doorway. The engine is a Baldwin 2-6-2T built around 1903. Cooper later went on to be a fireman on the world-famous Blue Comet. (Courtesy of Loretta Pasko.)

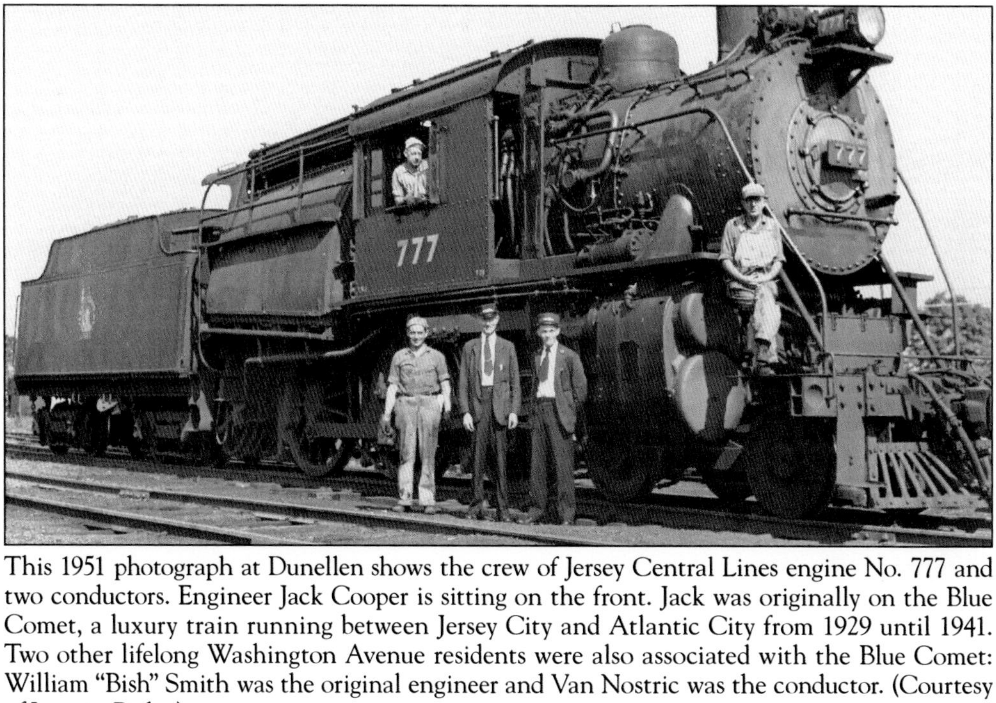


This 1951 photograph at Dunellen shows the crew of Jersey Central Lines engine No. 777 and two conductors. Engineer Jack Cooper is sitting on the front. Jack was originally on the Blue Comet, a luxury train running between Jersey City and Atlantic City from 1929 until 1941. Two other lifelong Washington Avenue residents were also associated with the Blue Comet: William "Bish" Smith was the original engineer and Van Nostric was the conductor. (Courtesy of Loretta Pasko.)

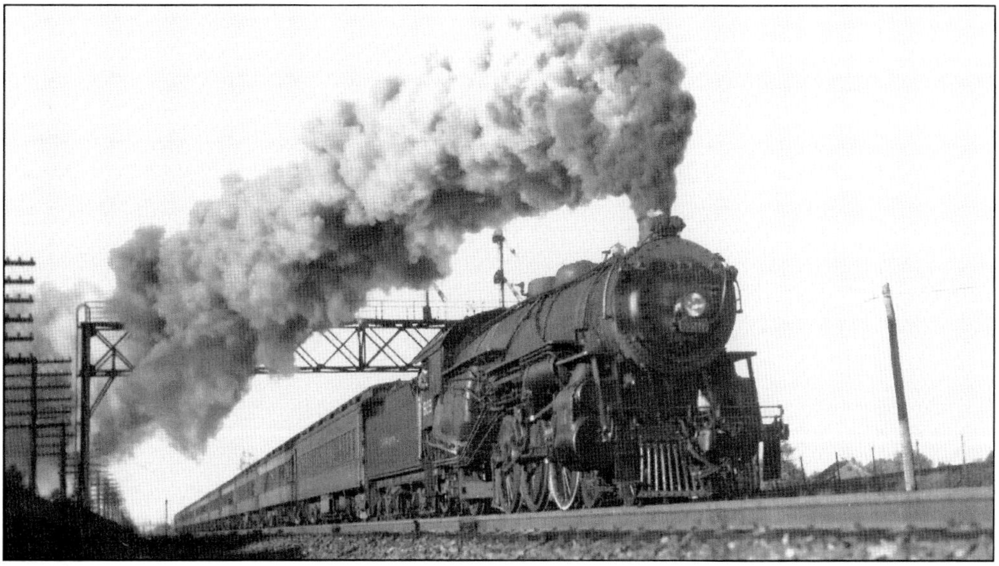

Steam locomotives were being phased out by the late 1940s and replaced by diesel engines. By 1949, there were 105 diesels in service. The last steam engine ran on April 23, 1954. Train No. 416 pulled by engine No. 829 are approaching Dunellen. Jersey Central Railroad's "Number One Woman Commuter" Grace Snyder rode the train everyday for 63 years commuting to New York City. Her retirement was marked by Eleanor Roosevelt, who presented her with a silver tray. (Courtesy of Yesteryear Depot, Eilenberger Collection.)

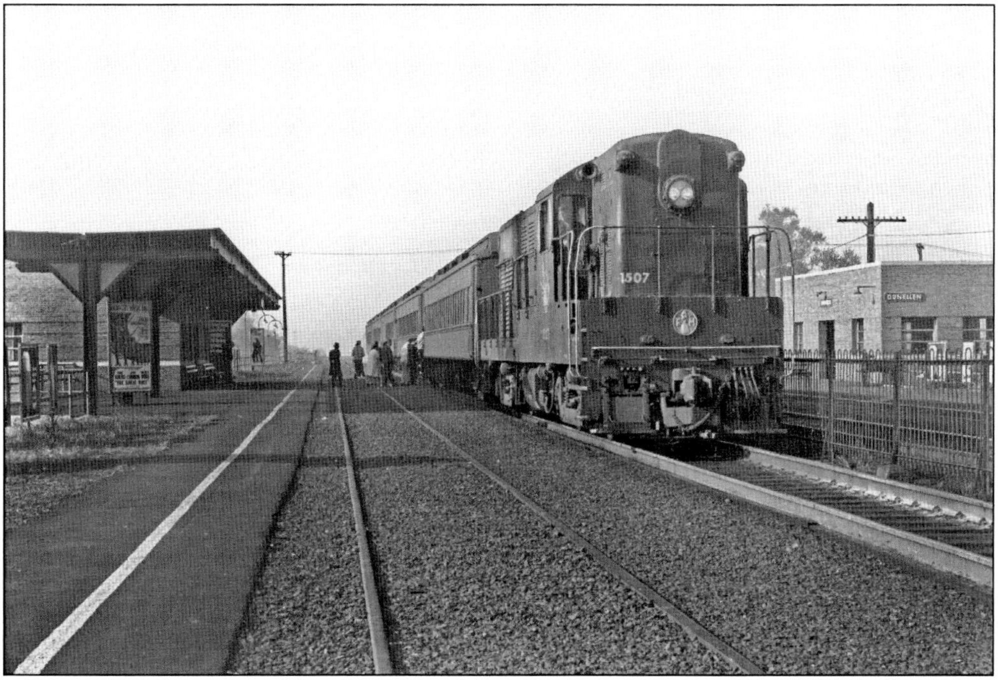


Commuters board cars for their trip to New York City on October 14, 1965. The tracks had been elevated for 10 years. This project was started on May 8, 1954. The old station, roundhouse, turntable, and tower, along with the passenger train yard, were all removed with the elevation of the tracks, and the town was literally cut in half. (Courtesy of Bob Pennisi, Railroad Avenue Enterprises.)

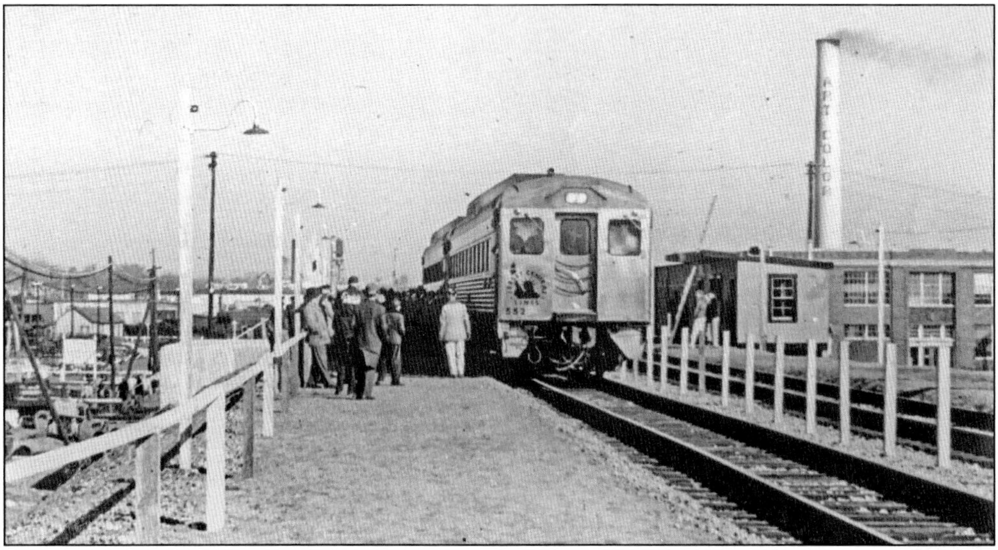

The work to elevate all the crossings was started on April 15, 1952. Shown here is No. 552, the first commuter train to use the elevated tracks on January 24, 1955. This Budd train carried regular commuters, railroad officials, politicians, and the press. A lifelong Dunellen resident, engineer Jack Cooper was at the throttle, honoring his lifetime of service to the railroad.

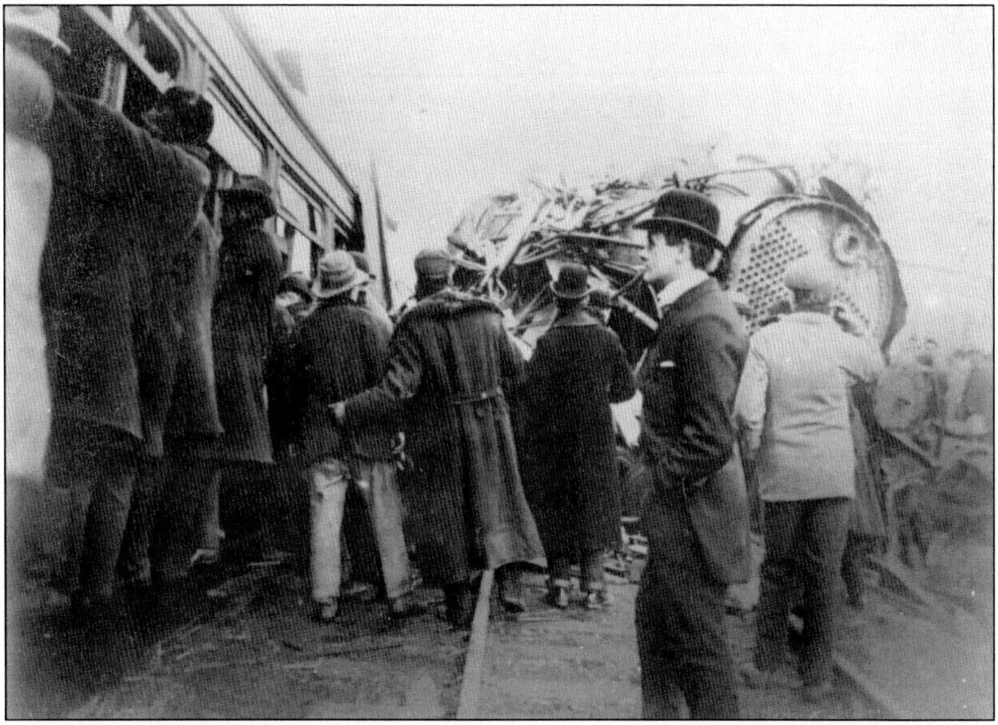

On January 9, 1899, the *New York Times* published an extensive article entitled "Fifteen Dead by Railroad Wreck; Two Trains Meet Head on in West Dunellen." A train was traveling west from South Plainfield, and the other was going east from Bound Brook. Witnesses said the two trains were approaching each other at high speed at the blind curve. Over 50 passengers were injured that day, and 17 eventually died.

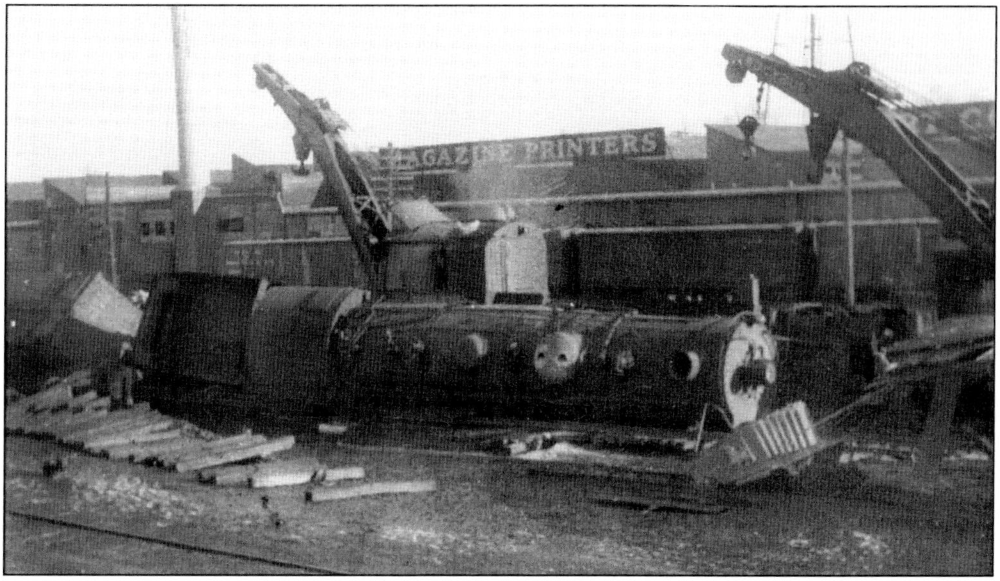

In this picture, two flatcar-mounted railroad cranes are working to remove the engine and debris at this 1929 derailment next to the Art Color Printing Company in Dunellen. The rail yard was six tracks wide with a staging area for passenger trains, and an accident of this size had to be cleaned up quickly to keep the tracks open to other rail traffic.

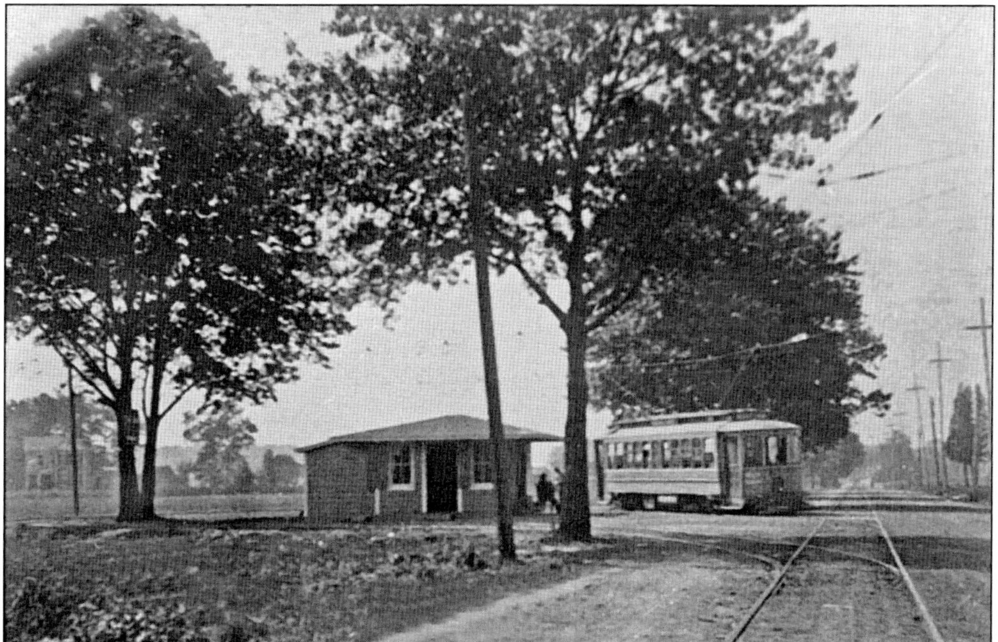

Dunellen's other railroad was the trolley. On September 22, 1898, the first trolley traveled through Dunellen. The Trolley Loop was in operation by July 1905 with a waiting room and refreshment stand opened by William Sanford. The circle of track was about 100 feet in diameter and located on the southerly side of Bound Brook Road near Sanford Avenue. Sanford leased six lots opposite his residence on Bound Brook Road to the trolley company for five years at $100 per year. (Courtesy of John Triolo.)

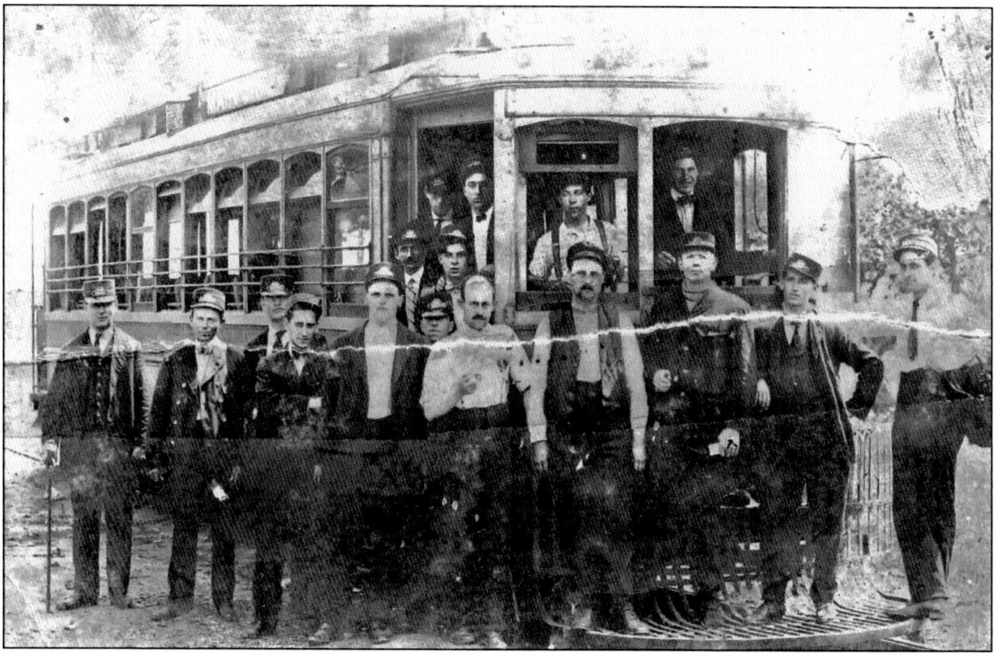

Ed Honig, a lifelong Dunellen resident and trolley operator, is pictured (with bow tie) inside the trolley on the right. This photograph was taken in 1910, the same year the Public Service Corporation started laying double track on North Avenue. A large car house and terminal called Dunellen was actually in Middlesex where the present-day Acme Supermarket now stands. (Courtesy of Loretta Pasko.)

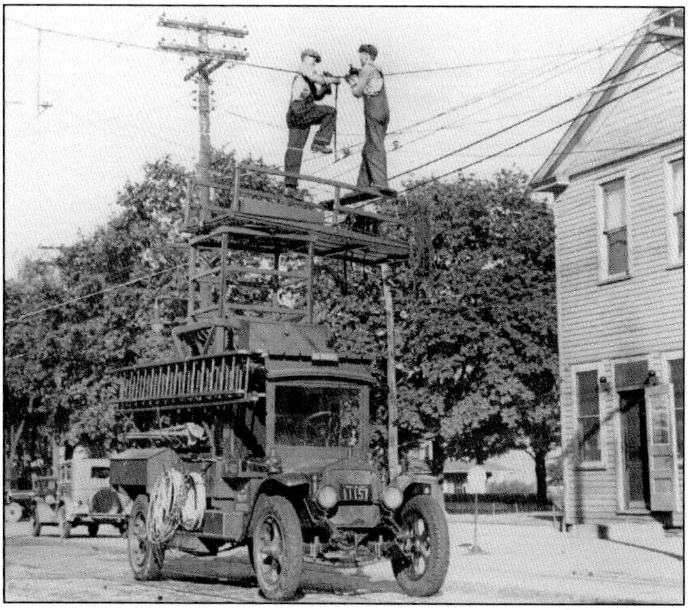

These two workmen are doing maintenance on trolley wires opposite borough hall at North Avenue and Prospect Street in 1925. On September 14, 1935, the Public Service Corporation discontinued trolleys and started rubber-tire (bus) trolleys the next day. The existing overhead wires were still used. The last power pole along the entire line was located in front of the present Quick Chek, but it sadly disappeared when new street lamps were installed in 2008.

# *Three*

# North Avenue

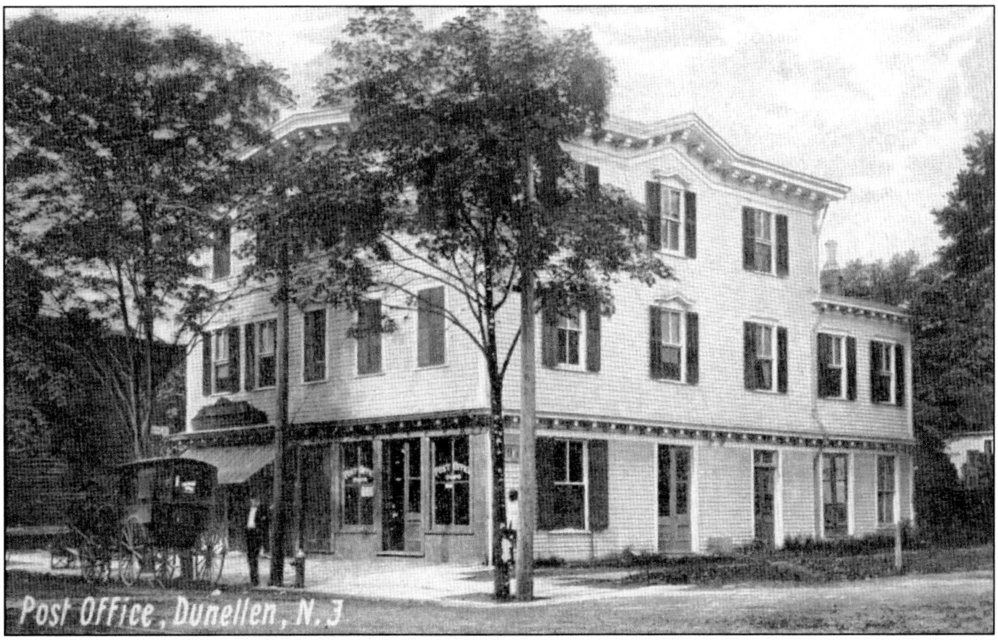


The Dunellen Post Office was in the Vars building at 300 North Avenue in 1896. In 1870, Charles Pope was appointed the first postmaster at Dunellen with his office located in the first railroad station at the intersection of Grove Street and the railroad. In 1885, the post office moved to the new postmaster's (Charles Boice) grocery store in the Vars building. From 1910 to 1919, it was located in the Runyon building at 340 North Avenue. The facilities then moved to the southeast corner of North and Washington Avenues in 1919. In 1929, it was located at 112 North Washington Avenue. It finally moved to its current location in November 1960. (Courtesy of John Triolo.)

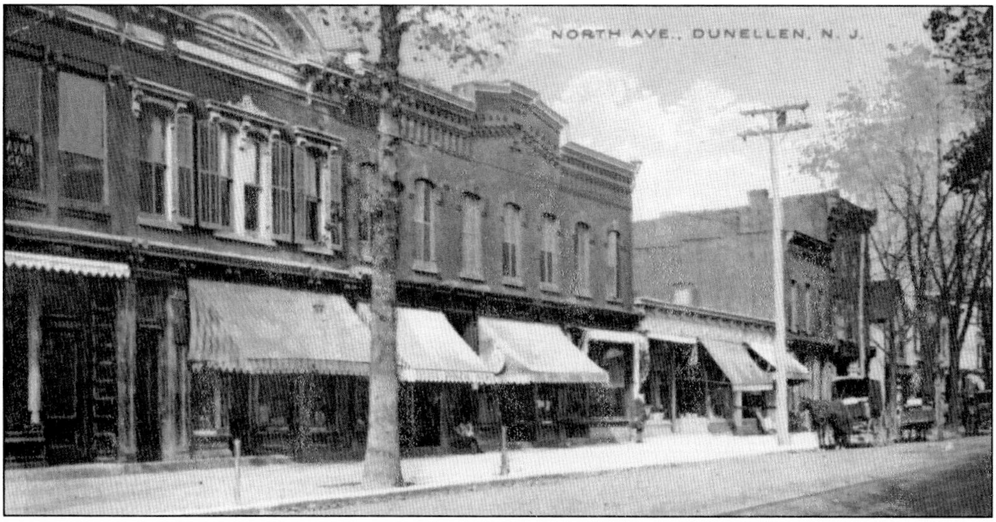


Dating back to the 1870s, the business district was predominantly located on the north side of the street between Washington and Madison Avenues. It contained the standard lineup of businesses over the years, such as the post office, groceries, butchers, banks, barbershops, hotels, and restaurants, just to name a few. A fire in 1875 destroyed much of the business district, but it was rebuilt better than before. The burned wood frame buildings were replaced with brick structures. (Courtesy of John Triolo.)

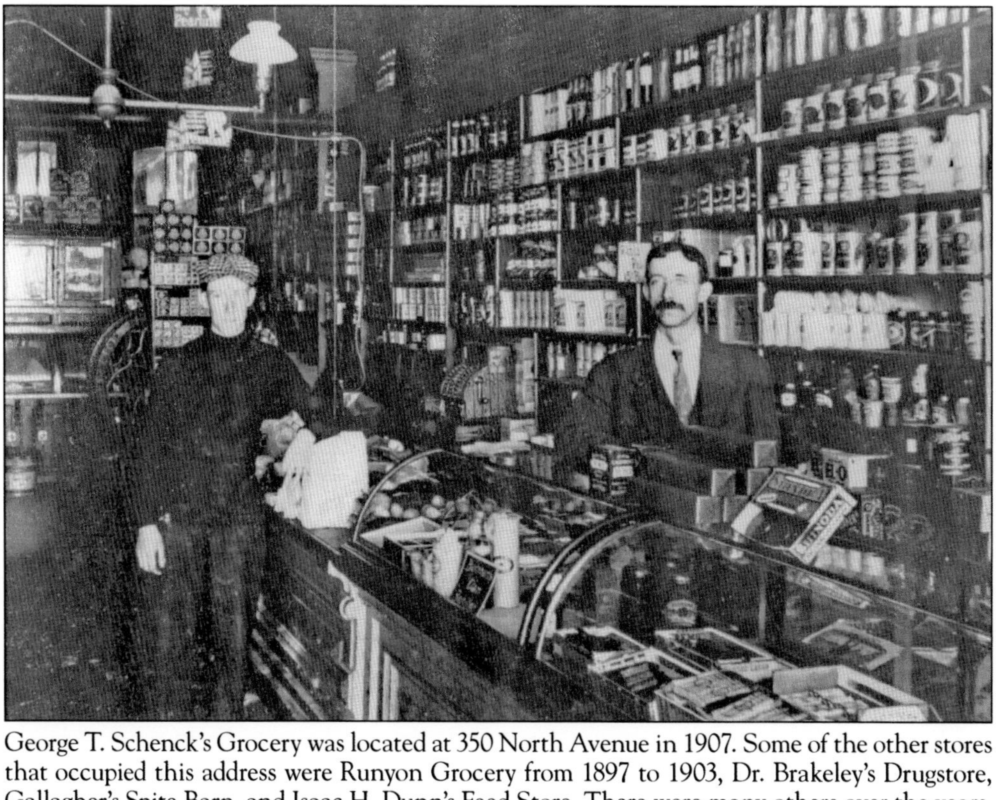

George T. Schenck's Grocery was located at 350 North Avenue in 1907. Some of the other stores that occupied this address were Runyon Grocery from 1897 to 1903, Dr. Brakeley's Drugstore, Gallagher's Spite Barn, and Isaac H. Dunn's Feed Store. There were many others over the years, including the Towne Shop in 1960.

The Kuldoshes building at 400 North Avenue in 1883 is shown here. The Plainfield Directory of 1885 records that Helen Kuldoshes, widow of Matthias, operated a grocery store at the corner of North and Lincoln Avenues. It housed the Bee Hive in 1915, the Imperial Barbershop in 1919, and the Great Atlantic and Pacific Tea Company (A&P) in 1929.

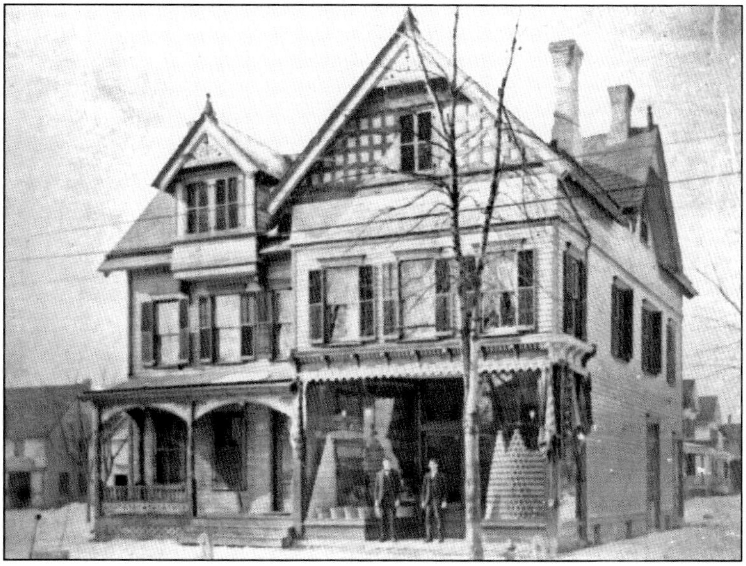

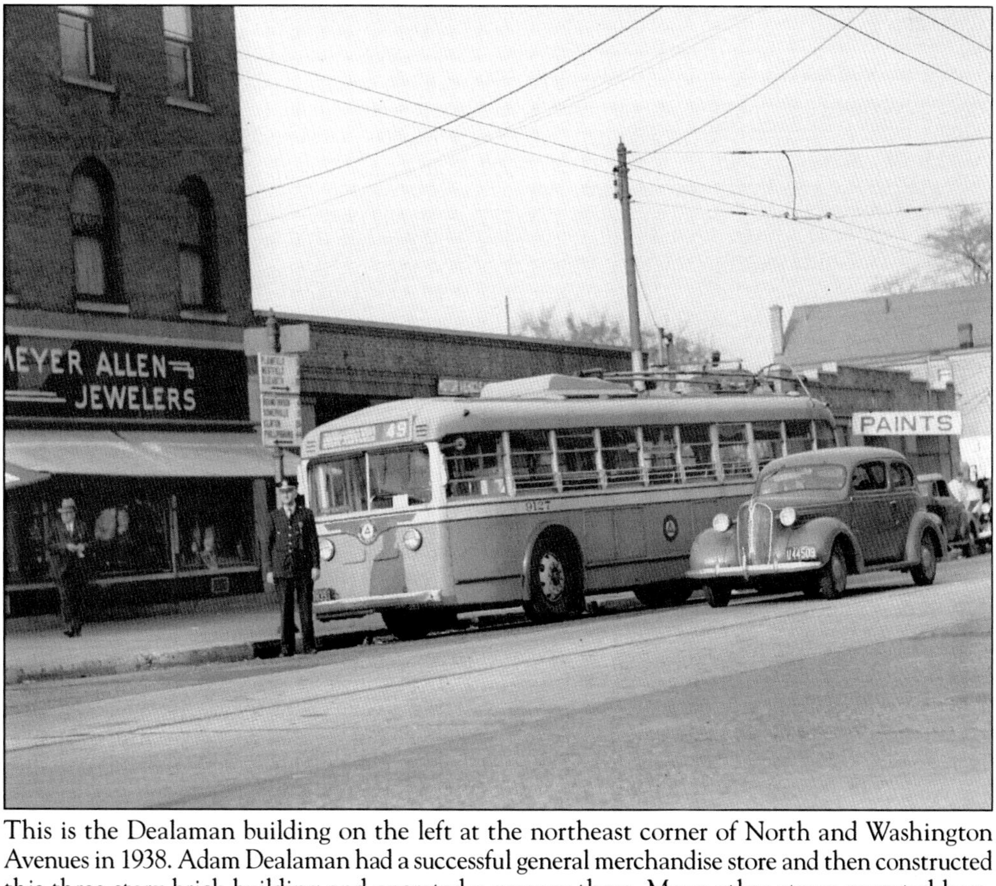


This is the Dealaman building on the left at the northeast corner of North and Washington Avenues in 1938. Adam Dealaman had a successful general merchandise store and then constructed this three-story brick building and operated a grocery there. Many other stores operated here, including the United States Stores in 1926 and Meyer Allen's Jewelry Store in 1934. The electric bus from Plainfield has just pulled up. Built to last, this structure still stands today.

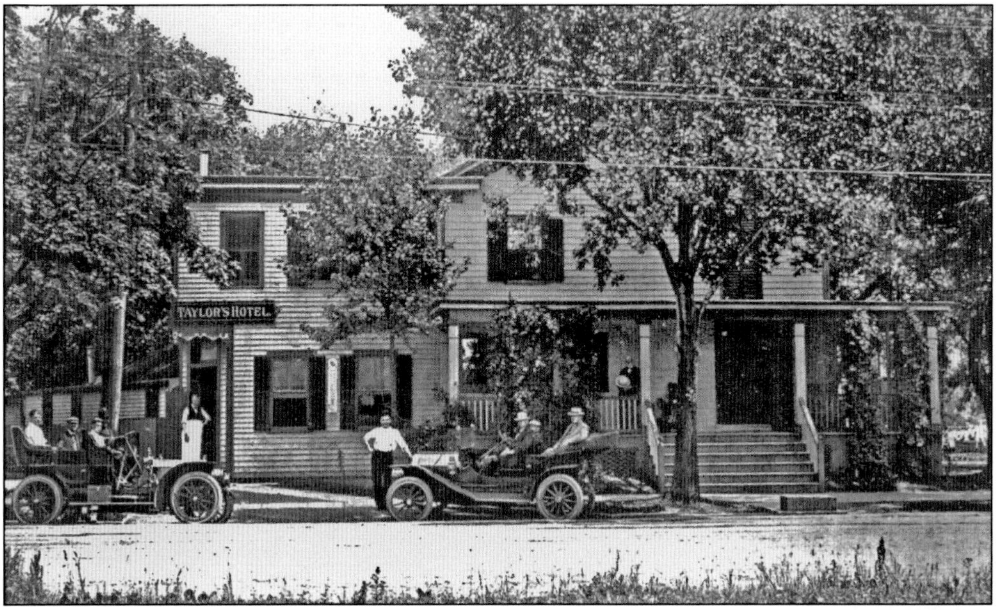


Pictured here in 1911, the Taylor Hotel started out as Charles Pope's store, railroad station, and post office in 1868. In 1874, it was moved to the southeast corner of North Avenue and Grove Street (now Madison Avenue) by John Emory. William Taylor converted it to a hotel in 1882, and it was in operation until 1918. Moved again and greatly altered, it is now located at 8 Madison Avenue. (Courtesy of John Triolo.)

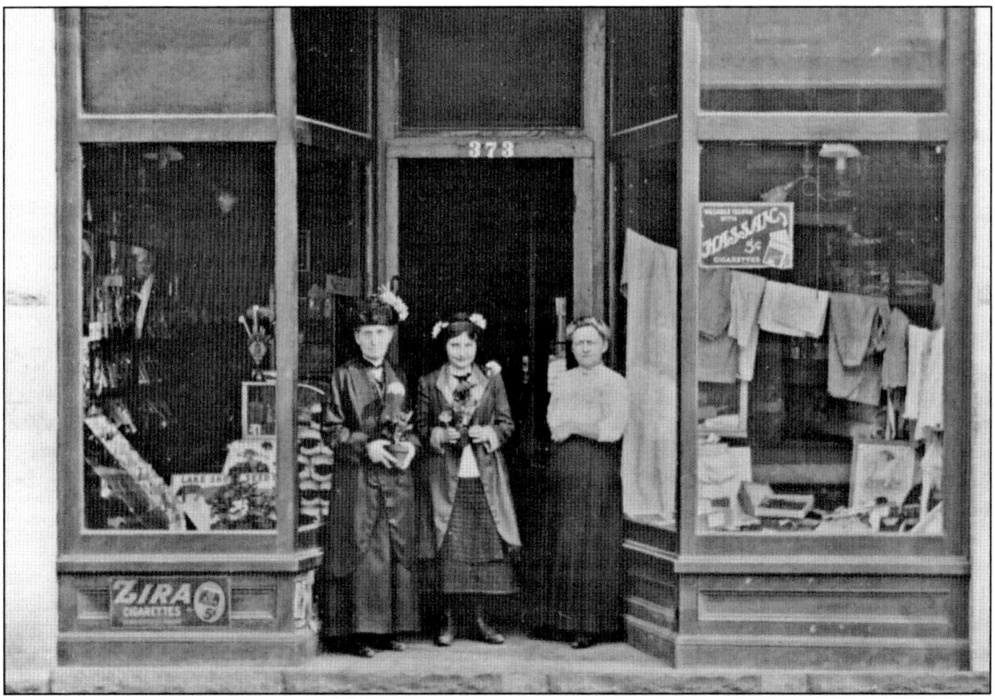


This dry goods store located at 373 North Avenue was owned and operated by Mrs. John Huff, seen at the right. Her two customers are Mrs. Giddes (left) and Ethel Lewis. This picture was taken about 1910.

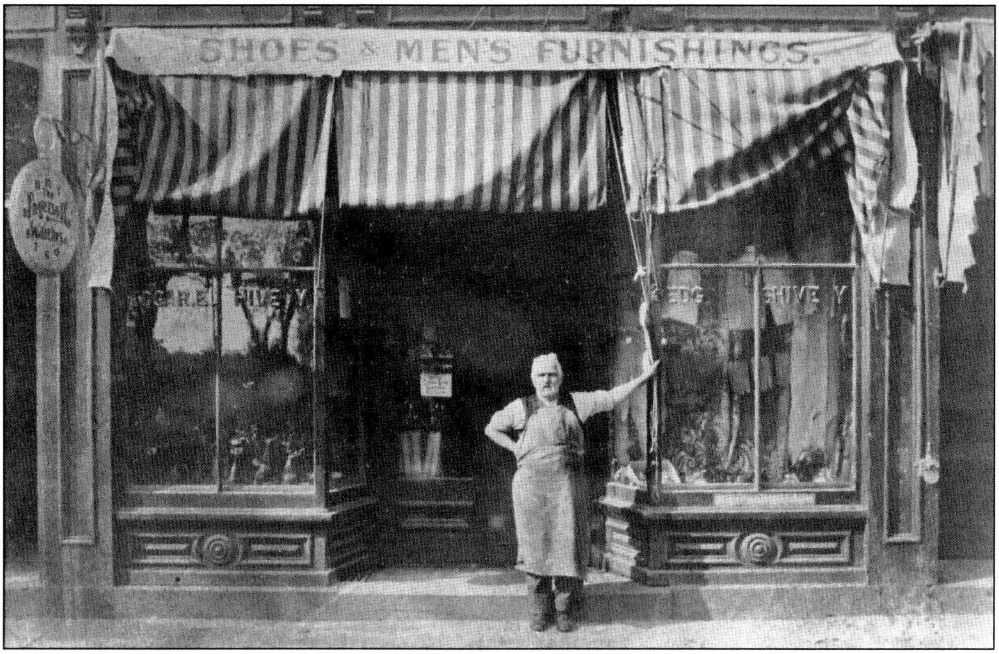


Edgar E. Shively poses for the camera in front of his menswear and shoe store in 1910. The store was previously Lewis' Men's Store in 1907. It was located in the Runyon building.

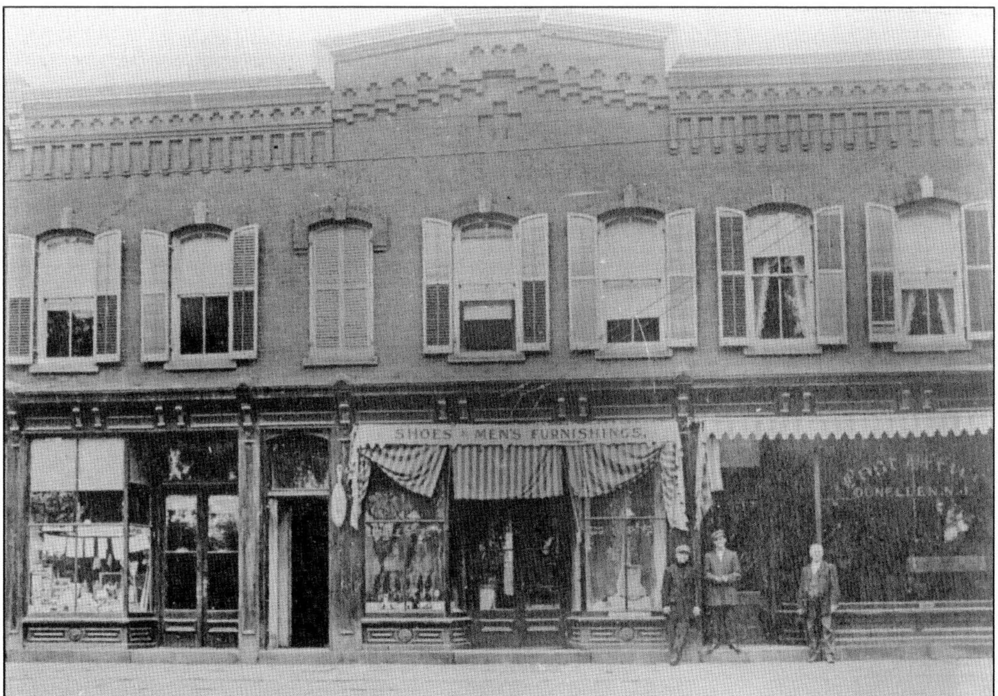


Stores in the Runyon building in 1910 include, from left to right, Mrs. Emma Pinza's Notions, Edgar Shively's Shoes and Men's Furnishings, and the Dunellen Post Office at yet another location. The post office was at this address from 1909 to 1919. This building was prominent in Dunellen then and still is today.

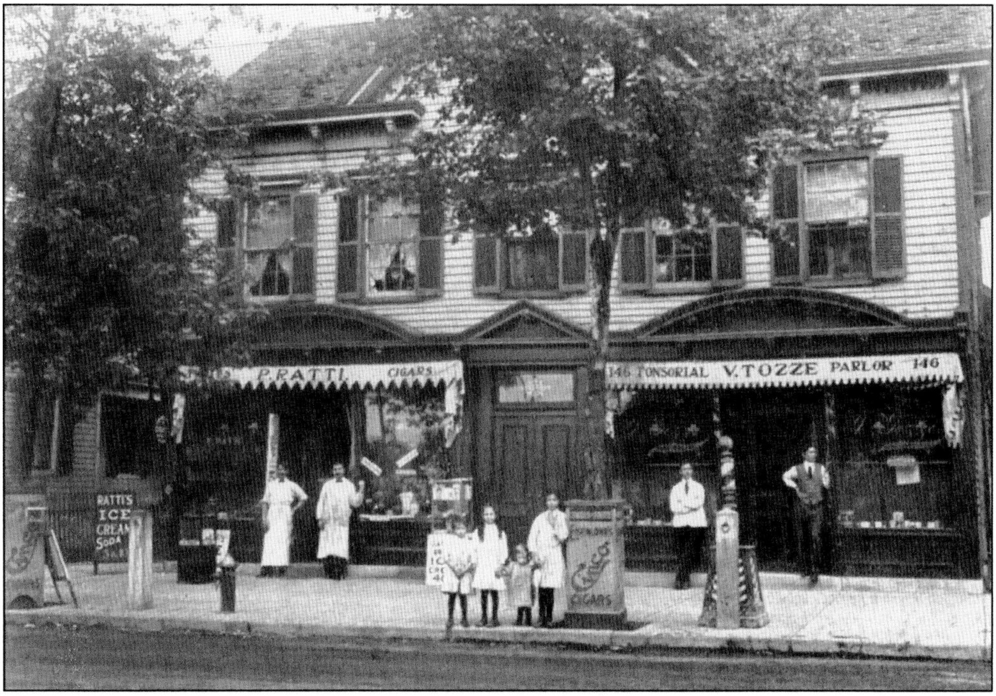


Here is the Ratti building at 364 North Avenue in 1910. Ratti's Ice Cream Parlor is on the left, and Tozze's Barbershop is on the right. In 1926, Ratti sold the building to Frank DiLonardo, who then opened the Bluebird Luncheonette, which continuously operated for almost 50 years.

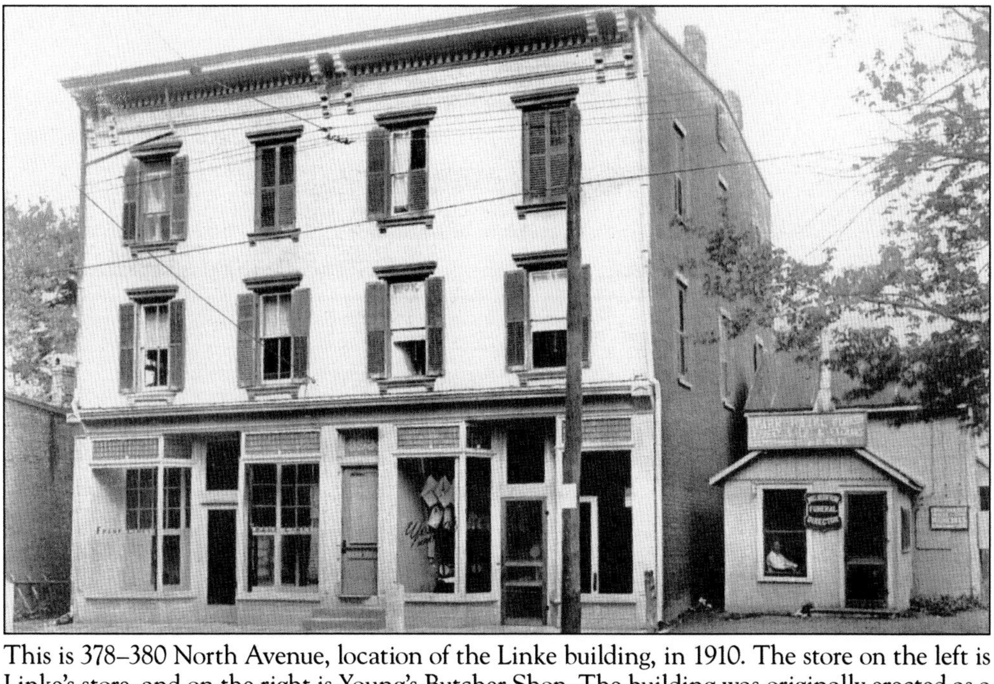

This is 378–380 North Avenue, location of the Linke building, in 1910. The store on the left is Linke's store, and on the right is Young's Butcher Shop. The building was originally erected as a two-story brick structure by butcher O.M. Hetfield in 1873. The first movie theater in Dunellen was located here in 1911 but only lasted four months; its doors closed on April 13, 1912.

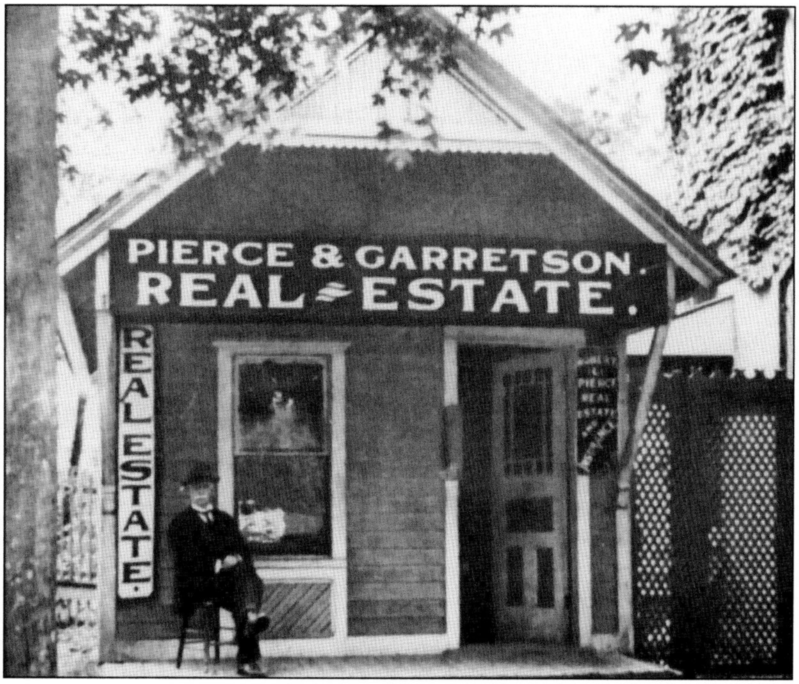


The Pierce & Garretson Real Estate office is seen in this 1910 photograph. A large number of building lots were still available for sale in Dunellen. There were even two building and loan associations operating at the same time. Auctions of large numbers of lots were common from 1910 through the 1920s.

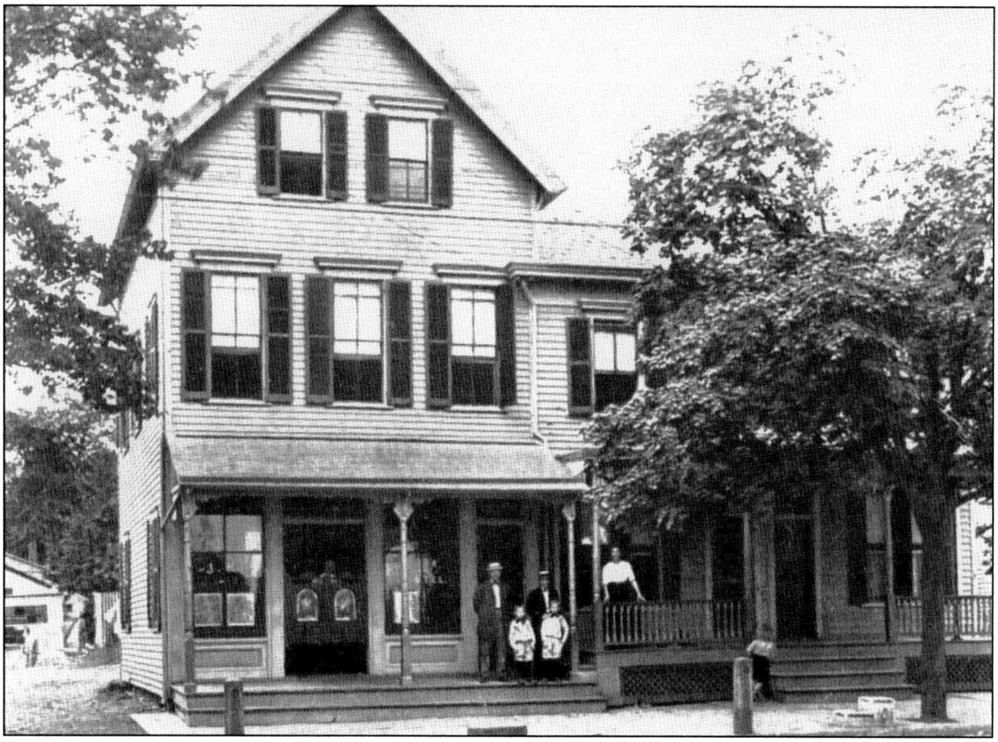

Joseph Maier's Park Hotel was located at 370 North Avenue. Maier came to America in 1857. He worked as a cobbler to earn enough money to buy two lots and erected a building in 1868. It was enlarged several times and became known as the Park Hotel, located directly across from the present Municipal Building.

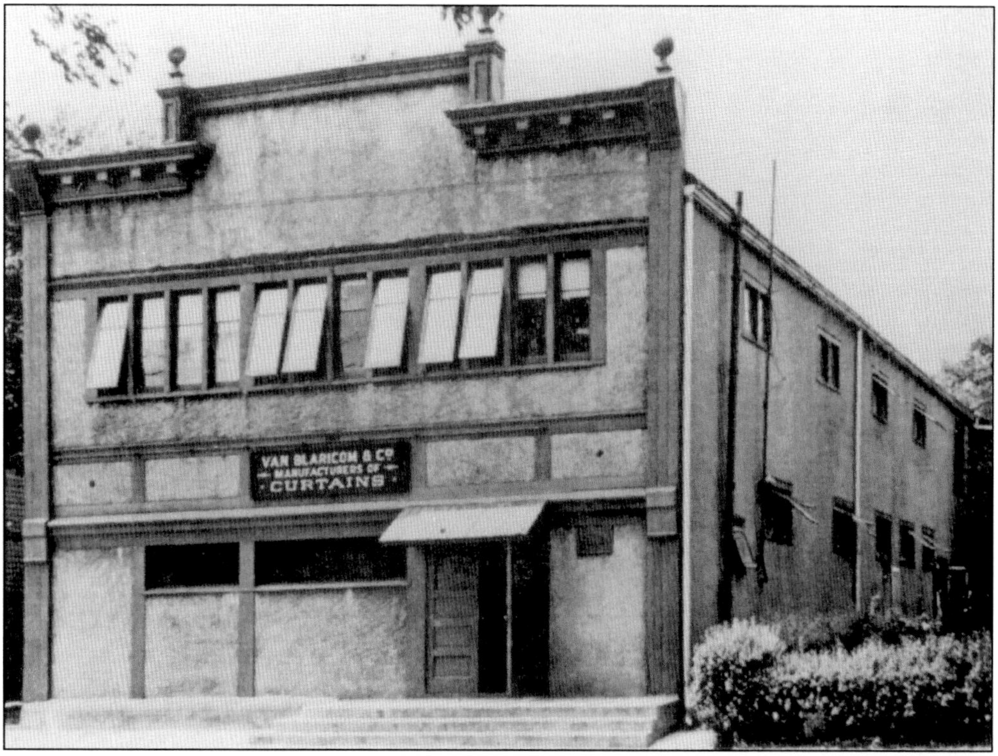


Pictured in 1937 is the Van Blaricom and Company building at 214 North Avenue. This building was erected and opened as a movie theater in 1913 and closed in 1915. No less than seven different owners tried unsuccessfully to continue operations of the theater. In 1918, Van Blaircom and Company purchased the building and operated it as a curtain factory for 68 years until closing in 1986.

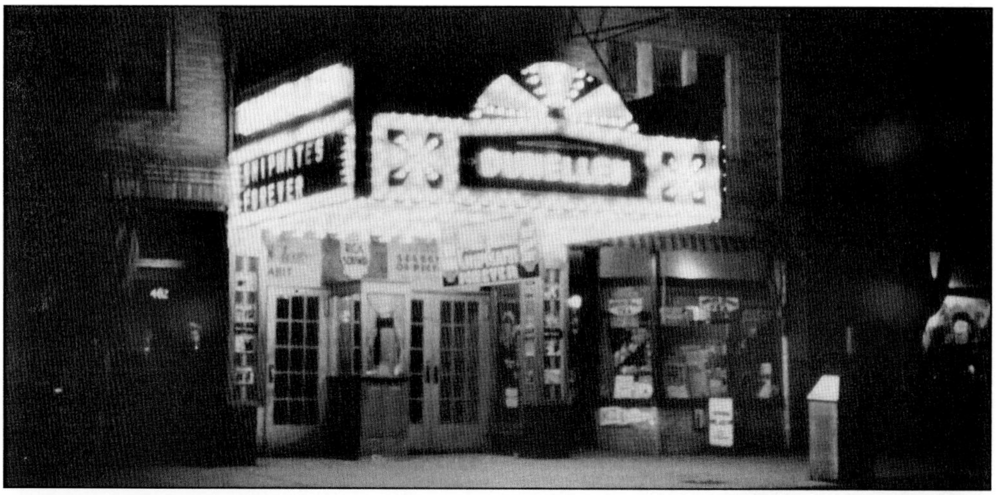

The present Dunellen Theater was built in 1922 and was called Hosford's Theatre. In 1927, it was sold and reopened as Dunellen's Cameo Theatre. Changing ownership in 1933, it was renamed the Dunellen Theater and has been operating as a movie theater to the present day. This nighttime photograph was taken in 1935 with a grocery store to the left and Joe Pasko's ice cream and candy store on the right, all in the same building.

This newspaper advertisement for the grand opening of Hosford's Dunellen Theatre in 1922 features a 28¢ admission price. The brand-new building located at the northeast corner of North and Madison Avenues housed the theater. In January 1927, Hosford opened the theater on a Sunday and he, his wife, and the projectionist were arrested for violation of the blue law.

# GRAND OPENING!

## HOSFORD'S

# DUNELLEN THEATRE

DUNELLEN, N. J.

SATURDAY, MAY 20th, 1922

UNDER THE AUSPICES OF

Dunellen Commandery, No. 70,

**P. O. S. of A.**

SHOWS 7:00 AND 9:00 p. m.

| | |
|---|---|
| ADMISSION | 25 Cents |
| TAX | 3 Cents |
| TOTAL | 28 Cents |

This is Salvin's store in 1928. Located at 704 Bound Brook Road, it was operated by Aaron Salvin for 50 years until closing in 1978. Pictured from left to right are Aaron (standing behind the counter), his daughter Bea, an unidentified customer, Anna (his wife), and baby Bob (in the wicker baby carriage). (Courtesy of Robert Salvin.)

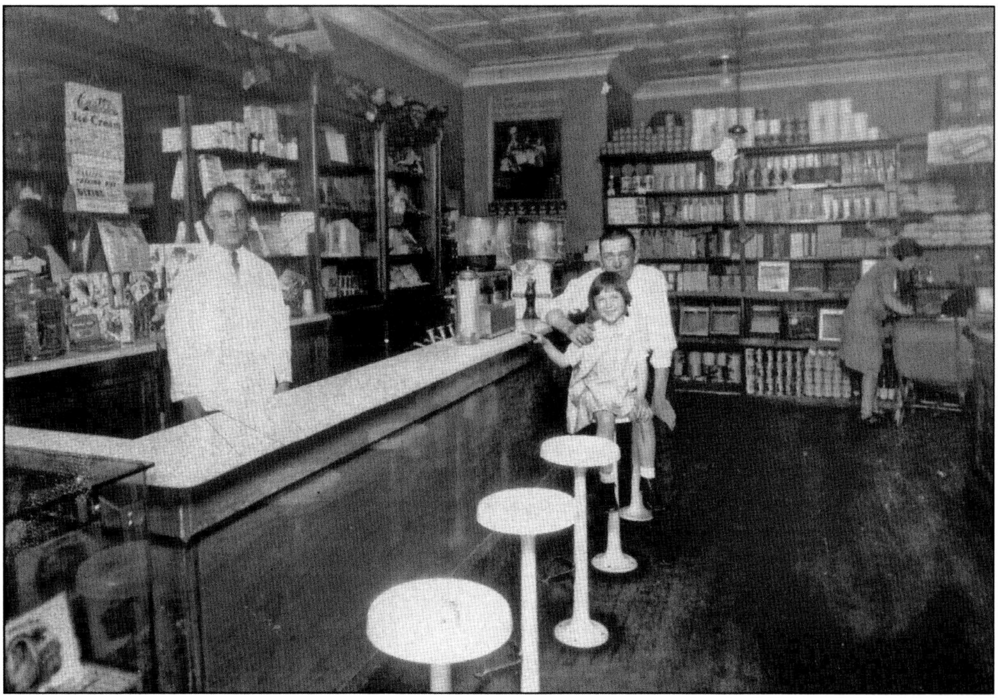

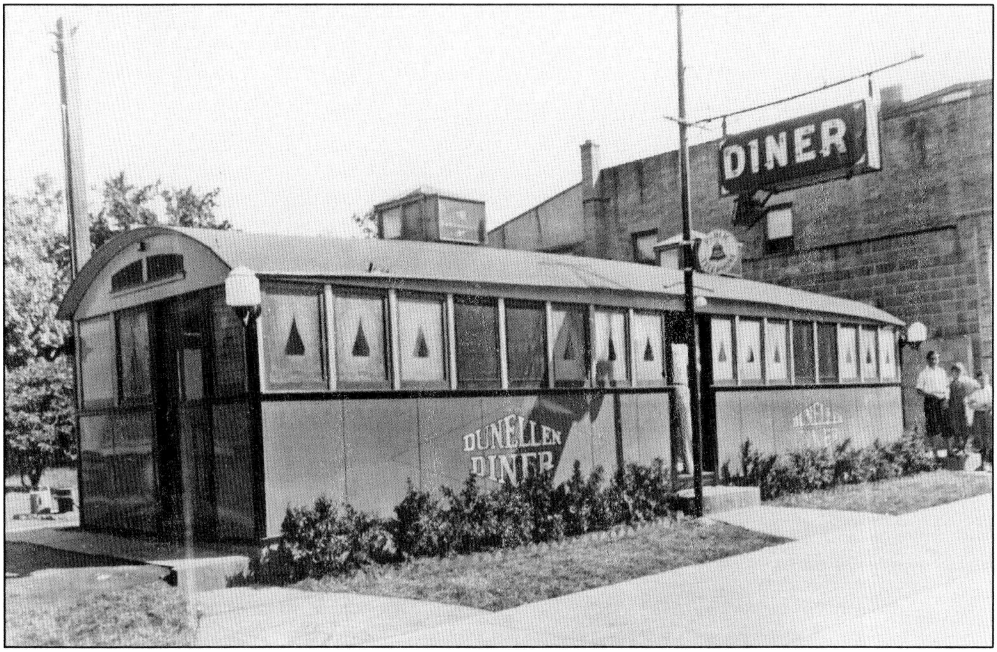


Shown here is the Dunellen Diner at the northeast corner of North and Lincoln Avenues in 1933. Jack Herman had moved the diner to this location from its original address at 376 North Avenue when he purchased it in 1933. Frank Stepko was the owner of the New Dunellen Diner in 1956, but it was torn down after a fire in 1977.

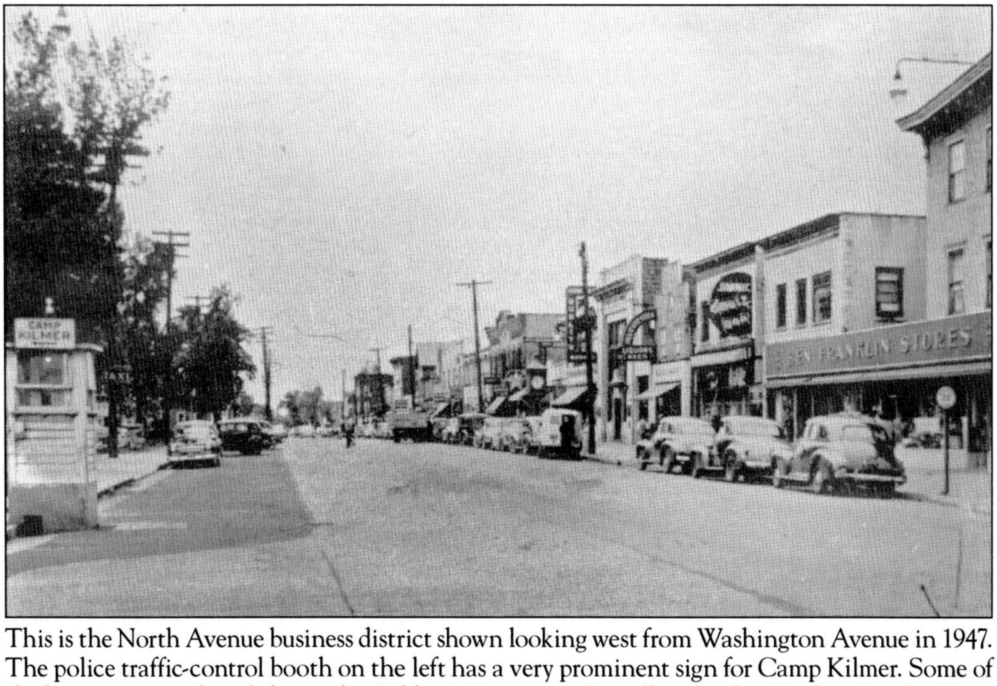


This is the North Avenue business district shown looking west from Washington Avenue in 1947. The police traffic-control booth on the left has a very prominent sign for Camp Kilmer. Some of the businesses are, from left to right, Seldow's Stationery, Dunellen Quality Market, Peoples Trust Company, Blocks Market, Jimnic Music Bar, and Ben Franklin Stores. Of note is the old clock on the sidewalk in front of the bank. A more modern clock stands at that exact spot today.

*Four*

# Homes and Residents

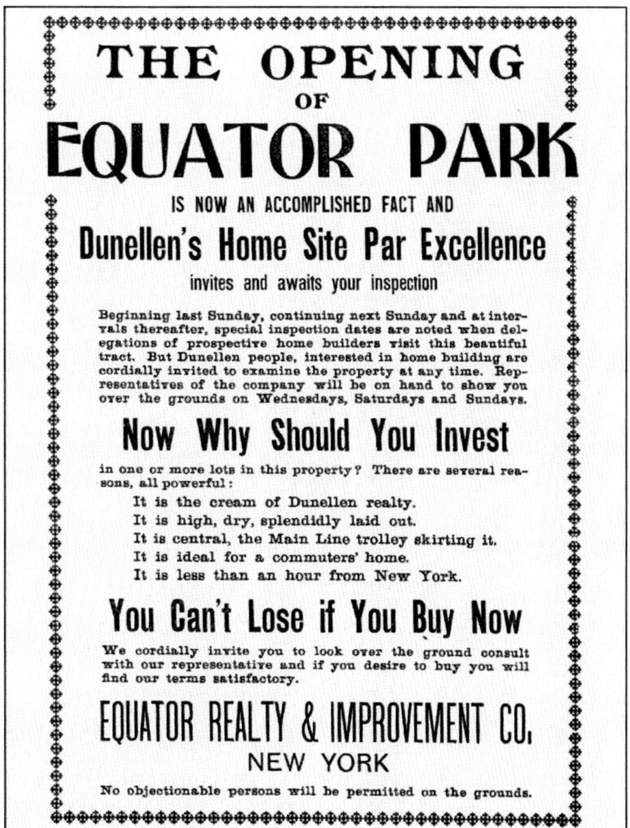

THE OPENING

OF

EQUATOR PARK

IS NOW AN ACCOMPLISHED FACT AND

Dunellen's Home Site Par Excellence

invites and awaits your inspection

Beginning last Sunday, continuing next Sunday and at intervals thereafter, special inspection dates are noted when delegations of prospective home builders visit this beautiful tract. But Dunellen people, interested in home building are cordially invited to examine the property at any time. Representatives of the company will be on hand to show you over the grounds on Wednesdays, Saturdays and Sundays.

Now Why Should You Invest

in one or more lots in this property? There are several reasons, all powerful:

It is the cream of Dunellen realty.
It is high, dry, splendidly laid out.
It is central, the Main Line trolley skirting it.
It is ideal for a commuters' home.
It is less than an hour from New York.

You Can't Lose if You Buy Now

We cordially invite you to look over the ground consult with our representative and if you desire to buy you will find our terms satisfactory.

EQUATOR REALTY & IMPROVEMENT CO,

NEW YORK

No objectionable persons will be permitted on the grounds.

This May 1910 newspaper article advertises a tract of land within Dunellen known as Equator Park. Previously, an auction on Wednesday, June 23, 1869, had sold 280 lots and two buildings for the Central Jersey Land Improvement Company. Years later, on Friday, September 11, 1925, auctioneer Joseph P. Day sold 250 residential lots in one night. Day was known as the greatest real estate auctioneer of the early 20th century. On December 21, 1921, he sold 1,574 houses and lots in Fairview, New Jersey.

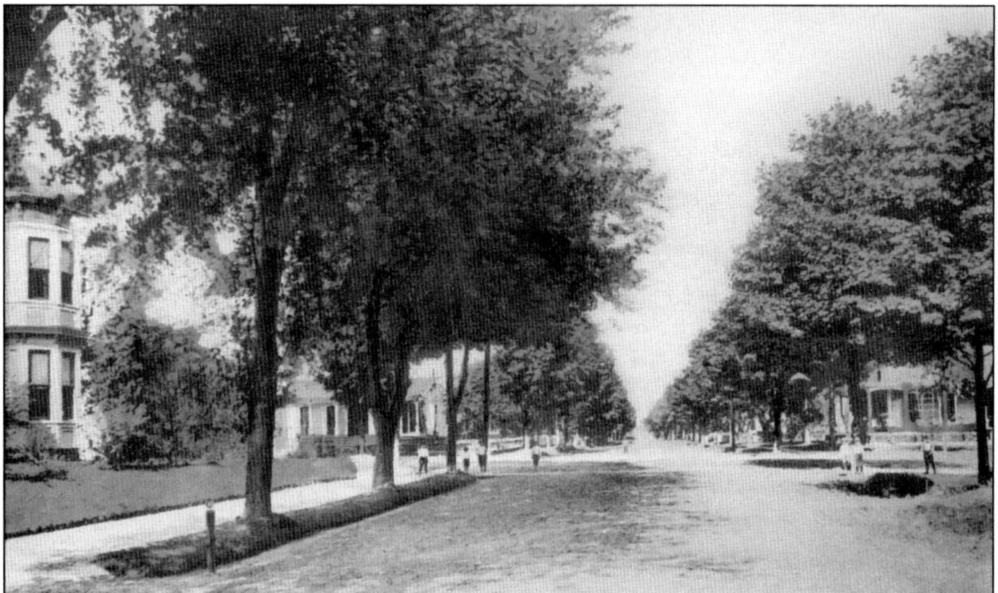

HIGH ST. EAST FROM WASHINGTON AVE., DUNELLEN, N. J.

Present-day Front Street was called High Street in 1893. This 1908 picture shows the view east from Washington Avenue. Pictured in the left foreground is not a parking meter, but a hitching post for horses. A block north was Church Street, or George Street, now Dunellen Avenue. Other street names have changed over the years. Fifth Street became Mountain View Terrace in 1906, and Whittier Avenue was Depot Street until 1909. (Courtesy of John Triolo.)

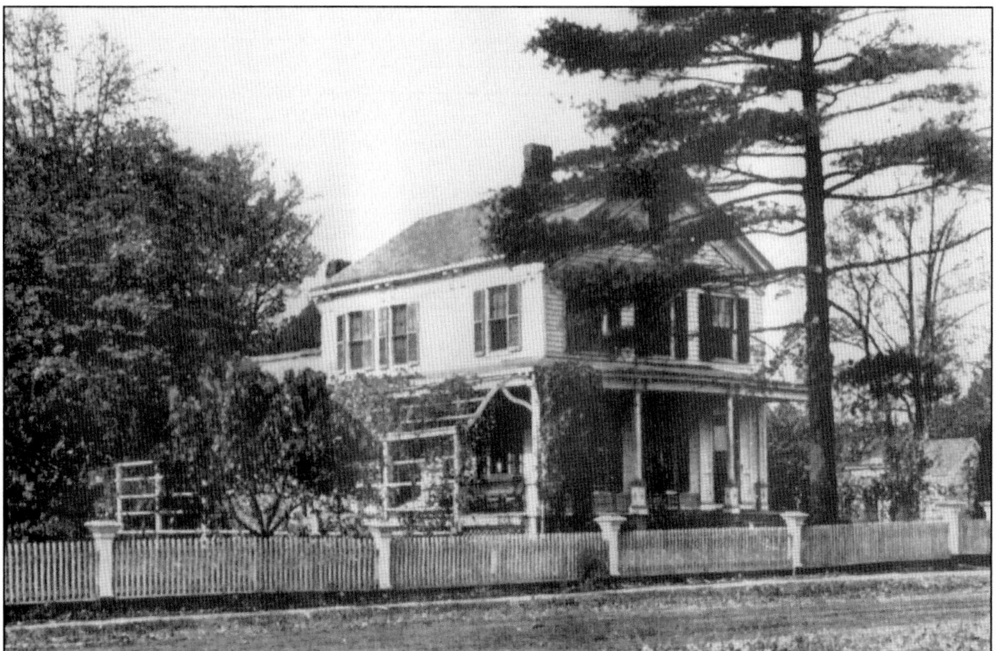

Pictured in this 1911 photograph is one of the oldest homes still standing in Dunellen. Known as the Campbell house at the time of the picture, it was owned by John R. Campbell, a local judge. It is located at the northwest corner of Prospect Avenue and Grove Street.

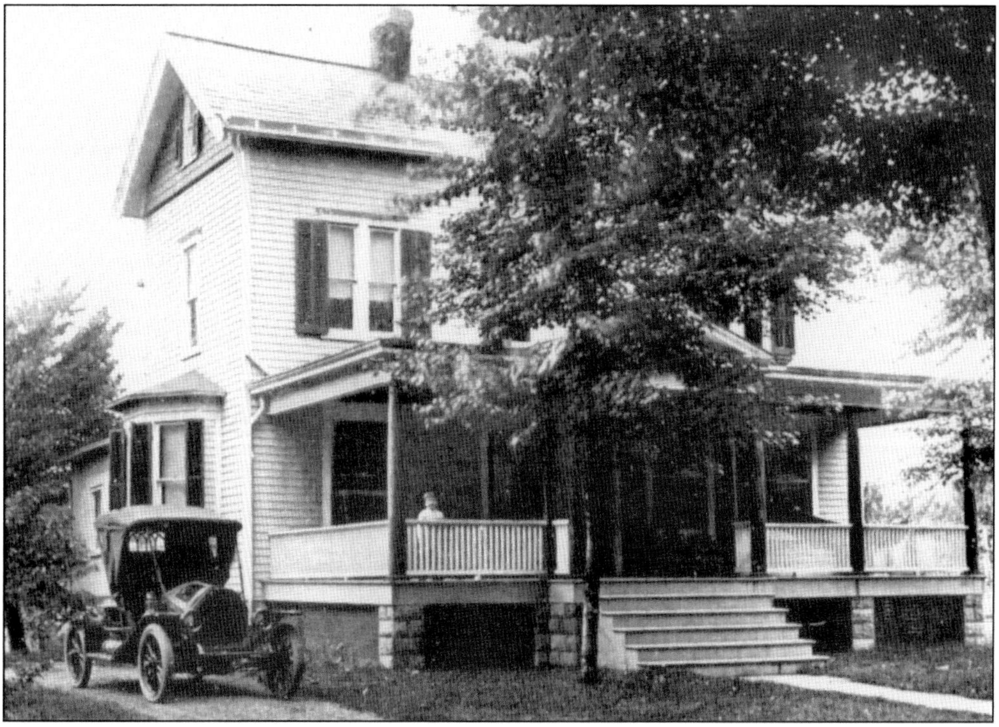

This is a 1910 photograph of Dr. Thomas J. Platt Jr.'s home at 134 Dunellen Avenue. Dr. Platt was one of two doctors in town at that time. He also invested in and was an officer of the Dunellen Pure Ice Manufacturing Company. The plant was located on Grove Street where the property adjoined the Central Railroad tracks.

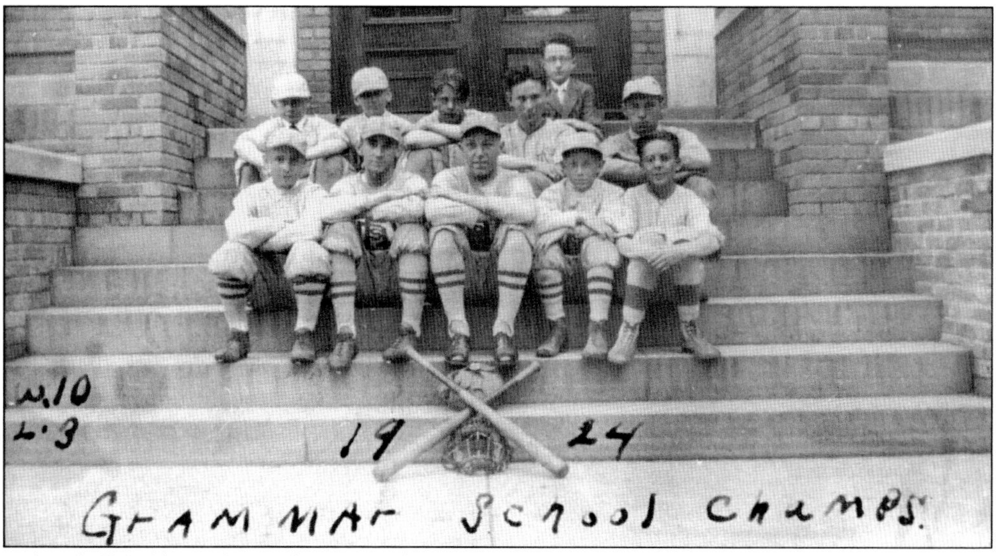


A baseball field was located on Lincoln Avenue in 1894 and was moved to Madison Avenue, complete with grandstands, and used until 1913. Dr. Platt owned property on part of this field and built a house. The field was moved again. In 1920, a sports field was located near the corner of Third Street and Washington Avenue. The 1924 Whittier School team in the picture played on that field.

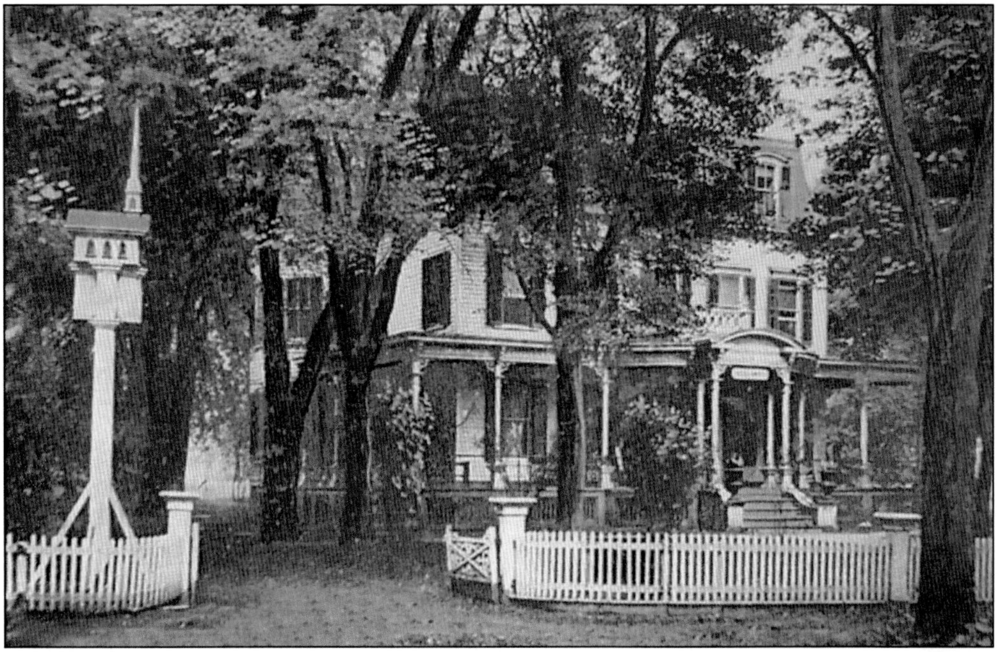

This picture is of the Ellsworth, located at 620 Grove Street, in 1910. It was the residence of Mrs. G. Sumner Smith and was run as a boardinghouse with many recreational activities. She advertised it as, "A Delightful Place to Spend a Summer." In 1930, the Ellsworth featured a miniature golf course, which was all the rage at that time.

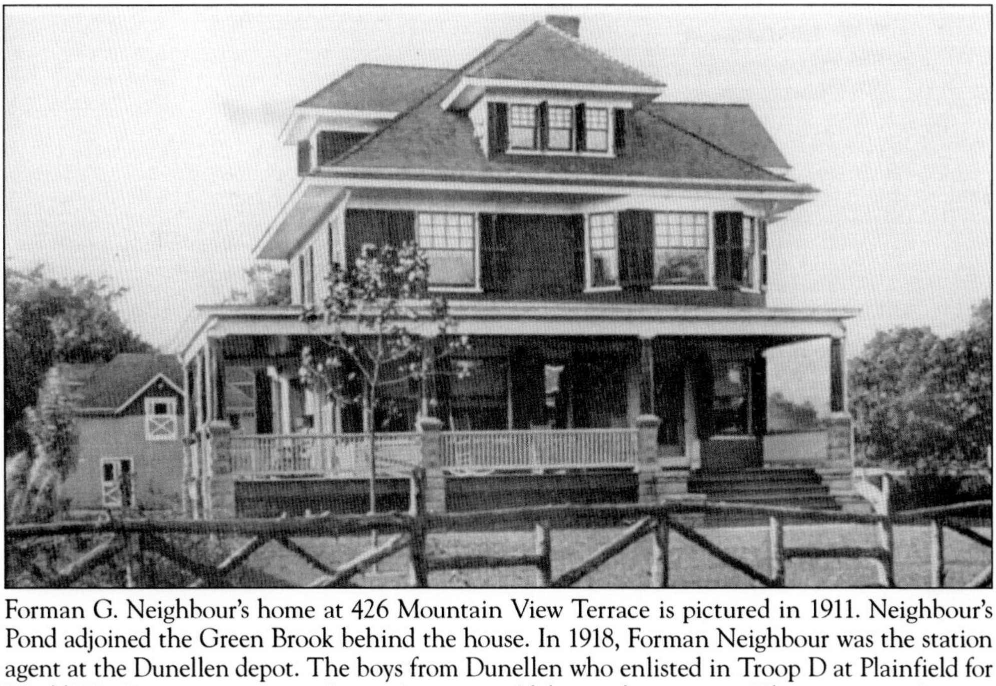

Forman G. Neighbour's home at 426 Mountain View Terrace is pictured in 1911. Neighbour's Pond adjoined the Green Brook behind the house. In 1918, Forman Neighbour was the station agent at the Dunellen depot. The boys from Dunellen who enlisted in Troop D at Plainfield for World War I were en route to Camp Anniston, Alabama, for training. The troop train's route went through Dunellen, and Neighbour alerted the town by sounding the fire bell so that residents could gather at the rails and cheer for the troops.

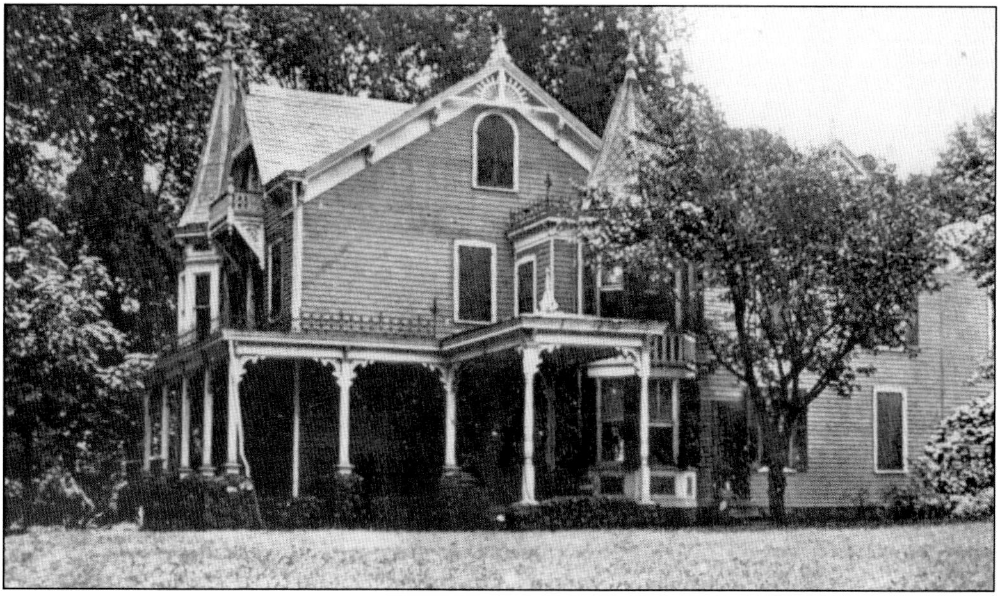

Lewis T. Churchill, a civil engineer, lived in this home at 205 Washington Avenue. In 1913, as the borough engineer, he found 12 acres of lost real estate. It was deeded, wooded land in Dunellen, which bordered Plainfield and Piscataway. Up until that time, everyone assumed it was town property, and it was never taxed. Unfortunately, the Churchill home no longer exists.

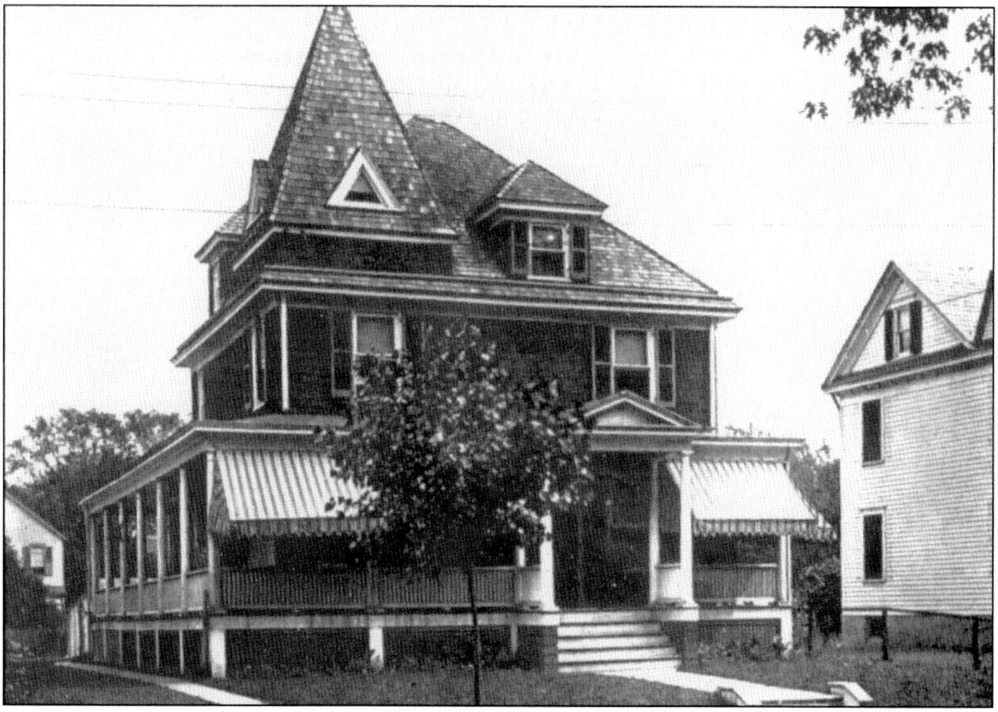

This is the home of Henry S. Garretson at 229 Front Street in 1911. Born in Piscataway in 1856, he farmed until he was 45 years old. In 1897, he partnered with Alvah Gray in the quarry business and later in the Dunellen Lumber and Stone Company and the Dunellen Lumber and Coal Company. His wife was Lily, and his children were Ethel, Russell, and Lillian.

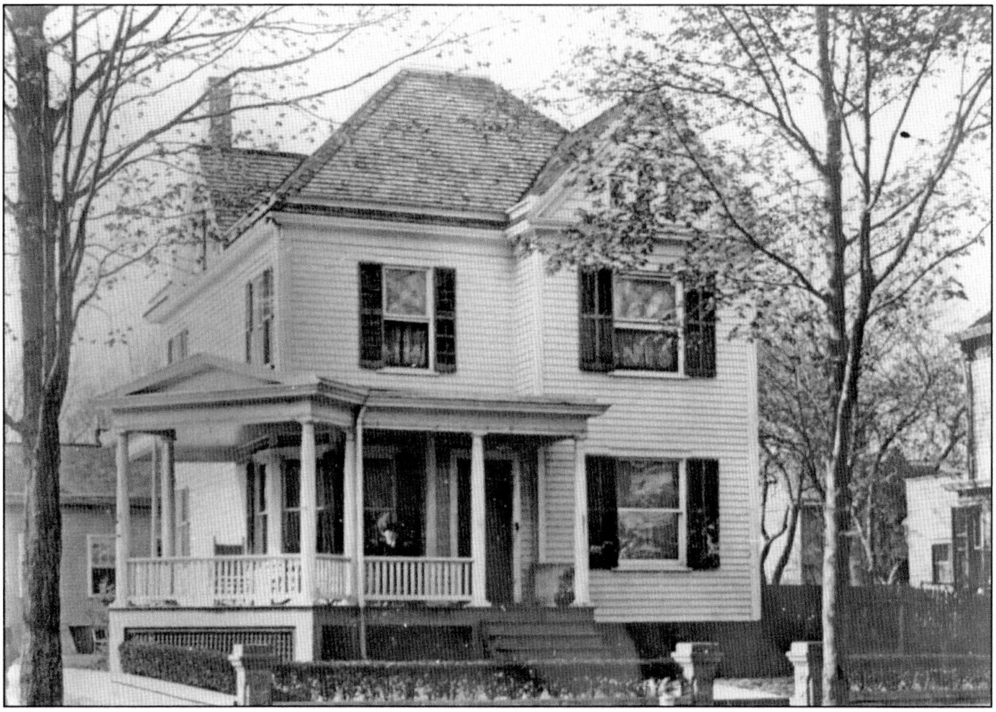

The house above is at 316 Front Street in 1901. George W. Day, his wife, Laura, and son Alfred lived here in 1924. George Day published the *Weekly Call* newspaper from 1892 until 1935. The print shop is visible behind the house.

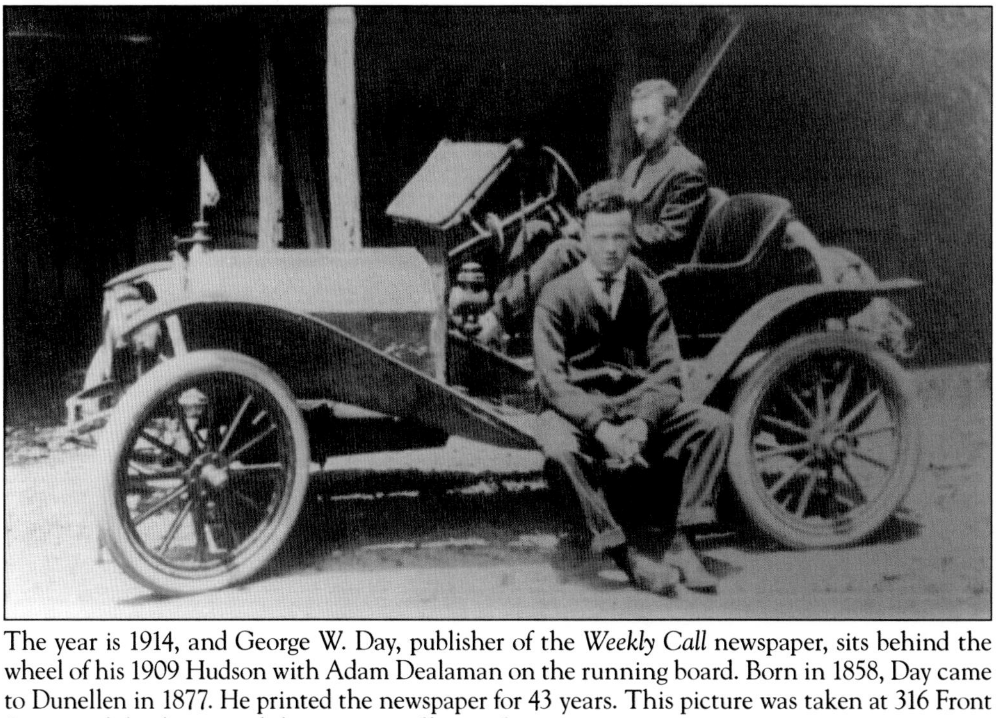

The year is 1914, and George W. Day, publisher of the *Weekly Call* newspaper, sits behind the wheel of his 1909 Hudson with Adam Dealaman on the running board. Born in 1858, Day came to Dunellen in 1877. He printed the newspaper for 43 years. This picture was taken at 316 Front Street with his home and the printing office at the rear.

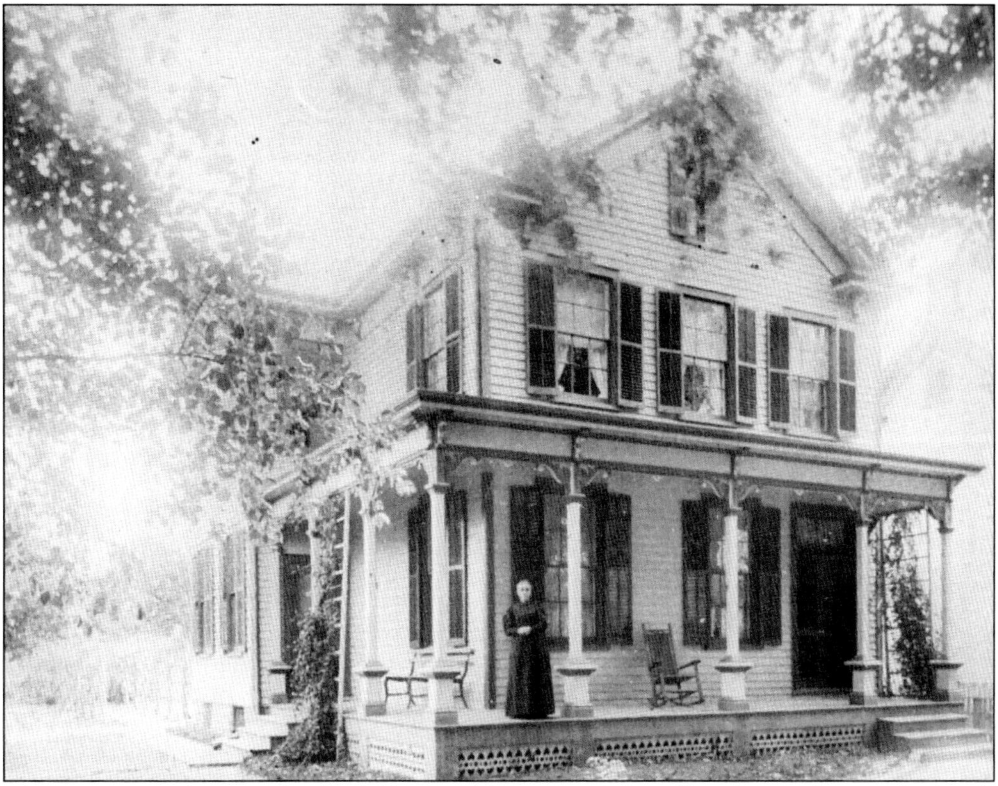

This is an 1890 photograph of Ruliff J. Swackhamer's 227 Dunellen Avenue home, which still exists today. Swackhamer was born in 1826. He worked for the Central Railroad of New Jersey and was superintendent of bridges until 1899. He was one of the first borough commissioners and later became mayor of Dunellen from 1899 until 1903.

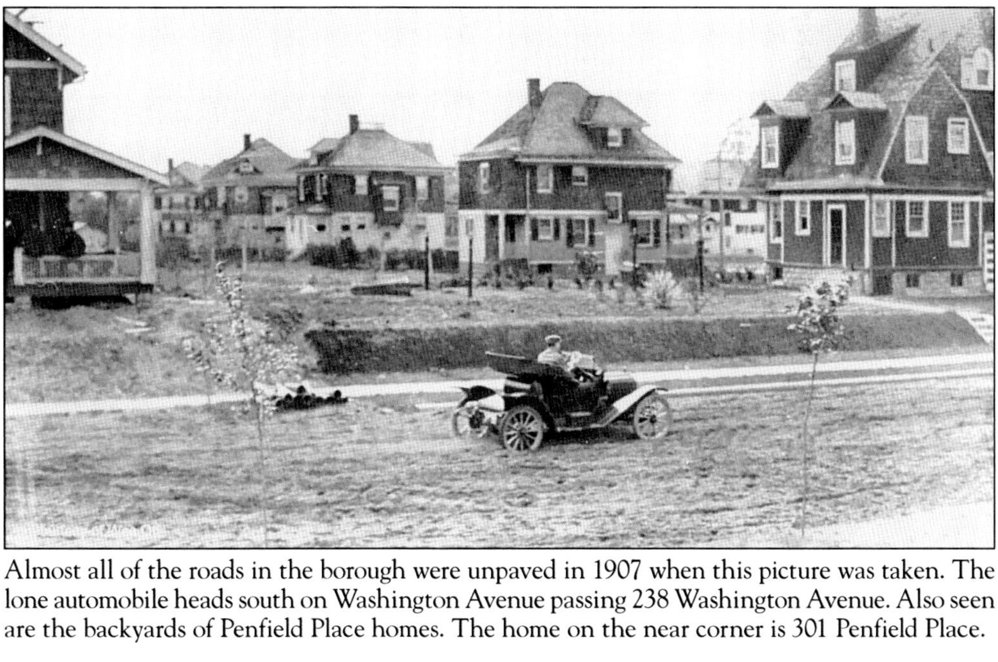

Almost all of the roads in the borough were unpaved in 1907 when this picture was taken. The lone automobile heads south on Washington Avenue passing 238 Washington Avenue. Also seen are the backyards of Penfield Place homes. The home on the near corner is 301 Penfield Place.

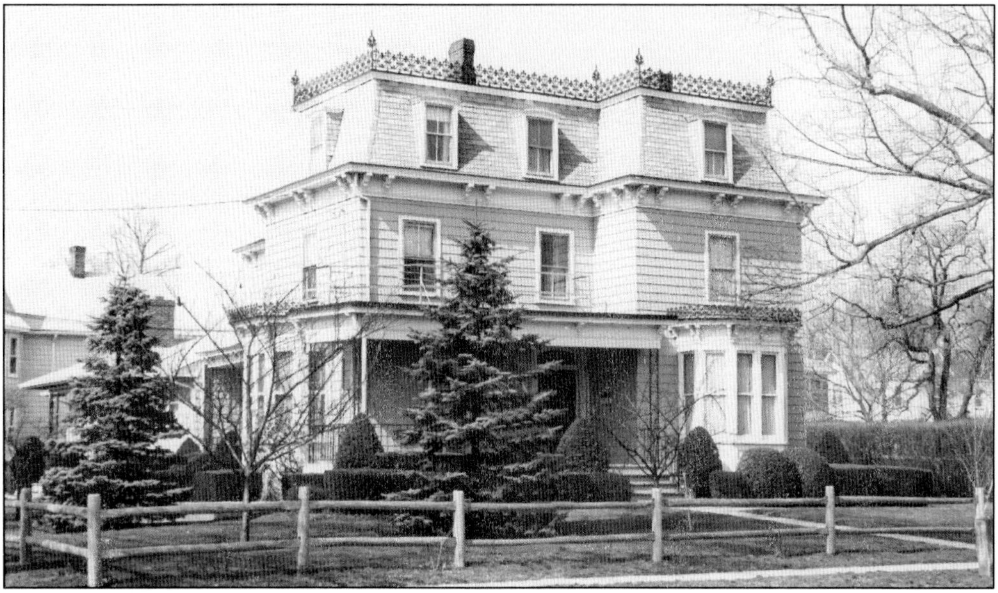

Augustus F. Todd, a stockbroker in New York City, lived in this house with his wife, Anna, and daughters Laura and Meribah. He was the president of the Dunellen Board of Education, a major stockholder in the *Weekly Call*, a councilman in town, and the mayor in 1912. In 1909, he owned the Todd building on the east side of the First National Bank on North Avenue. This house at the corner of Jackson Avenue and Front Street still stands today.

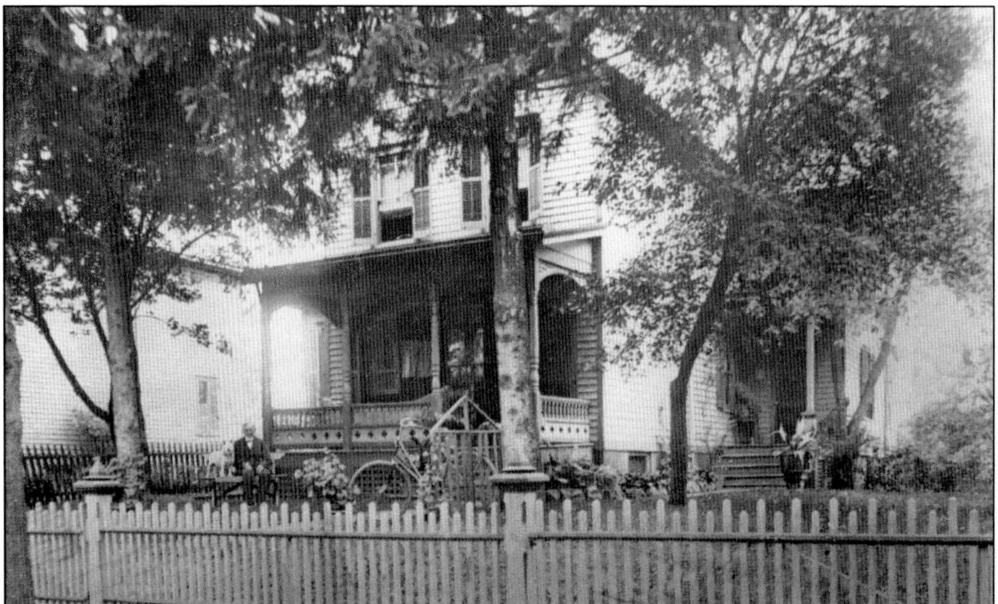

A man and his dog pose for this picture of his home at 440 Front Street in 1910. The house still stands at this address, minus the white picket fence. Of note is the bicycle in the front yard. Bicycling dropped off dramatically in the United States between 1900 and 1910. Automobiles became the preferred means of transportation. Bicycles gradually became considered children's toys, and by 1940, most bicycles were made for children.

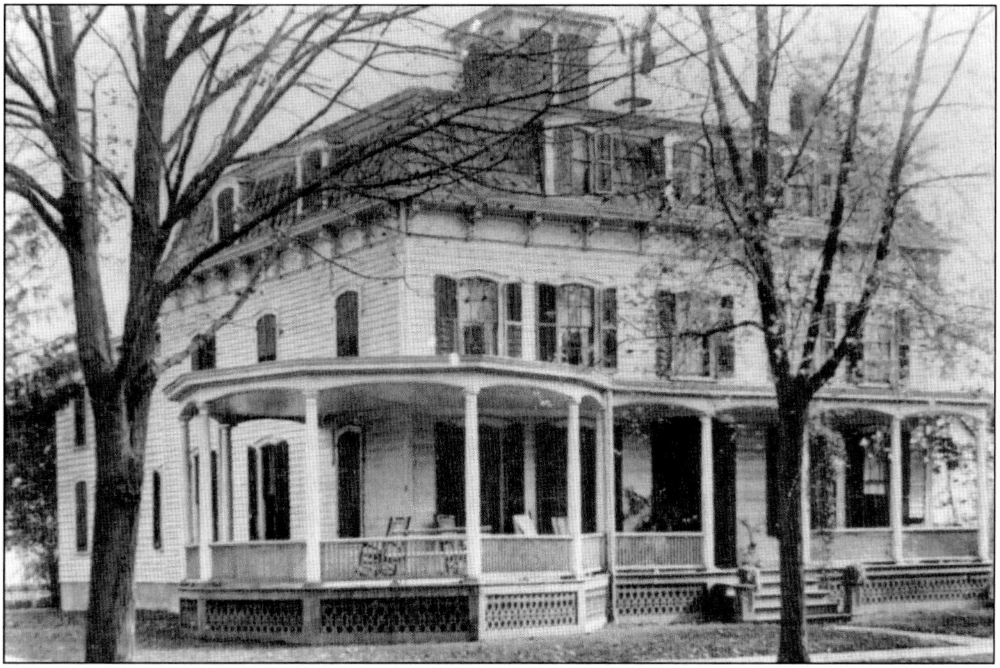

The picture shows the Alvah Gray house at the southeast corner of Washington Avenue and Front Street in 1910. Originally built by W. Richardson in 1869, it became Gray's home in 1884. Gray operated quarry, coal, and lumber businesses for many years. He was one of the organizers of the First National Bank of Dunellen in 1907 and was its president for 11 years. The renovated building is now the Dunellen Hotel.

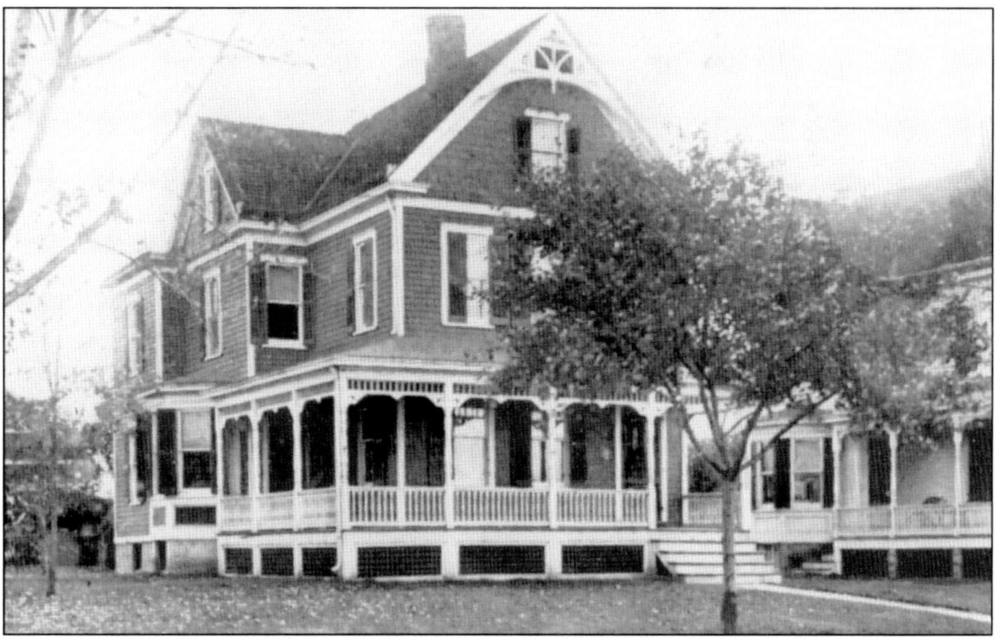

The 1911 home of the Apgar brothers at 248 Dunellen Avenue is shown here. Corvin Apgar was a clerk, and his brother Melancthon was an engineer for the Central Railroad of New Jersey. The much-altered house still stands at this address today.

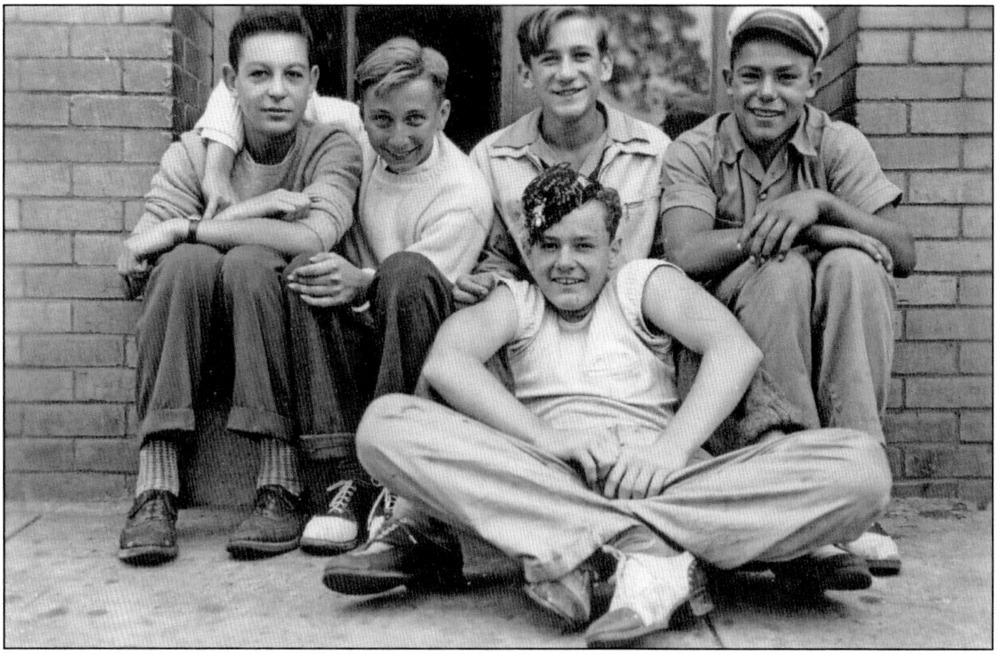

Here is a picture of Dunellen's answer to *Our Gang*. In this c. 1939 picture taken in front of 704 Bound Brook Road are, from left to right, (seated on sidewalk) "Bunny" Eelman; (second row) Robert "Sonny" Salvin, Francis "Franny" Setnicky, Edward "Shrimpy" Horvath, and Anthony "Tony" DeBiase. (Courtesy of Robert Salvin.)

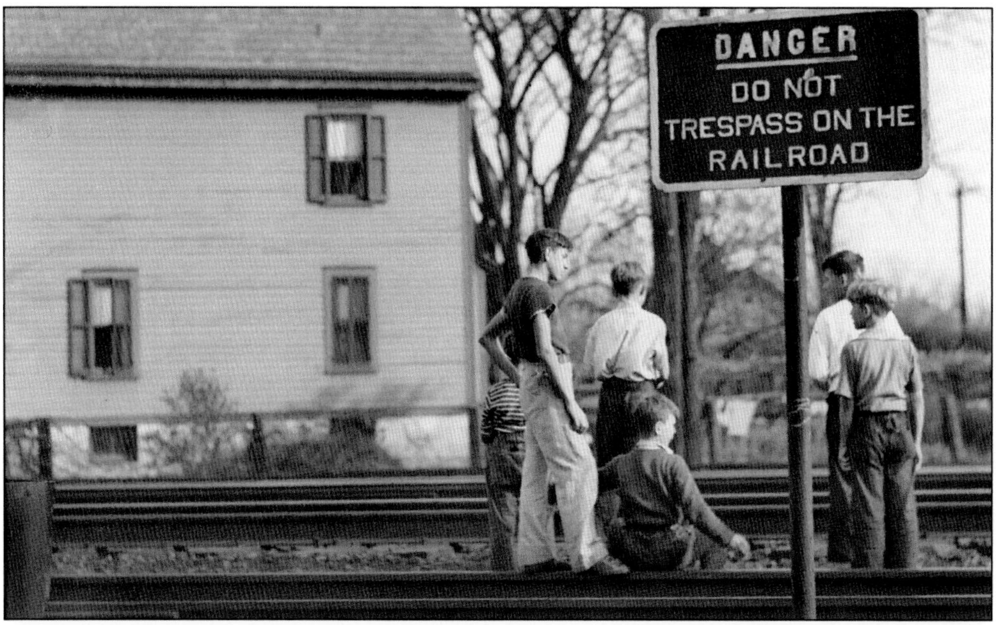


The expression, "A picture is worth a thousand words," is depicted in this 1939 photograph. During the years, over 50 trains came through Dunellen daily. The tracks were a very dangerous place to be, but sometimes children have no sense of danger. "Boys will be boys." Edward "Shrimpy" Horvath is the tall boy at the extreme left. The other boys are unidentified. (Courtesy of Schuyler family collection.)

Dunellen postman Henry Rankin is shown picking up letters from the mailbox at the southeast corner of Madison Avenue and Mountain View Terrace. Rankin's four-legged "helper" is unidentified, but the dog always waited for his friend. The picture is dated January 16, 1940. (Courtesy of Schuyler family collection.)

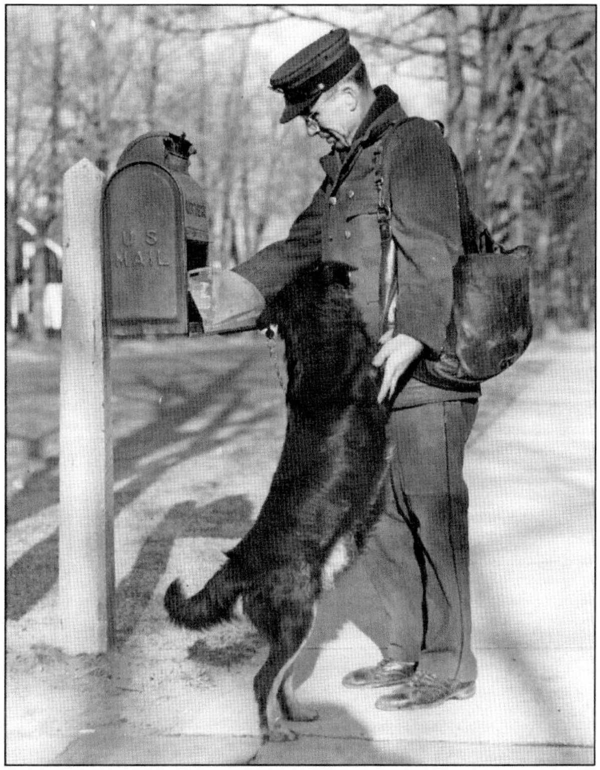


This picture of the great American love affair—a man and his car—was taken in 1950, and the Dunellen man is unidentified. (Courtesy of Schuyler family collection.)

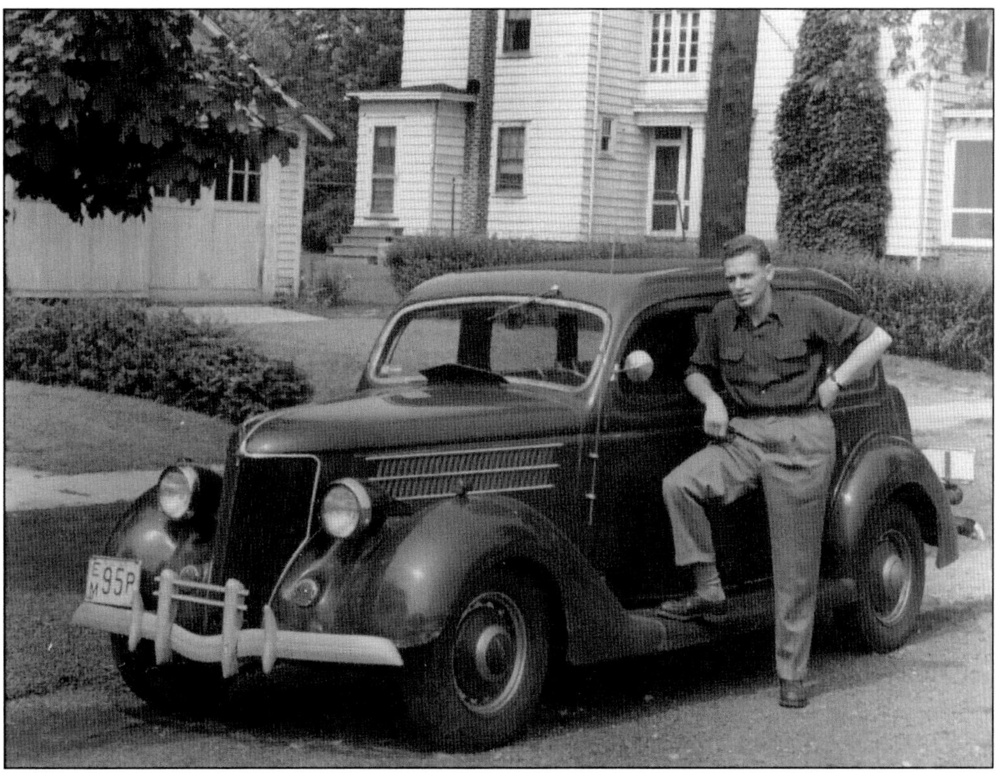

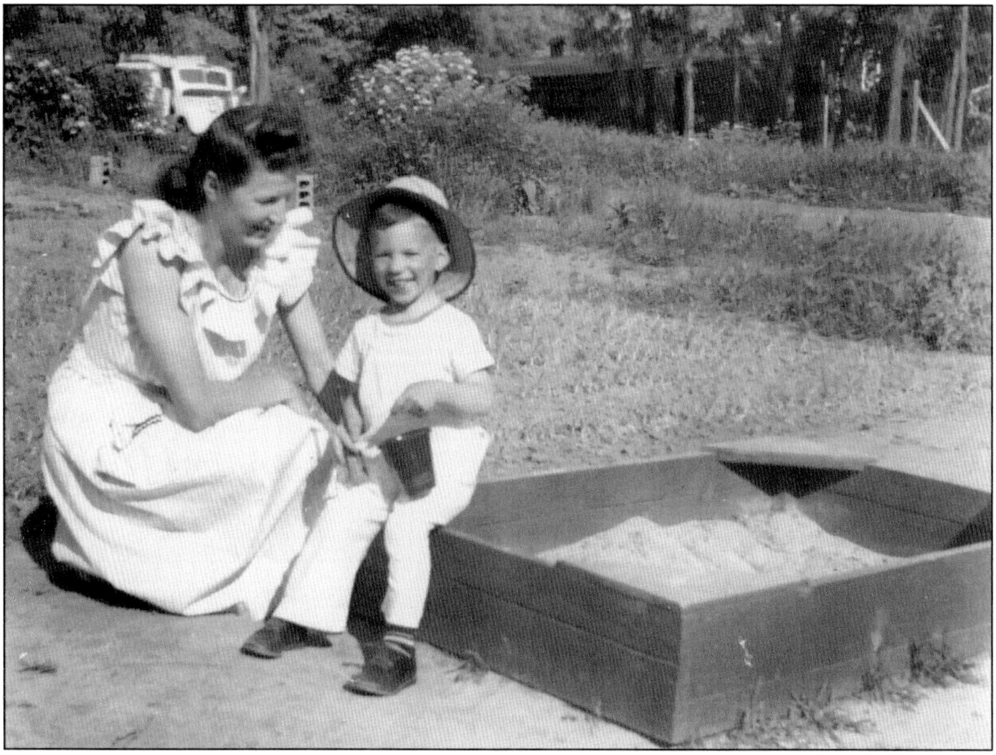

In this 1949 photograph, Anne Triolo and her son John are pictured in the backyard of 545 Fourth Street. This property abutted Third Street, and it was almost entirely woods from Sanford Avenue to the west end of the street. To the left, a Good Humor truck approaches. At the right in the background, a chicken coop the size of a small house is seen. (Courtesy of John Triolo.)

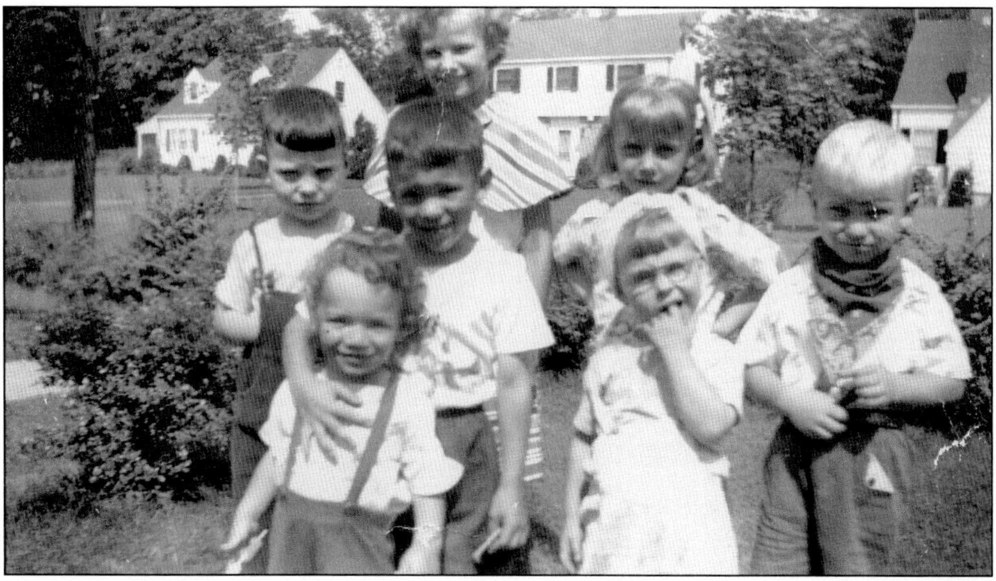

On the front lawn of 545 Fourth Street is this group of baby boomers in 1952. From left to right are (first row) Eddy Triolo, John Triolo, and Elaine Wisnewski; (second row) Tom Wisnewski, Joan Pelchar, Sue Nelson, and Don "Bunny" Nelson. (Courtesy of John Triolo.)

*Five*

# Churches and Organizations

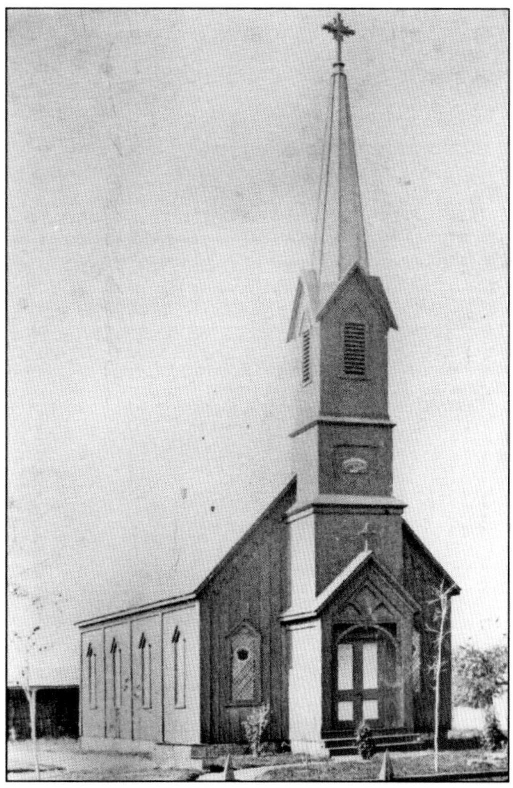

St. Francis Episcopal Church has been located at 400 New Market Road since 1872 when it was purchased from the United Methodist Church. The Episcopal Church of the Holy Innocents was originally formed from their Piscataway parish. In 1870, they held their services in the Methodist church and then purchased it two years later. The building was the oldest church in Dunellen, constructed in 1866. In 1980, Holy Innocents and St. Andrews of Plainfield joined to form St. Francis Episcopal Church. (Courtesy of John Triolo.)

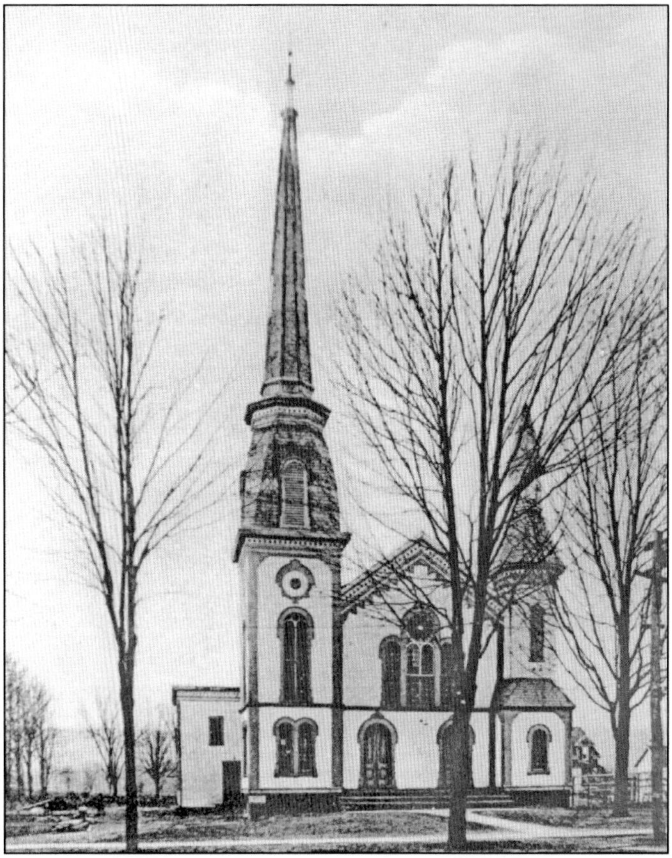

The cornerstone for the First Presbyterian Church of Dunellen was laid May 15, 1871, and the church was dedicated January 26, 1872. The land had been donated by the New Jersey Land Improvement Company. While the church was being completed, the services were held in the railroad station. This picture shows the church with its original steeple in 1909.

Here is a picture of the First Presbyterian Church without its original steeple around 1923. Because of structural weakness, the tall, original steeple of the west tower was removed by a steeplejack from Newark in 1922. The first parsonage was at 340 Dunellen Avenue. The Sunday school was added in 1892 and another addition in 1922.

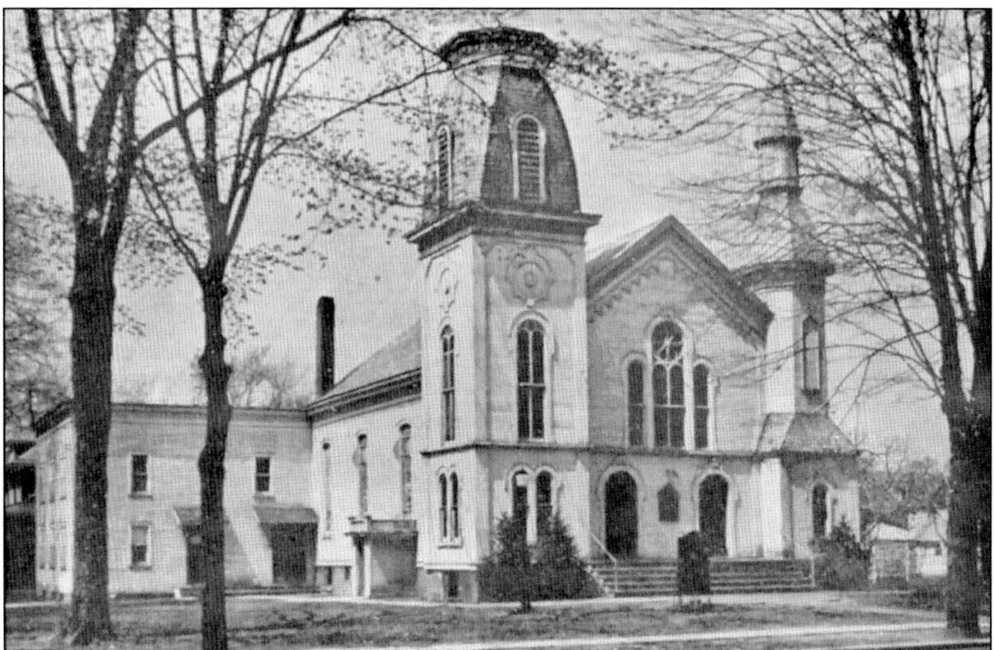

The United Methodist Church had its beginning in the 1850s in the old Academy Building on Center Street in New Market. The Academy Building hosted the Methodist Episcopal Church since its formation in 1866. The Methodist congregation's church building, the first in Dunellen, was at 400 New Market Road. While plans were made for their new church on the corner of Jackson and Dunellen Avenues, services were held in a hall across from Depot Park. (Courtesy of John Triolo.)

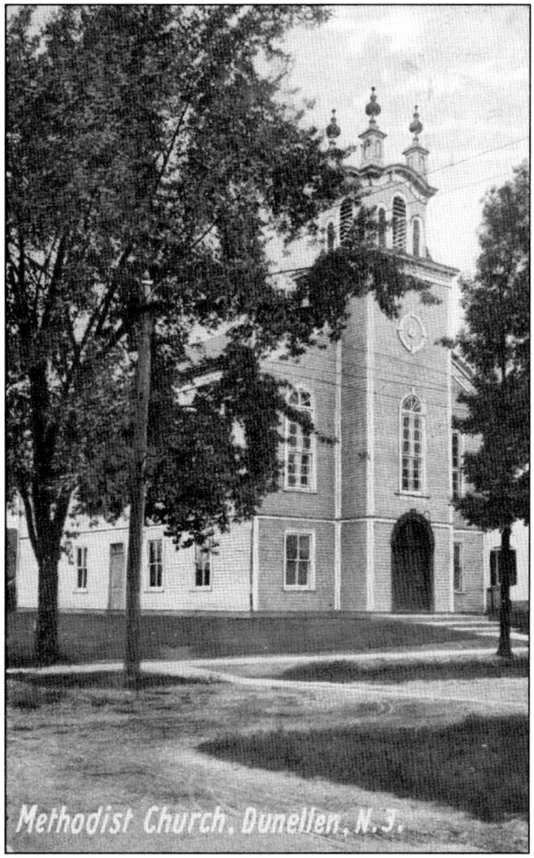


The new United Methodist Church was completed in 1876. The religious education building behind the church was dedicated on January 31, 1932. The property the education building occupies consisted of six lots that were donated in 1925 by the children of Mr. and Mrs. Jacob Fisher in memory of their parents.

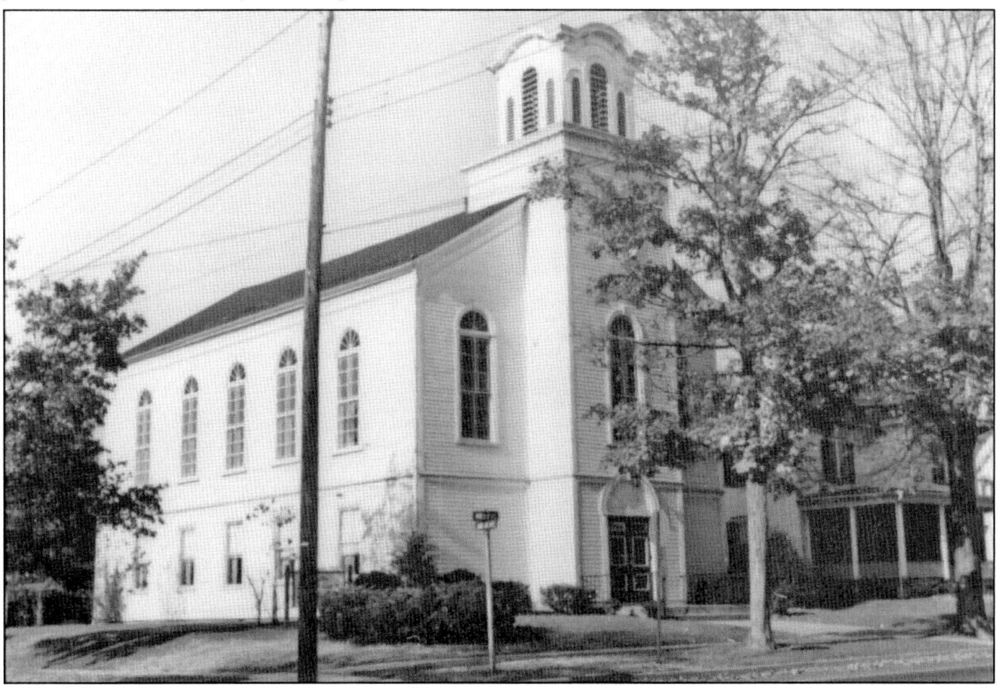

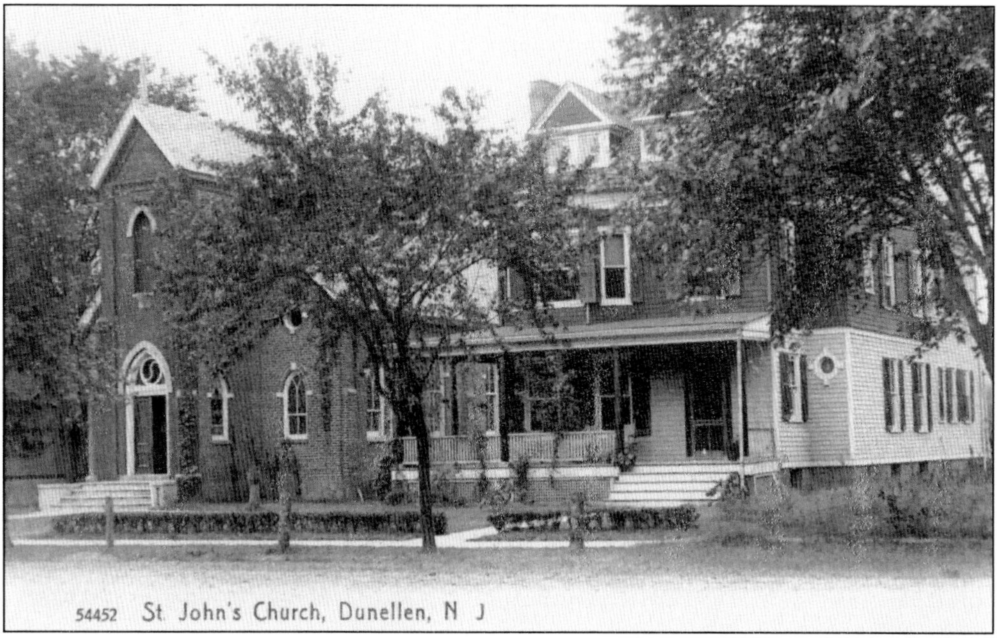


St. John's Catholic Church was dedicated on October 24, 1880. Prior to that, Catholics from Dunellen attended St. Mary's Church in Plainfield. William Moore of Plainfield donated a large lot on Washington Avenue near First Street for the church and a small rectory. In 1910, improvements were completed and a handsome new altar of regalico stone was installed. A nine-room rectory was built next to the church in 1903, shown in this picture. (Courtesy of John Triolo.)

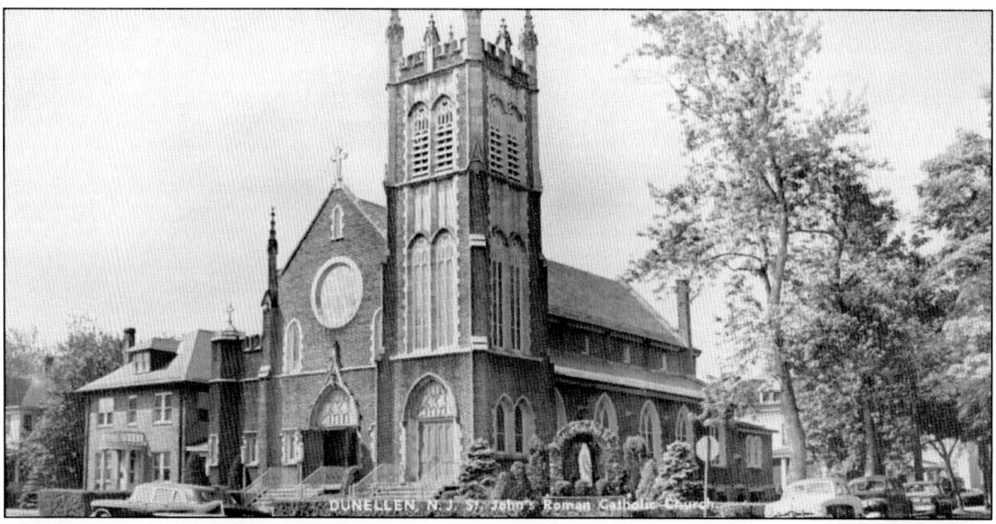


The rectory was moved to a new location on First Street to make room for this new, Early English Gothic–style brick church that was dedicated on November 30, 1916. The basement auditorium was excavated by hand by the men of the congregation. The 12-room brick rectory was added, and the old rectory on First Street was used as a convent for the Sisters of St. Francis in 1924. (Courtesy of Patricia Leuschner.)

St. Nicholas Byzantine Catholic Church is located at 119 Madison Avenue. The church building was completed in 1927. In the early 1930s, the onion-shaped dome was installed on the church, and a bell for the tower was donated by R. Hoe & Company. Metro Sedon and Theodore Grapp were instrumental in the completion of the dome and bell.

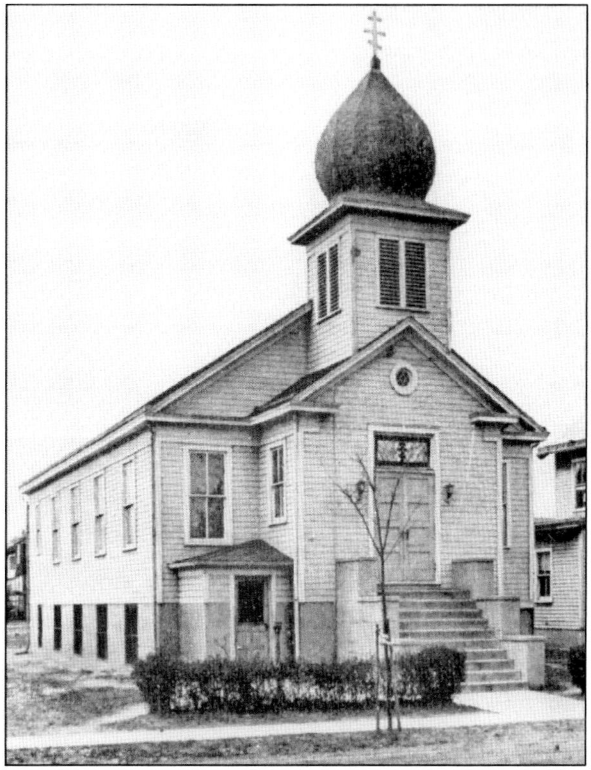

Pictured here is St. Luke's Lutheran Church on New Market Road and Walnut Street. In 1927, St. Peter's Lutheran Church of North Plainfield had a Sunday school for children of Dunellen at the Patriotic Hall on North Washington Avenue. In 1929, the Dunellen congregation was formed, and in 1947, its permanent home was established on New Market Road. The parsonage was on Mountain View Terrace in the early 1950s.

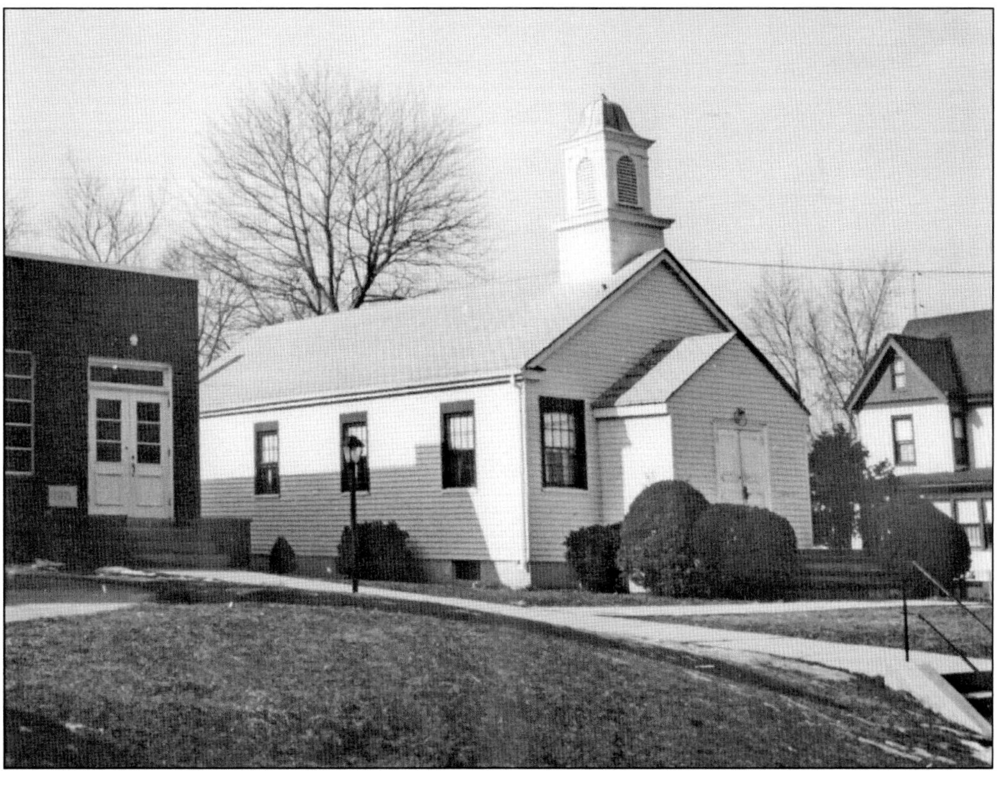

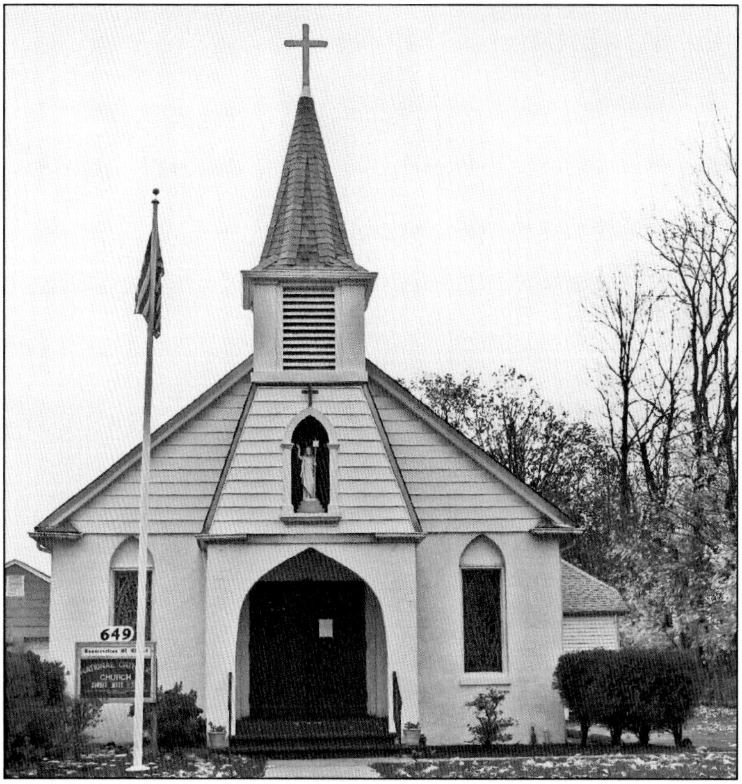


The Resurrection of Christ National Catholic Church at 649 Bound Brook Road is pictured here. The church was organized as an independent parish in 1939. In January 1953, it joined the Polish National Catholic Church of America. In 1954, the building was renovated. The property is held by the parish, and the people have a voice in the general administration of the church. A parish hall is located behind the church building. (Courtesy of Liz Marren-Licht.)

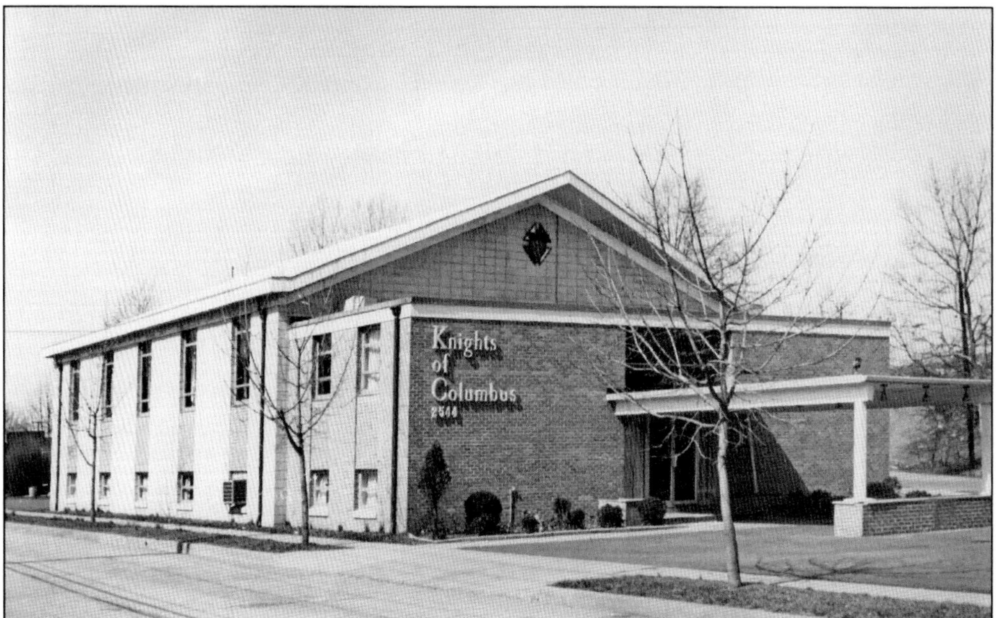


The Knights of Columbus is located at the corner of South Avenue and Grove Street. They were nationally founded in New Haven, Connecticut, in 1882. The Knights were formed to render financial aid to sick, disabled, and needy members and their families. Dunellen's Council No. 2544 was formed in 1924. The current building was dedicated May 31, 1966.

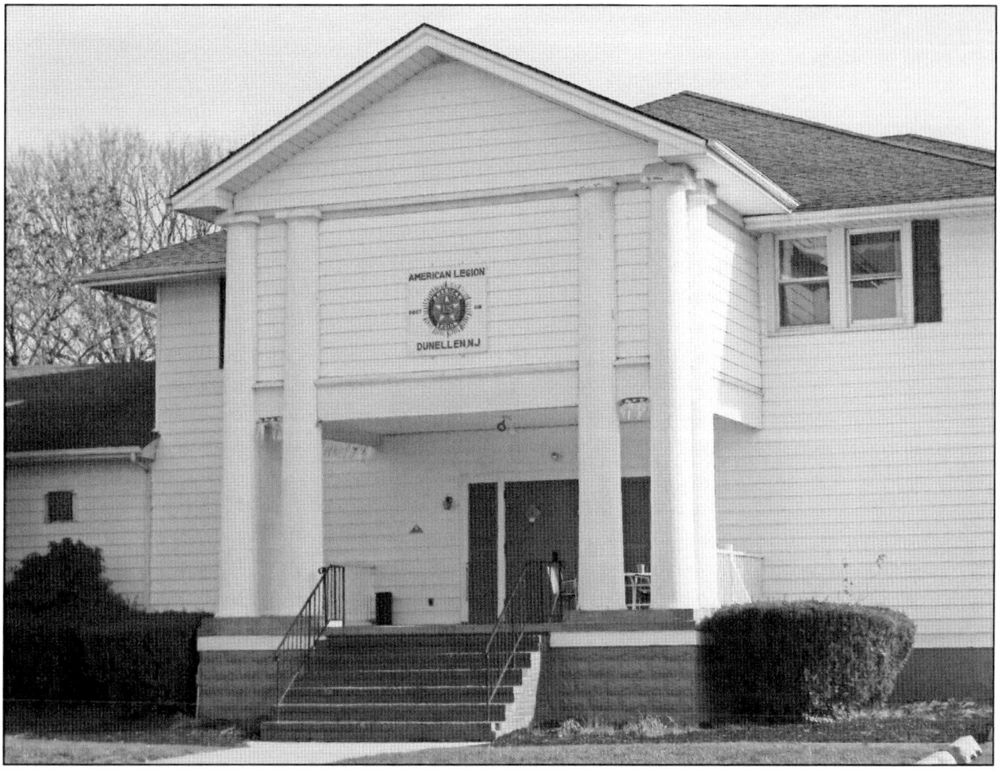


American Legion Post No. 119 is located at the corner of New Market Road and Orange Street. It was formed in September 1919, and fundraising to build the present hall continued; its dedication was on Washington's Birthday, February 22, 1923. (Courtesy of John Triolo.)

After World War I, the US government made available to New Jersey Legion Posts cannon and other war trophies captured from Germany. Distribution of these items had to be secured by proper application. In 1925, Dunellen was awarded a seven-ton Krupp cannon. This cannon was on display until it was returned to the government during World War II to aid in the war effort.

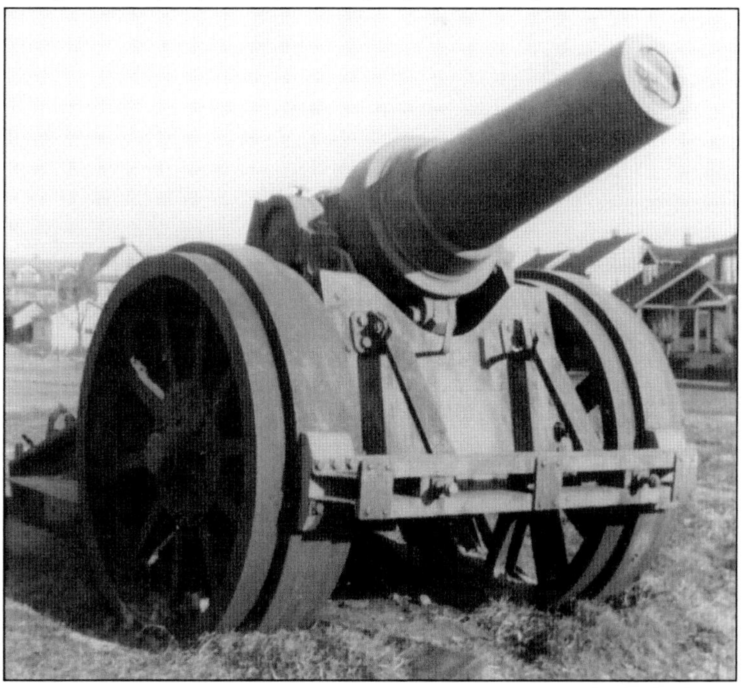

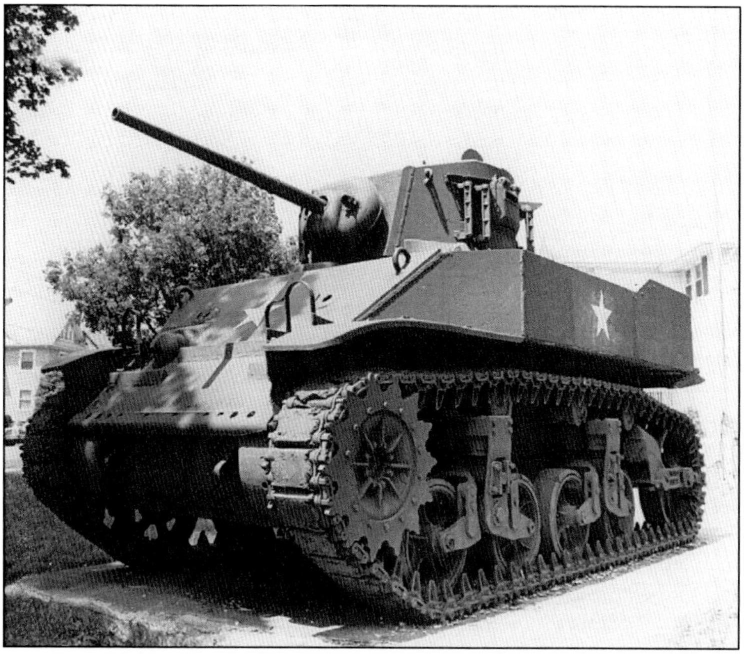

This Stuart M5-A1 light tank was given to Dunellen Post No. 119 after World War II to replace the cannon that was donated to the war efforts. Every year on Memorial Day, refreshments served to all parade-goers are alternately hosted by the American Legion and the Veterans of Foreign Wars (VFW). At the American Legion in the 1950s, the hatches on the tank were opened so boys and girls could crawl inside the tank.

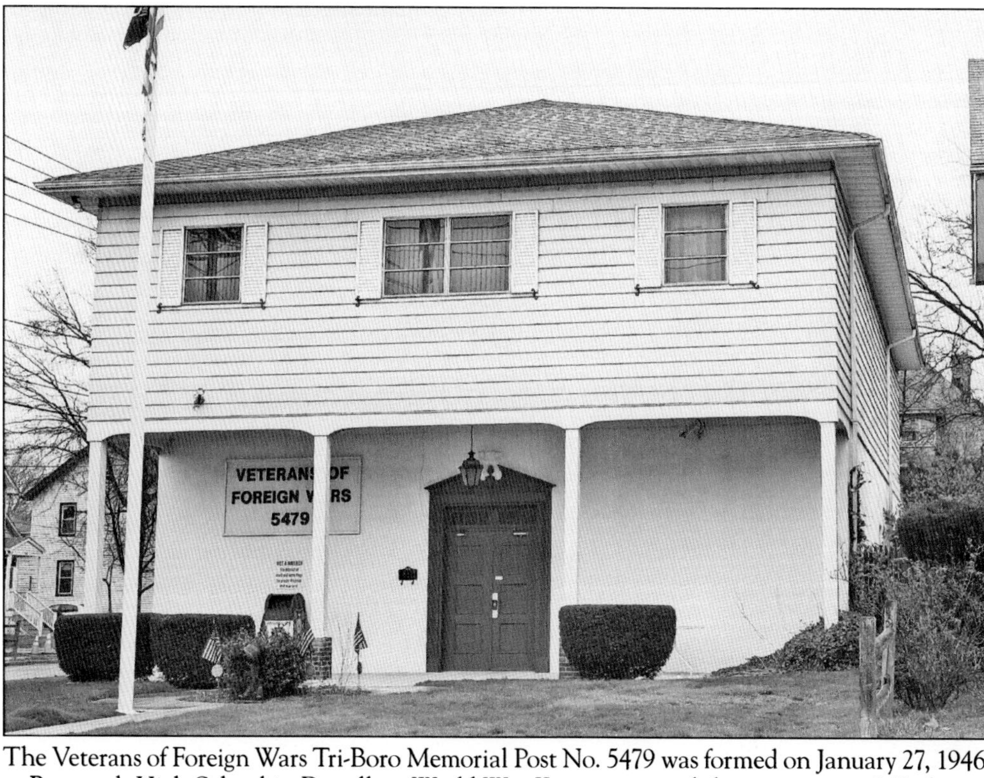


The Veterans of Foreign Wars Tri-Boro Memorial Post No. 5479 was formed on January 27, 1946, at Roosevelt High School in Dunellen. World War II was over, and there were over 250 charter members. The post members met at various temporary locations until a small building was erected on the southeast corner of Grove Street and Prospect Avenue in 1952. A few years later, the building was enlarged, and a second story was added. (Courtesy of Liz Marren-Licht.)

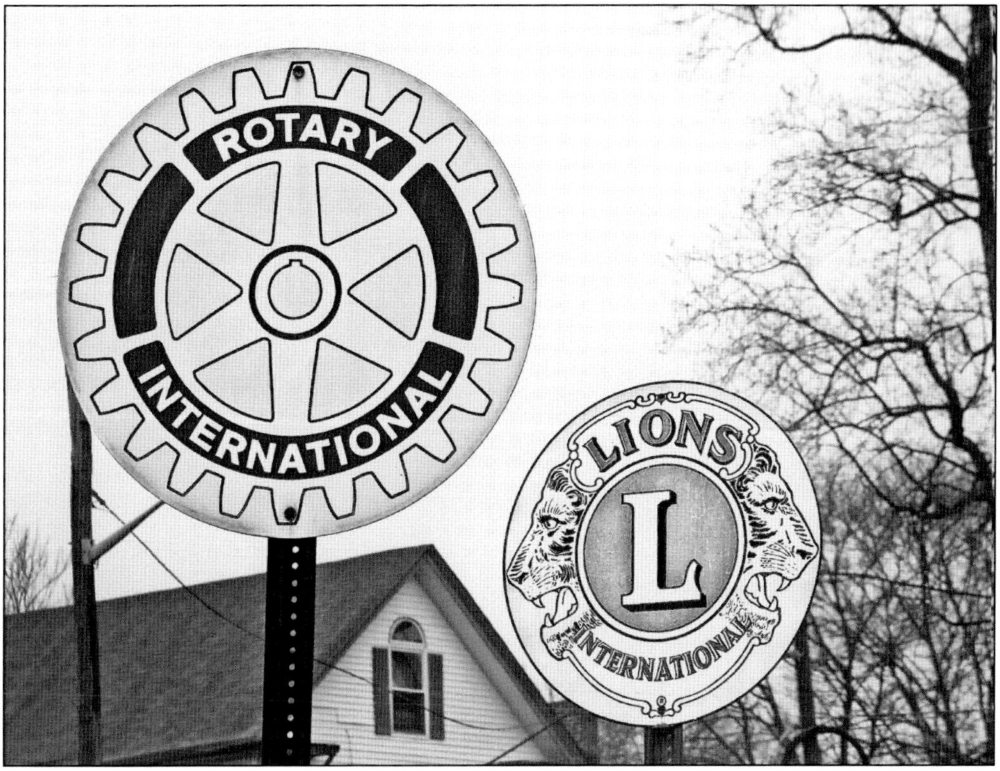


The Dunellen Rotary Club was chartered in 1924. Their motto, "Service Above Self," had contributed to hundreds of community projects. The Lions Club was chartered in Dunellen in 1936 with 26 members, including residents from both Dunellen and Green Brook. The Lions is a service organization for sight conservation and other community projects. (Courtesy of Liz Marren-Licht.)

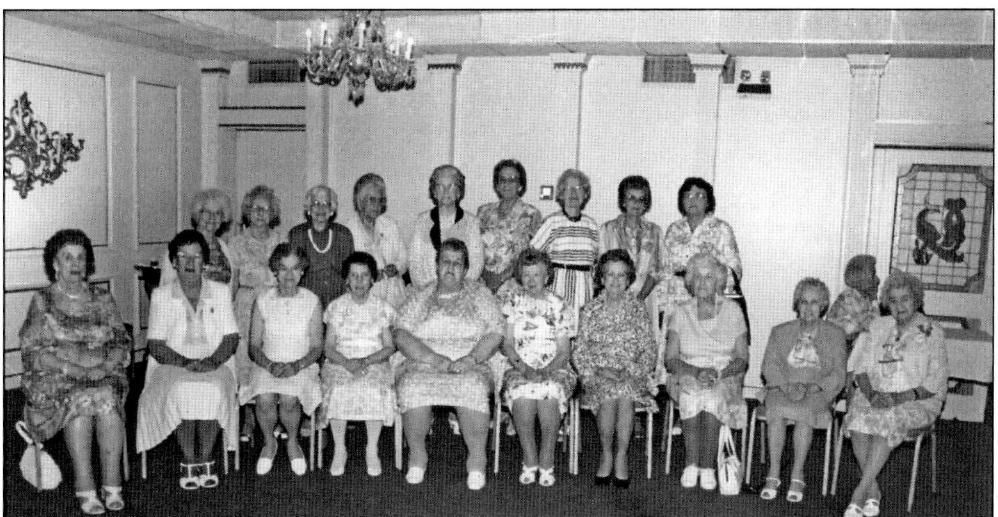

The ladies of the New Market–Dunellen Women's Club are pictured in 1989. The club was originally a Red Cross unit during World War I. It became a unit of the New Jersey State Federation of Women's Clubs in November 1919.

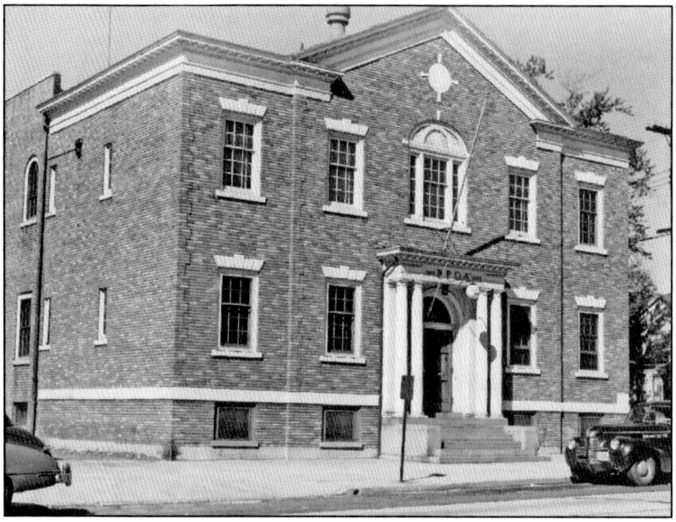

This is the Elks Lodge No. 1488 on the southeast corner of Washington Avenue and Front Street in 1949. The cornerstone for this building was laid on December 4, 1926, and dedicated on October 27, 1927. At that time, there were 238 members in this Elks Lodge. The Benevolent and Protective Order of Elks of the United States of America (BPOE) was established in 1868. (Courtesy of Schuyler family collection.)

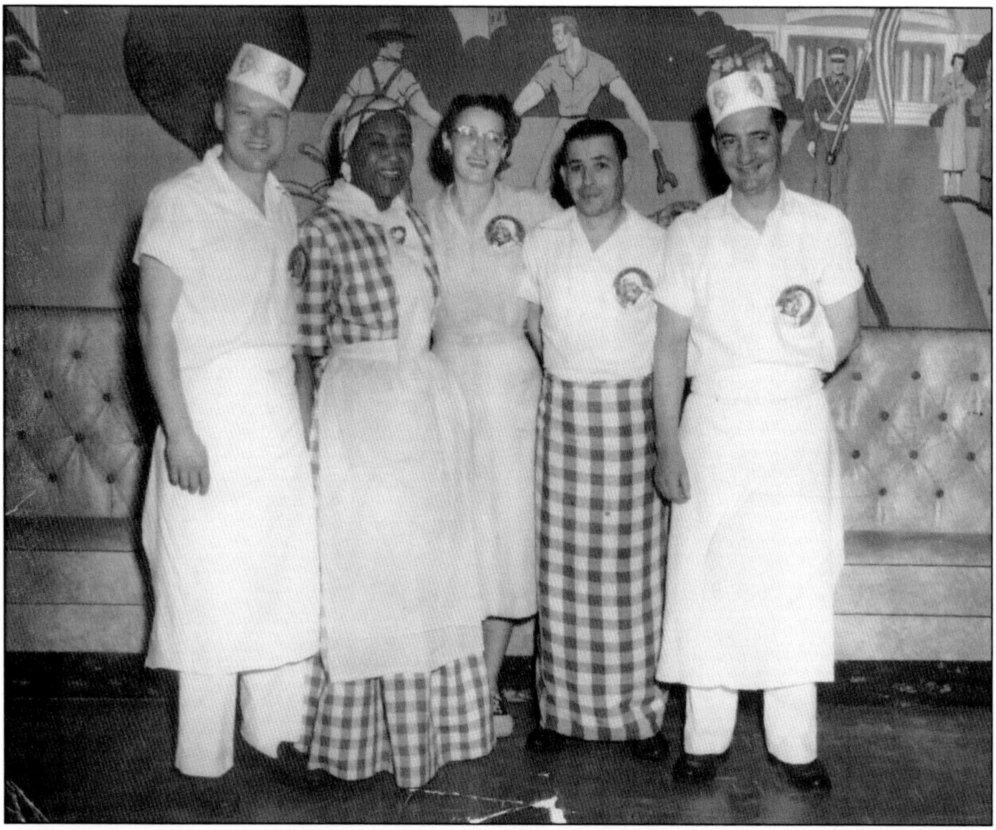

This picture was taken on February 6, 1955, at an Elks pancake breakfast to benefit their Crippled Children Fund. From left to right are Lee Doushal, Aunt Jemima, Mary Eskesen, and Julie and Moe Yengst. The Elks are well known for their interest in disabled children and commitment to veterans. They have supplied many worthy causes with money for medical help, equipment, and surgery. (Courtesy of Ron Eskesen.)

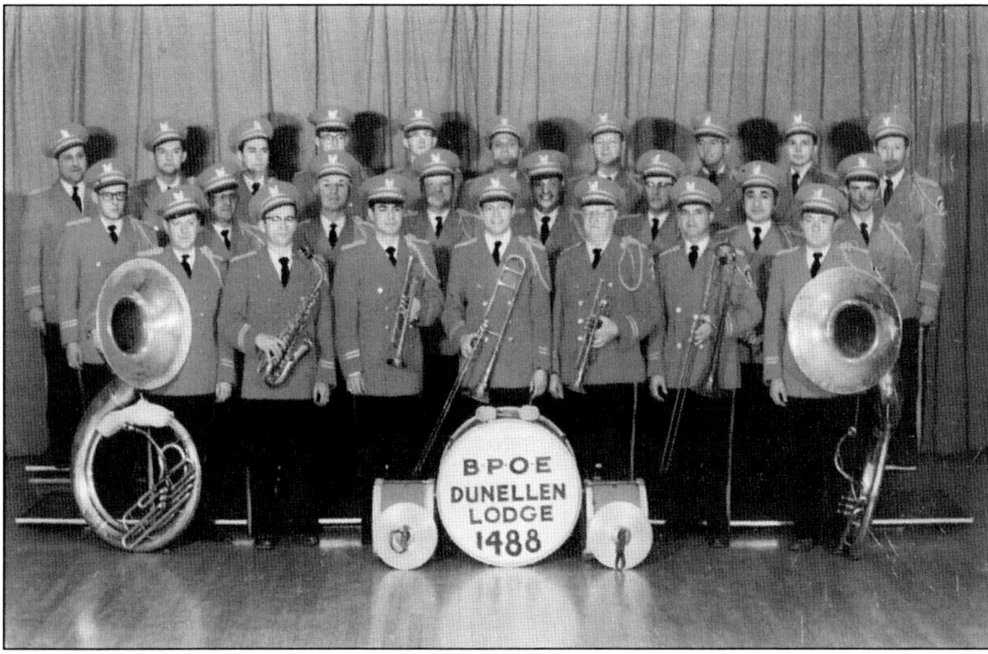


This is the Dunellen Elks Band c. 1955. In times past, almost every club and organization had a marching band. A few years ago, because of lack of membership and rising expenses, the Dunellen Elks sold their beautiful Elks Lodge and merged with the Middlesex Borough charter. (Courtesy of John Triolo.)

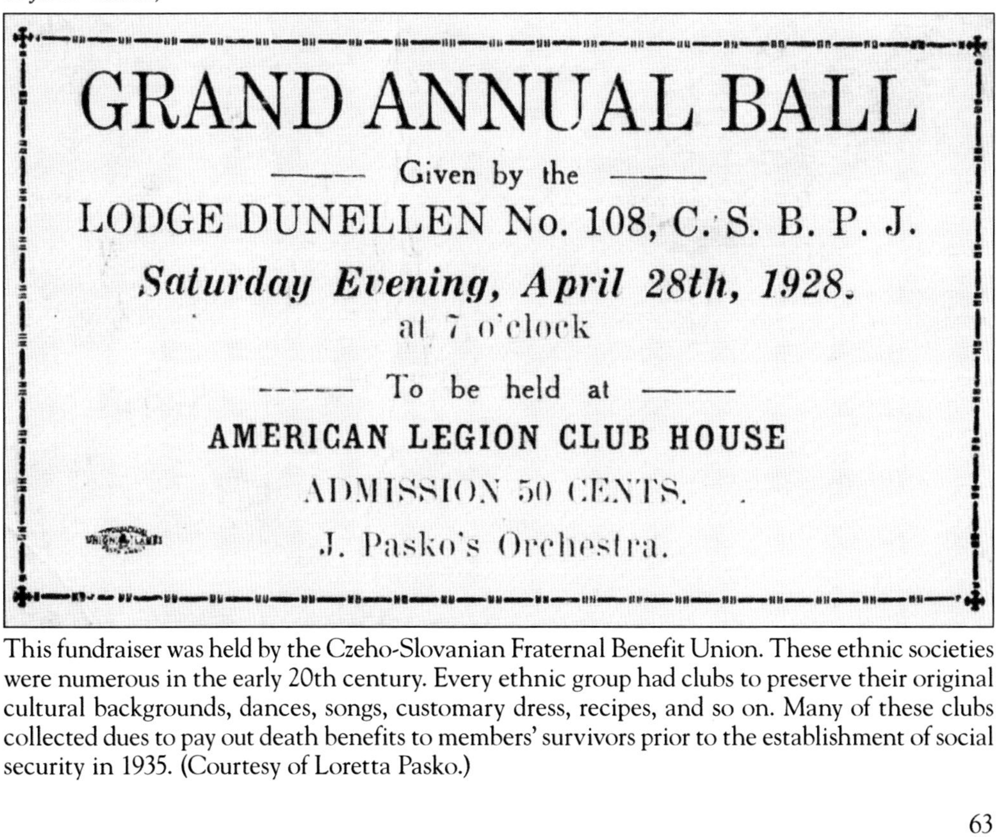

GRAND ANNUAL BALL

Given by the

LODGE DUNELLEN No. 108, C. S. B. P. J.

*Saturday Evening, April 28th, 1928.*

at 7 o'clock

To be held at

AMERICAN LEGION CLUB HOUSE

ADMISSION 50 CENTS.

J. Pasko's Orchestra.

This fundraiser was held by the Czeho-Slovanian Fraternal Benefit Union. These ethnic societies were numerous in the early 20th century. Every ethnic group had clubs to preserve their original cultural backgrounds, dances, songs, customary dress, recipes, and so on. Many of these clubs collected dues to pay out death benefits to members' survivors prior to the establishment of social security in 1935. (Courtesy of Loretta Pasko.)

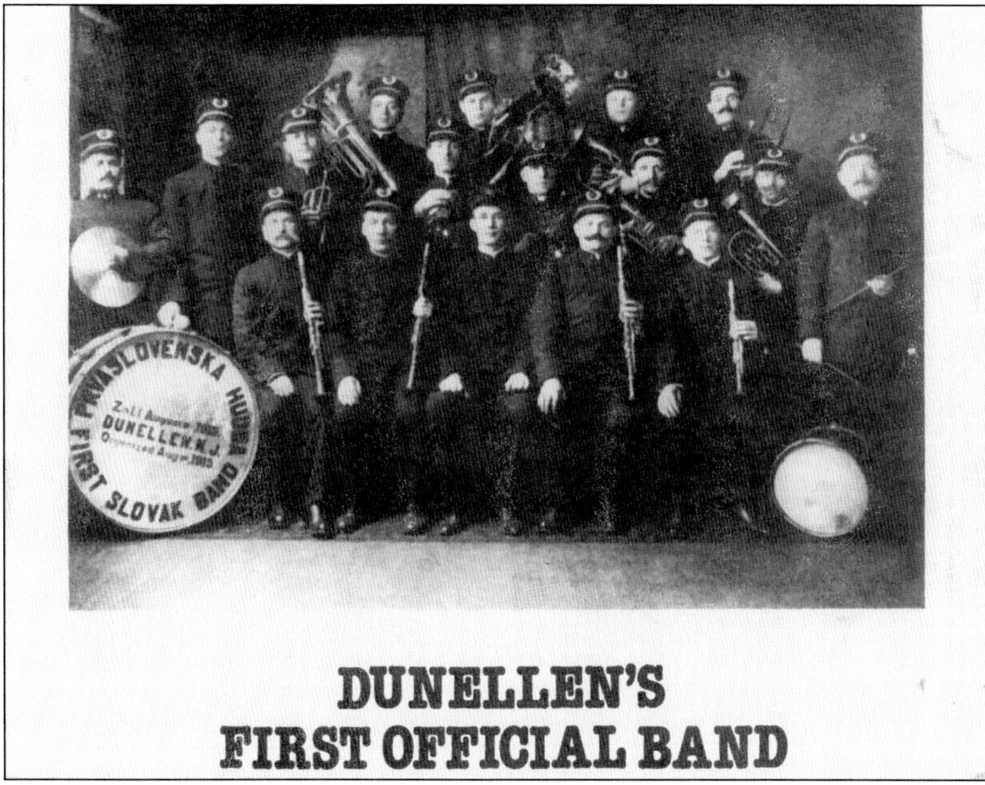


Dunellen's first official band was the First Slovak Bank, organized by Joseph Pasko in August 1915. From left to right are (first row, seated) unidentified, Paul Sadlow, Joseph Pasko (the leader and founder), unidentified, and Steve Heldt; (second row) unidentified, Tom Lenner, Frank Pasek, Henry Gazi, Libor Gazi, Steve Danek, Tony Hoffman, and unidentified; (third row) Steve Stribrany, Ben Blazo, Joseph Samek, and unidentified.

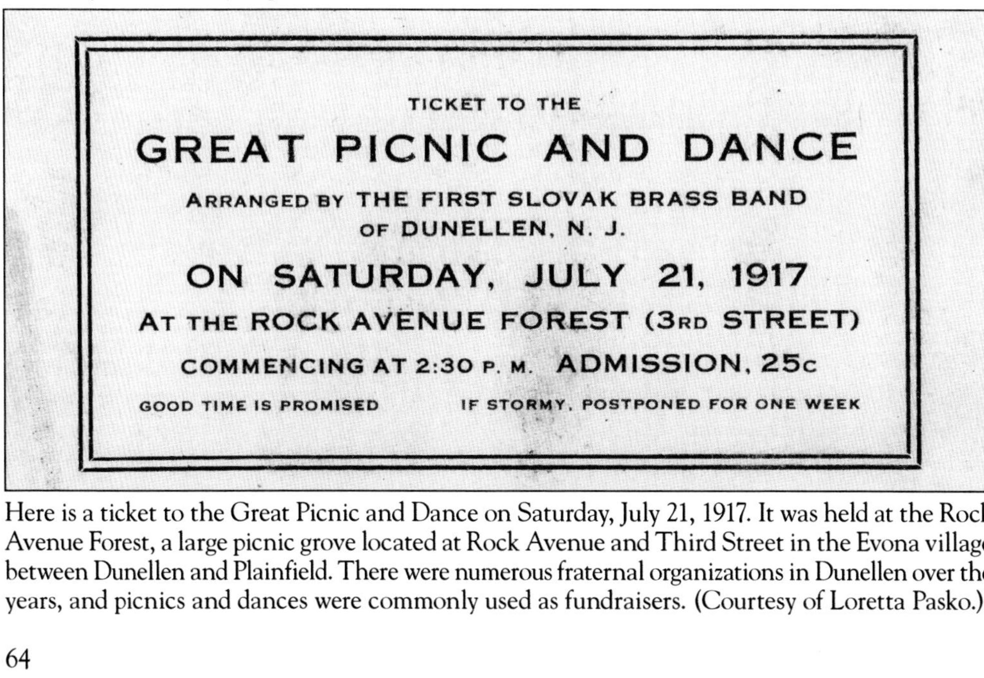

TICKET TO THE

GREAT PICNIC AND DANCE

ARRANGED BY THE FIRST SLOVAK BRASS BAND
OF DUNELLEN, N. J.

ON SATURDAY, JULY 21, 1917

AT THE ROCK AVENUE FOREST (3RD STREET)

COMMENCING AT 2:30 P. M. ADMISSION, 25c

GOOD TIME IS PROMISED IF STORMY, POSTPONED FOR ONE WEEK

Here is a ticket to the Great Picnic and Dance on Saturday, July 21, 1917. It was held at the Rock Avenue Forest, a large picnic grove located at Rock Avenue and Third Street in the Evona village between Dunellen and Plainfield. There were numerous fraternal organizations in Dunellen over the years, and picnics and dances were commonly used as fundraisers. (Courtesy of Loretta Pasko.)

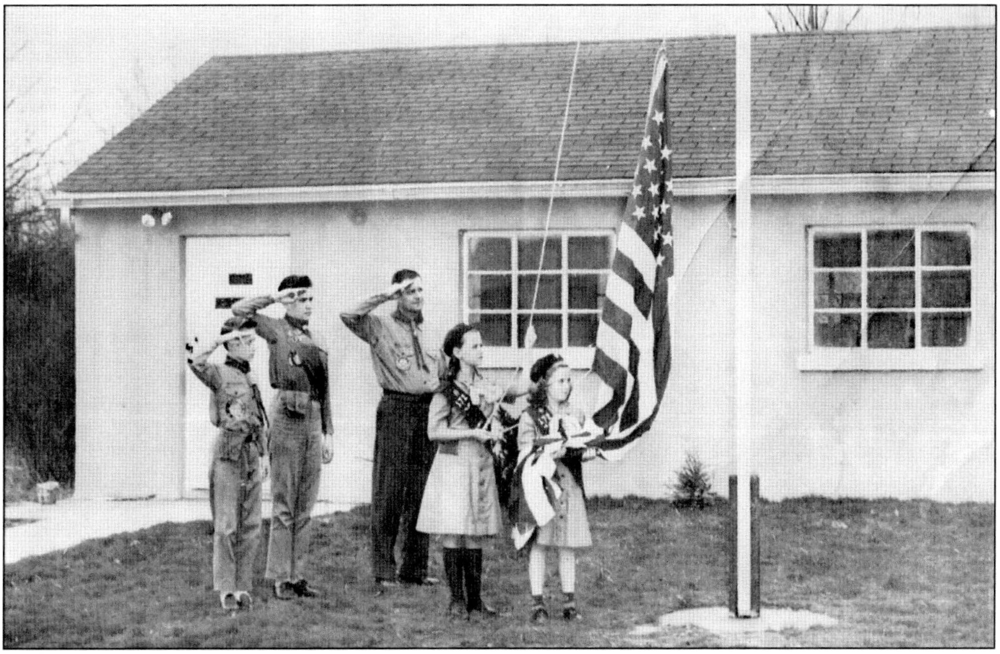

Boy Scouts of Troop 127 and Girl Scouts of Troop 172 raise the American flag at the Sponsors Club building on Pulaski Street. At the time of this photograph, there were 15 Girl Scout troops in Dunellen comprised of about 300 girls. From left to right are Dale Jaquish, Chuck Bender, Bob MacLernnan, Sue Ramsberger, and Janine Bauman. (Courtesy of Boy Scout Troop 127.)

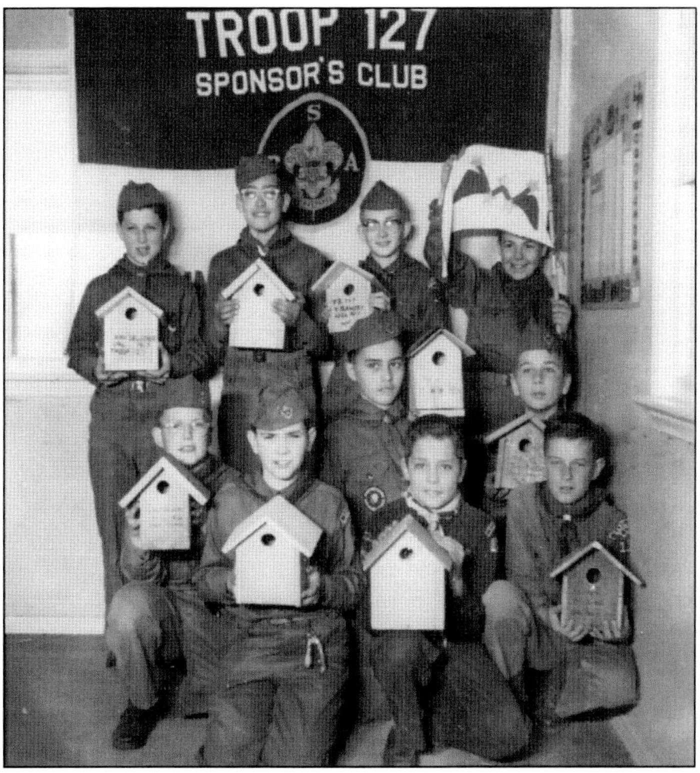


The first Boy Scout troop founded in Dunellen was in 1913. Presently, there are two troops in town: Troop 29 of the Presbyterian Church, formed in the 1930s, and Troop 127 of the Sponsors Club. Shown here around 1958, Troop 127 Scouts include, from left to right, (first row) Chuck Bender, Dave Bauman, and unidentified; (second row) Pete Rutan, Bob Reid, and John McCloud; (third row) Ray Dellecker, Jay Bauman, Tom Slehetka, and Bob Wainwright. (Courtesy of Chuck Bender.)

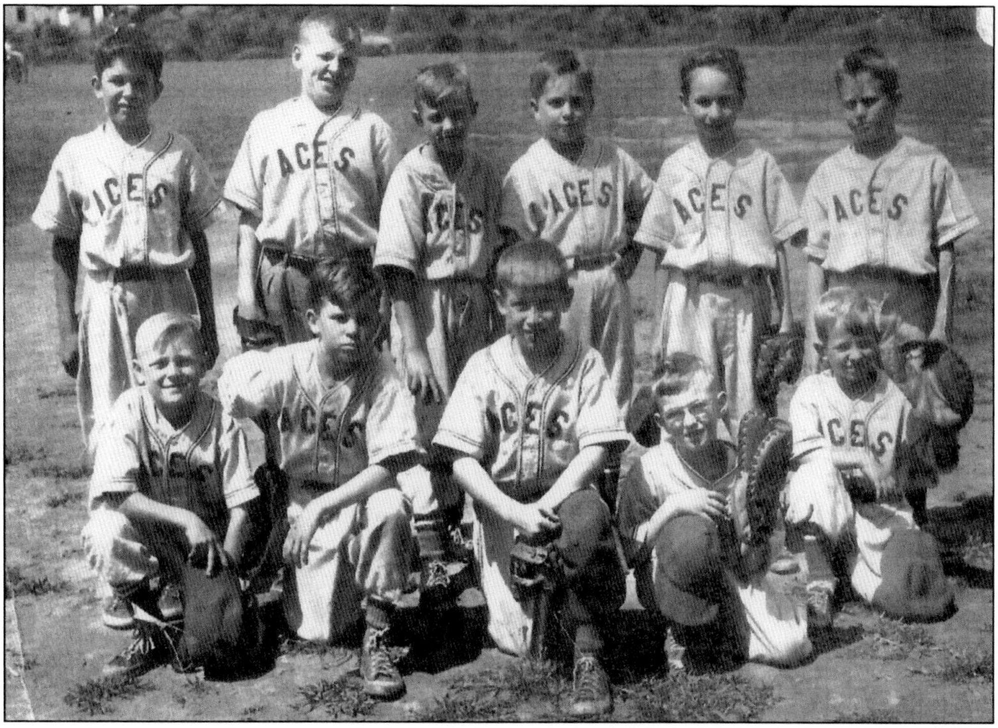

Little League Baseball was organized in Dunellen in 1940. The Dunellen Recreation Commission has provided services and programs since that date. There are four playgrounds and playing fields in the borough. Shown here, the 1950 Aces Little League team includes, from left to right, (first row) Mike Feno, Robert Watkinson, George Deene, and two unidentified players; (second row) Ron Rathborne, Bud Terry, unidentified, Charlie Batcha, Ed Parr, and Ritchie Matt. (Courtesy of Ron Eskesen.)

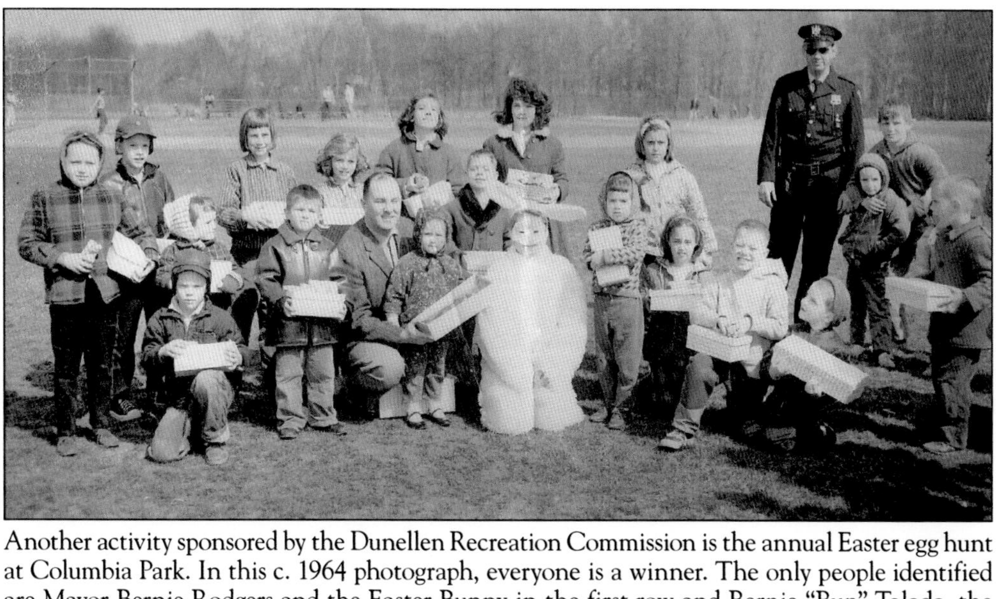

Another activity sponsored by the Dunellen Recreation Commission is the annual Easter egg hunt at Columbia Park. In this c. 1964 photograph, everyone is a winner. The only people identified are Mayor Bernie Rodgers and the Easter Bunny in the first row and Bernie "Bun" Talada, the police officer at right. (Courtesy of Ron Eskesen.)

# *Six*

# Schools and Parks

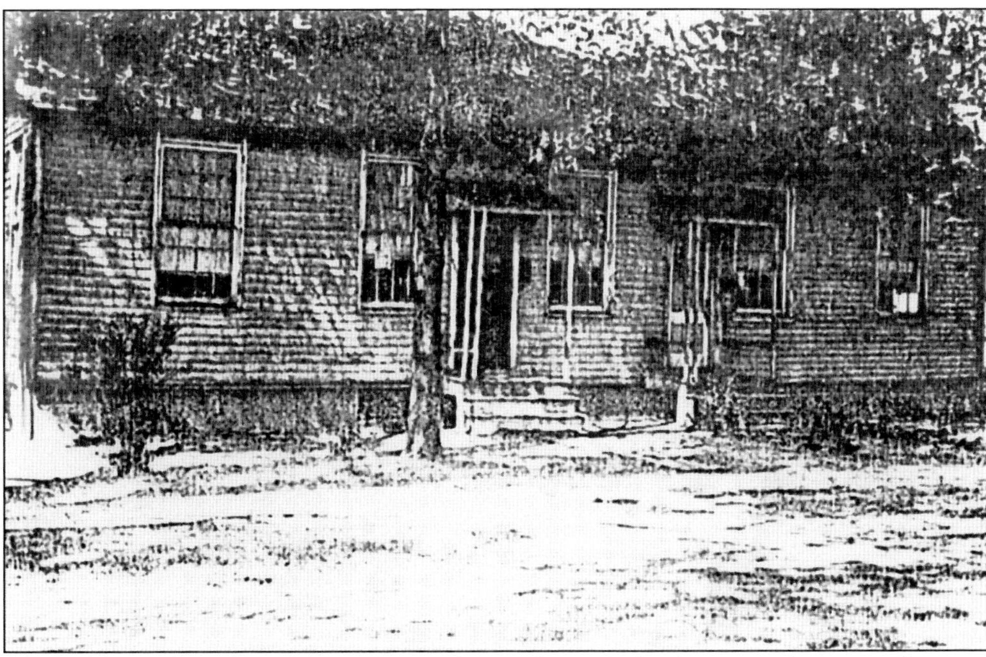

A 1777 Erskine map shows a schoolhouse where Whittier School now stands. It started out as a 16-foot log cabin, and a one-room school replaced it in 1838. In 1871, a second room was added. This two-room schoolhouse, pictured here, was moved to the rear of the school property when construction commenced on the new Whittier School, a two-story, four-room building, in 1875. The original two-room school still exists today as a residence on New Market Road. The other school in the borough in 1868 was Miss Child's Academy, a private school on Dunellen Avenue across the street from Washington Park.

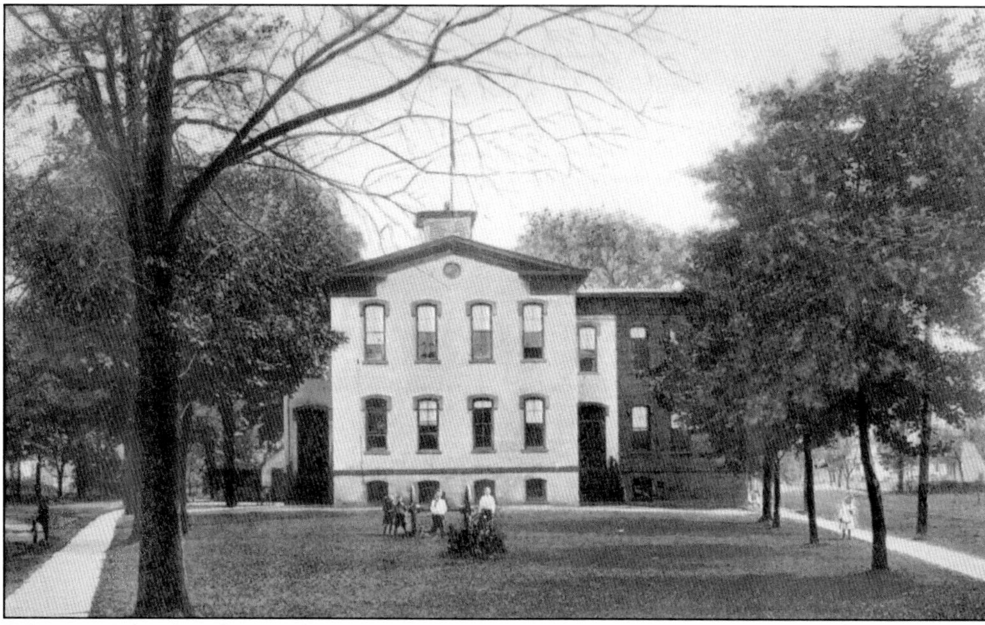

Whittier School is shown above around 1909. A two-room addition was made in 1901, and another two-room addition was completed in 1909. Of note is the cannon in front of the school. Application was submitted to the US War Department and a Civil War cannon and 40 shells were delivered to the school in 1908. It remained in place until World War II when it was donated to the war effort for scrap. (Courtesy of John Triolo.)

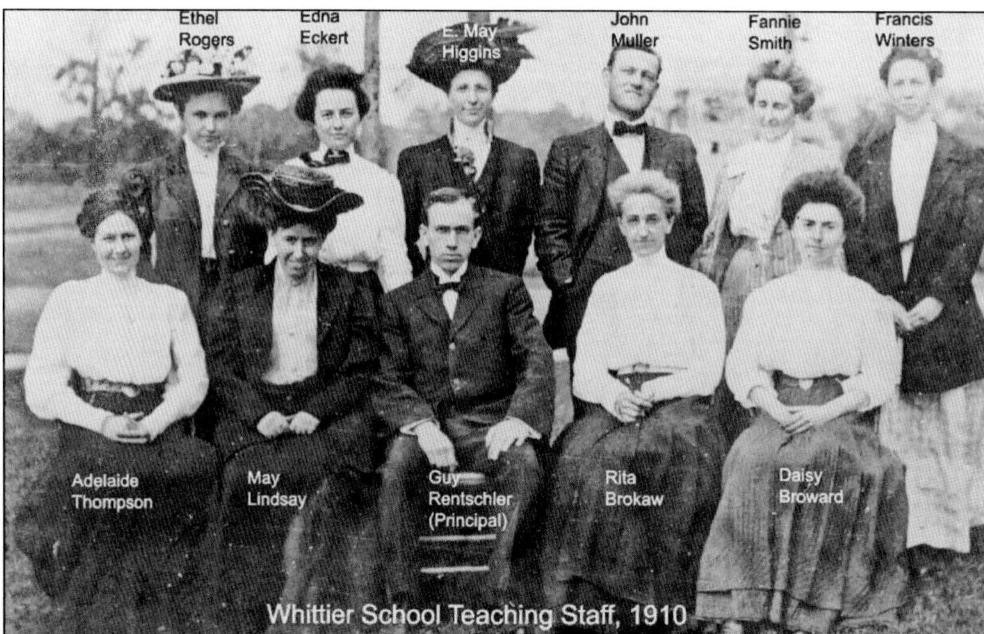


The Whittier School teaching staff in 1910 consisted of 10 teachers and the principal. Very strict rules applied to teachers in those days. They could not be married or even keep company with men. They could not dress in bright colors or wear a dress shorter than two inches above their ankles. Did all these rules apply to the male teacher in the back row?

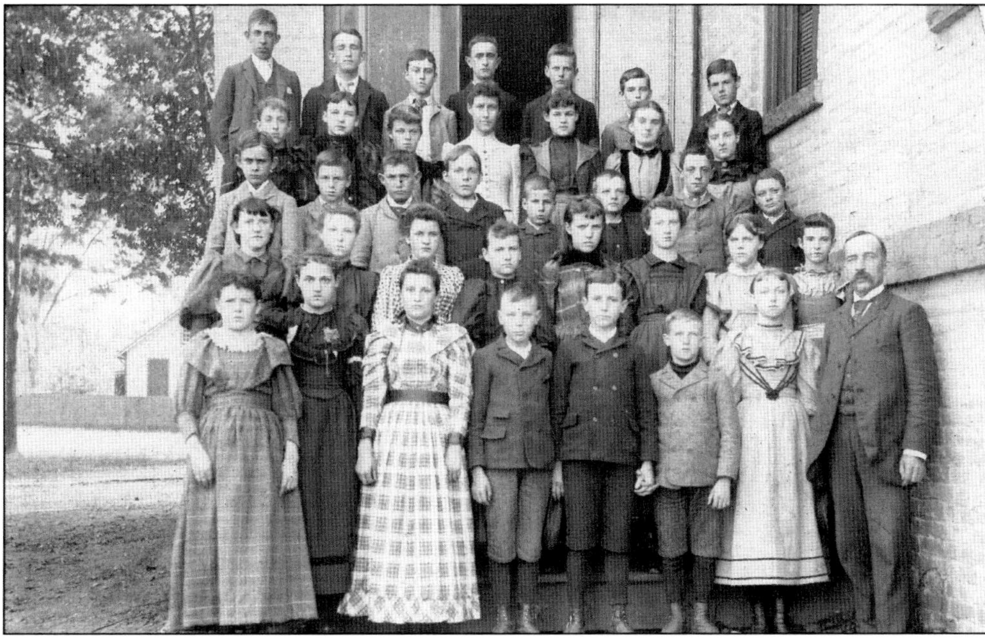

The entire c. 1892 student body is shown here at Whittier School. The three boys in the front row are Charles Vail (left), Arthur Vail (center), and Fred Vail (right). Visible in the left background is the original two-room schoolhouse, which was moved to that location to construct the new Whittier School. Records show that a picket fence enclosed the school grounds but was removed and sold at public auction in 1893. (Courtesy of Lawrence Anzavino.)

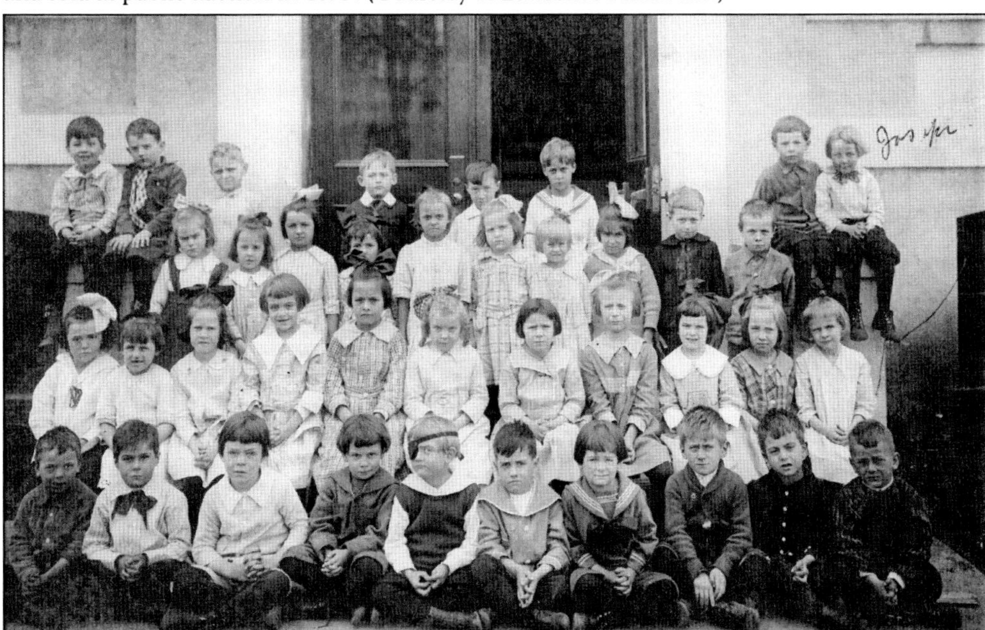

In this c. 1920 Whittier School class picture is the final rendition of the school with the two main entries at the front. The additions and renovations were funded by raising $82,000 in 1919. The original Whittier School cost $10,000 in 1875. Little Joseph Pasko is sitting in the fourth row, farthest right. (Courtesy of Loretta Pasko.)

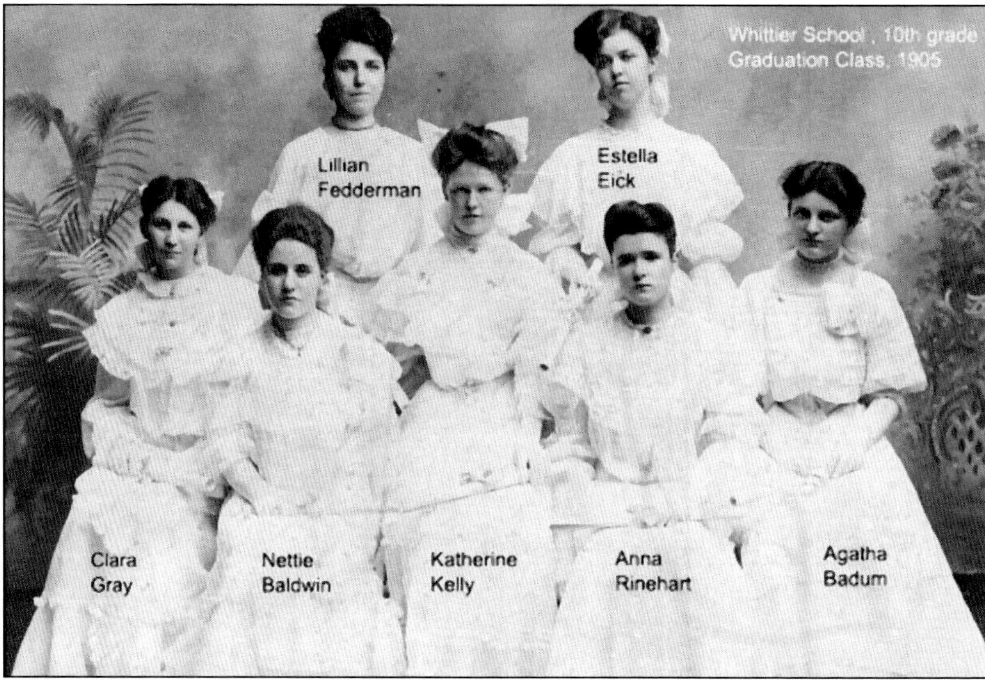


Pictured here are the Whittier School's class of 1905 graduates. Clara Gray, the first student on the left, was the 1905 valedictorian. Until 1906, Dunellen graduated pupils from ninth and 10th grades and considered them "high school graduates," complete with high school diplomas. After 1906, the school curriculum was changed, ending at eighth grade. For further studies, Dunellen students attended Plainfield High School.

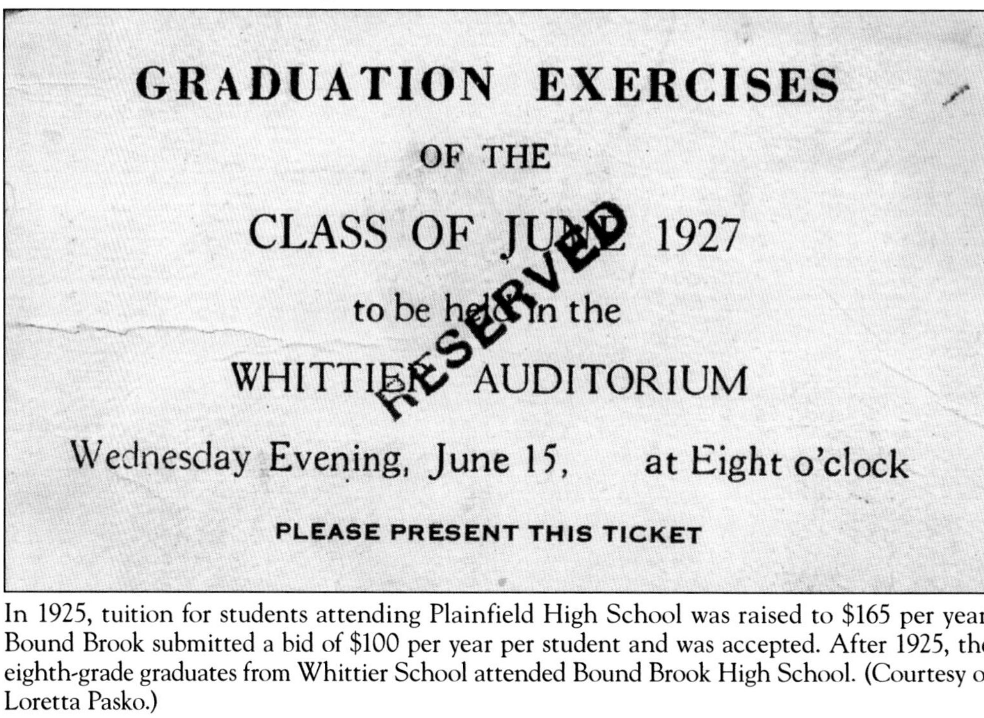

GRADUATION EXERCISES

OF THE

CLASS OF JUNE 1927

to be held in the

WHITTIER AUDITORIUM

Wednesday Evening, June 15, at Eight o'clock

PLEASE PRESENT THIS TICKET

RESERVED

In 1925, tuition for students attending Plainfield High School was raised to $165 per year. Bound Brook submitted a bid of $100 per year per student and was accepted. After 1925, the eighth-grade graduates from Whittier School attended Bound Brook High School. (Courtesy of Loretta Pasko.)

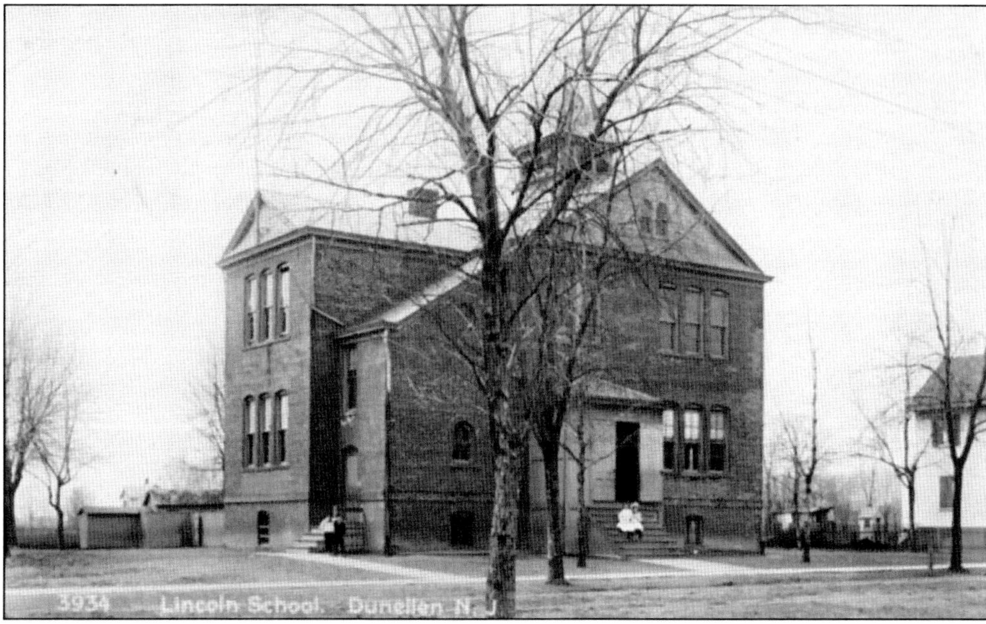


This postcard shows the expanded Lincoln School in 1915. Built in 1891 on land donated by the railroad, it contained four rooms and was enlarged to eight rooms in 1915 at a cost of $15,000. The school provided classrooms for kindergarten through fourth grade for all children on the north side of the borough. Much of the original school lies under the present-day construction at the corner of Lincoln and Dunellen Avenues. (Courtesy of John Triolo.)

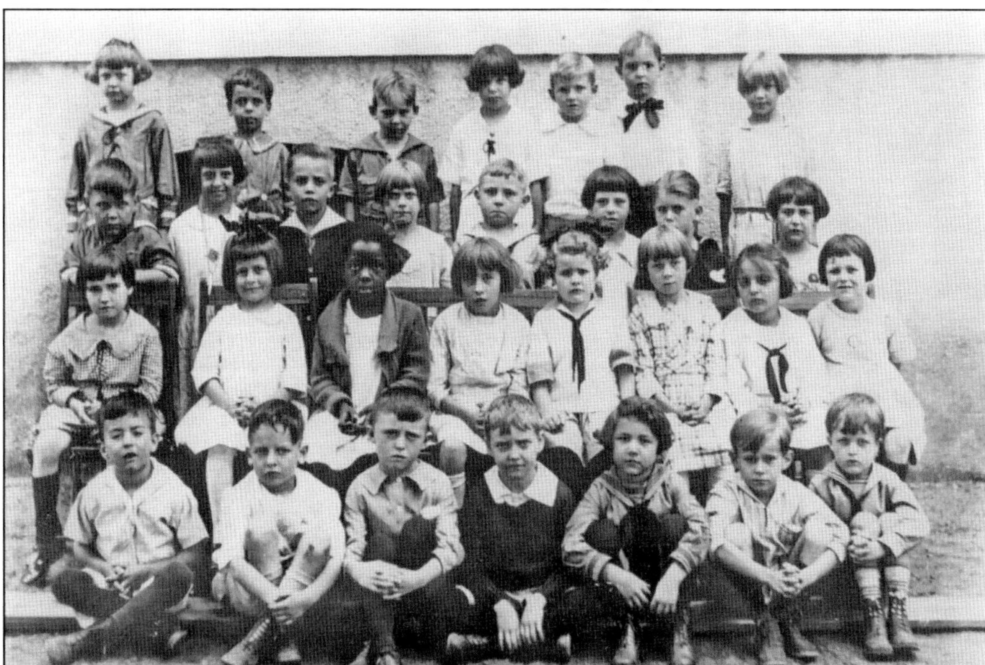

Students of the Lincoln School are shown in this 1920 photograph. During the renovation and expansion of the school in 1914, the first-grade pupils were schooled in the Presbyterian church hall until the remodeling was completed.

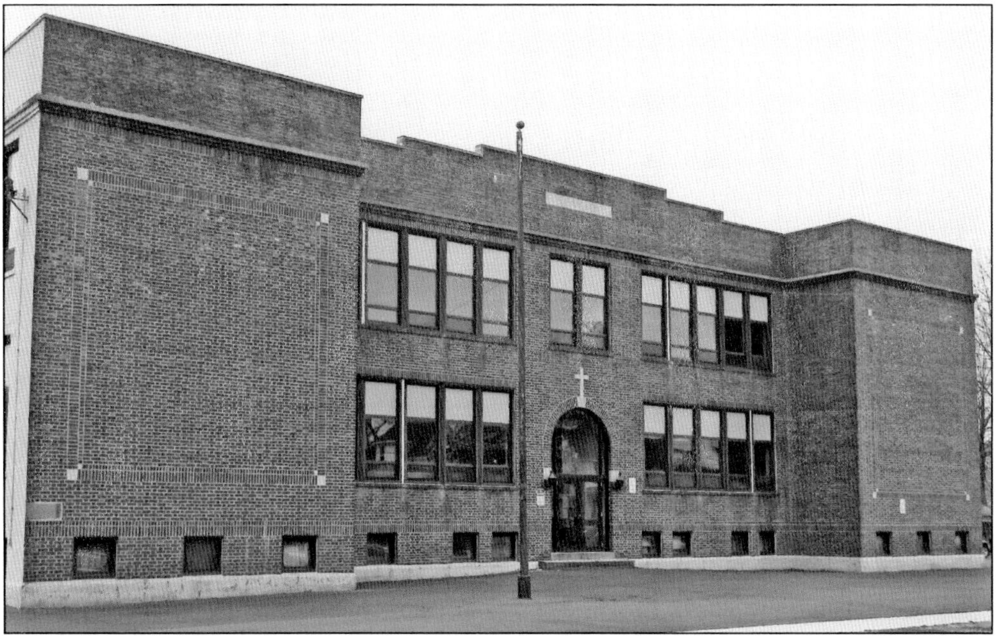

St. John's Parochial School was completed and opened in 1924. During the first year, the school enrolled 250 pupils in five grades. An additional grade was added for the next three years. By 1927, the school had 412 pupils in eight grades. St. John's School graduated more than 30,000 students from the date it opened until it closed in 1989.

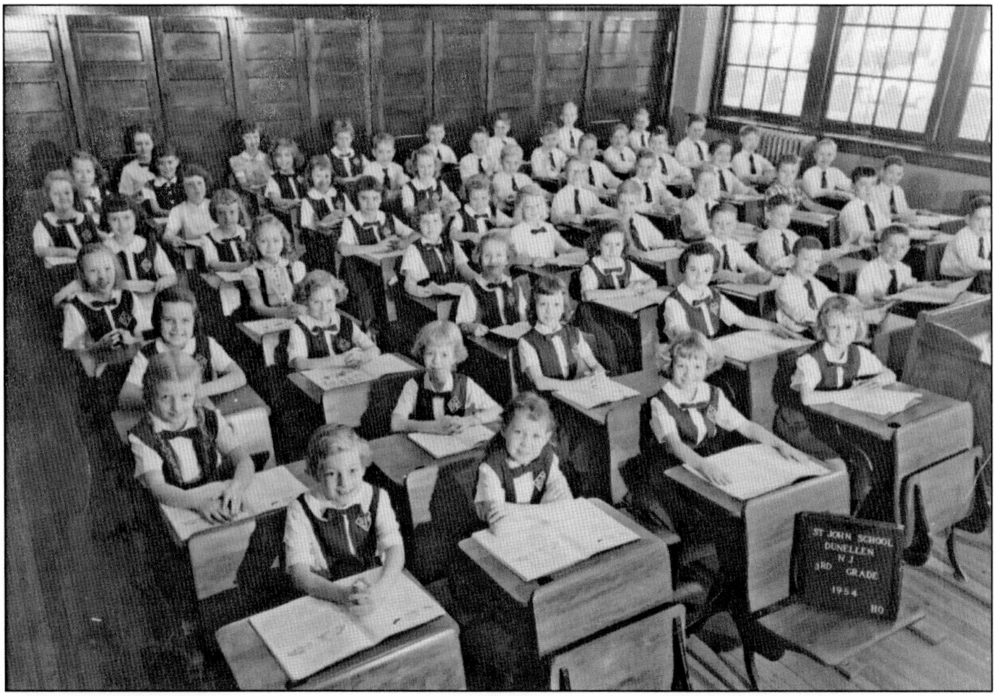


The third-grade class at St. John's School in 1954 boasted 54 students. This large class size was thanks to the first baby boomers, and all these students were born in 1946. The girls were seated on one side of the room and the boys on the other. (Courtesy of John Triolo.)

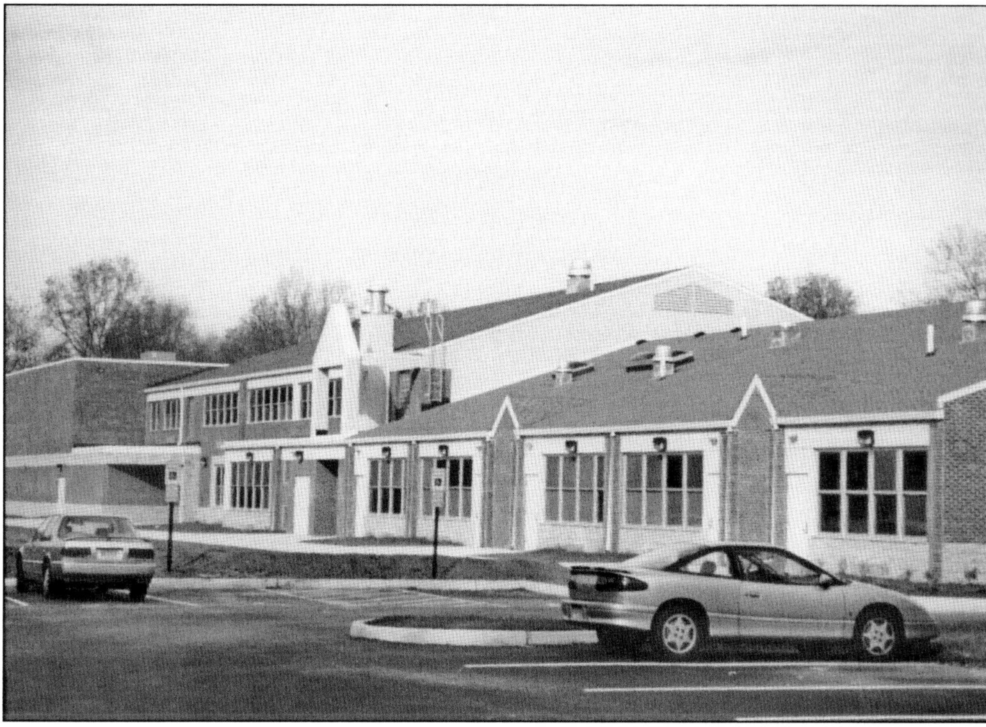

This photograph shows Faber School after its addition. The original building was completed in 1960. The school was named in honor of John P. Faber, who served on the board of education for 43 years and was president for 15 years. The building originally contained 12 classrooms, a library, and an all-purpose room.

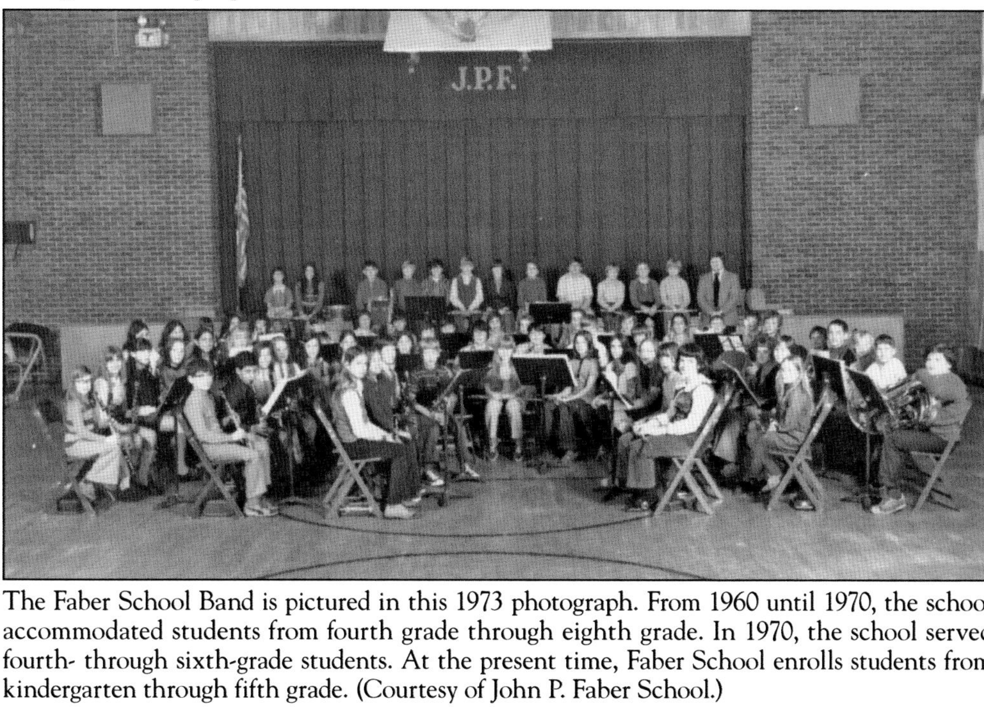


The Faber School Band is pictured in this 1973 photograph. From 1960 until 1970, the school accommodated students from fourth grade through eighth grade. In 1970, the school served fourth- through sixth-grade students. At the present time, Faber School enrolls students from kindergarten through fifth grade. (Courtesy of John P. Faber School.)

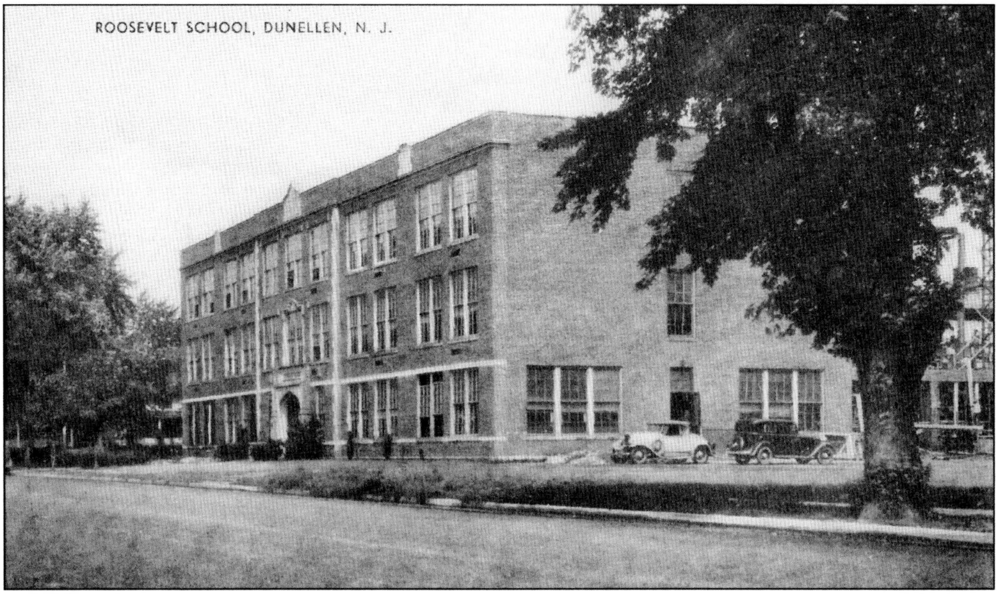


Building lots containing several homes were torn down, and Roosevelt School was built and opened in 1930. In 1935, an addition provided five more classrooms, a science laboratory, and a gymnasium. When completed, it was renamed Dunellen High School. From 1906 to 1925, Dunellen's high school students attended Plainfield High School, and from 1925 to 1935, they attended Bound Brook High School. From 1935 until 1969, students from Middlesex, Piscataway, Manville, and Green Brook periodically attended Dunellen High School. (Courtesy of John Triolo.)

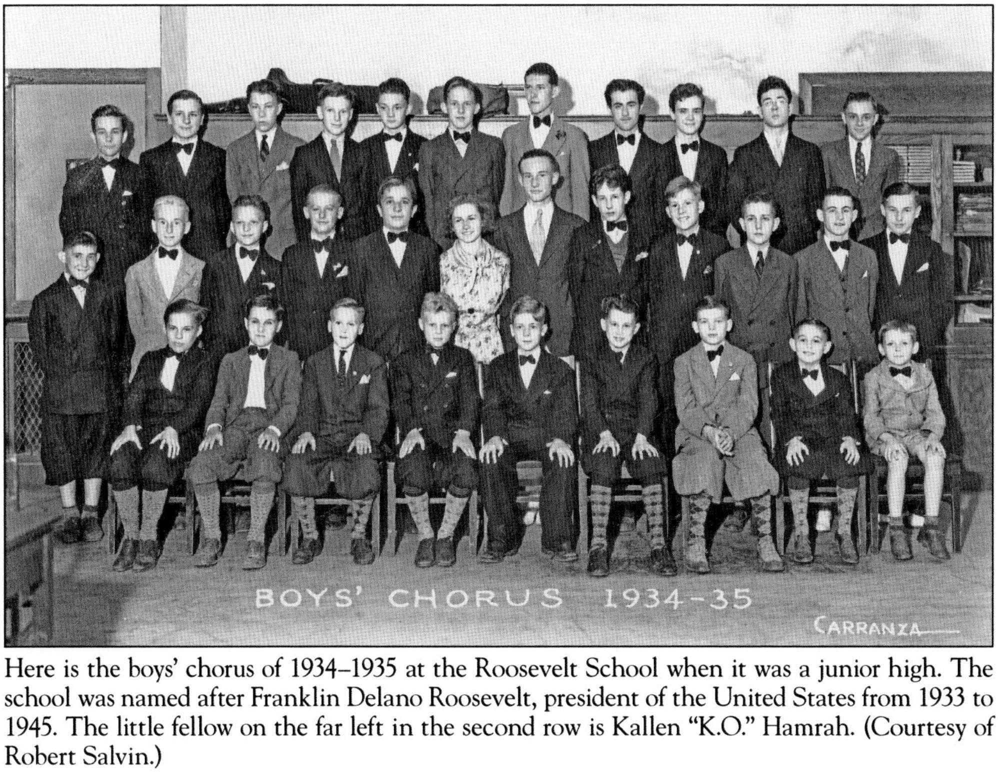


Here is the boys' chorus of 1934–1935 at the Roosevelt School when it was a junior high. The school was named after Franklin Delano Roosevelt, president of the United States from 1933 to 1945. The little fellow on the far left in the second row is Kallen "K.O." Hamrah. (Courtesy of Robert Salvin.)

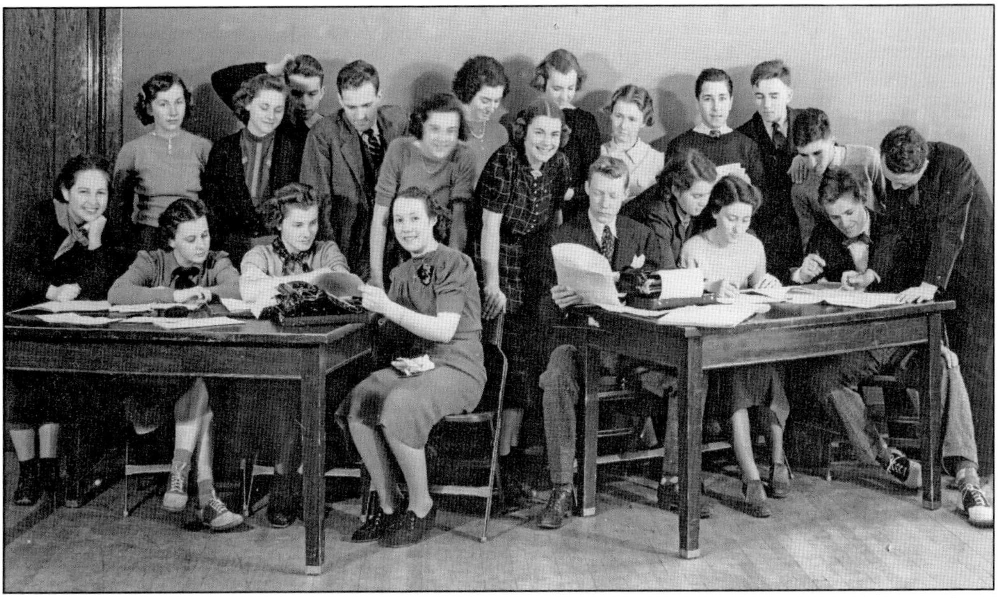

Shown here is the yearbook staff of Dunellen High School hard at work in 1939. They are working on the 1940 edition of the *Exodus*. The yearbook of Dunellen High School to this day is still called the *Exodus*. (Courtesy of Bea Salvin.)

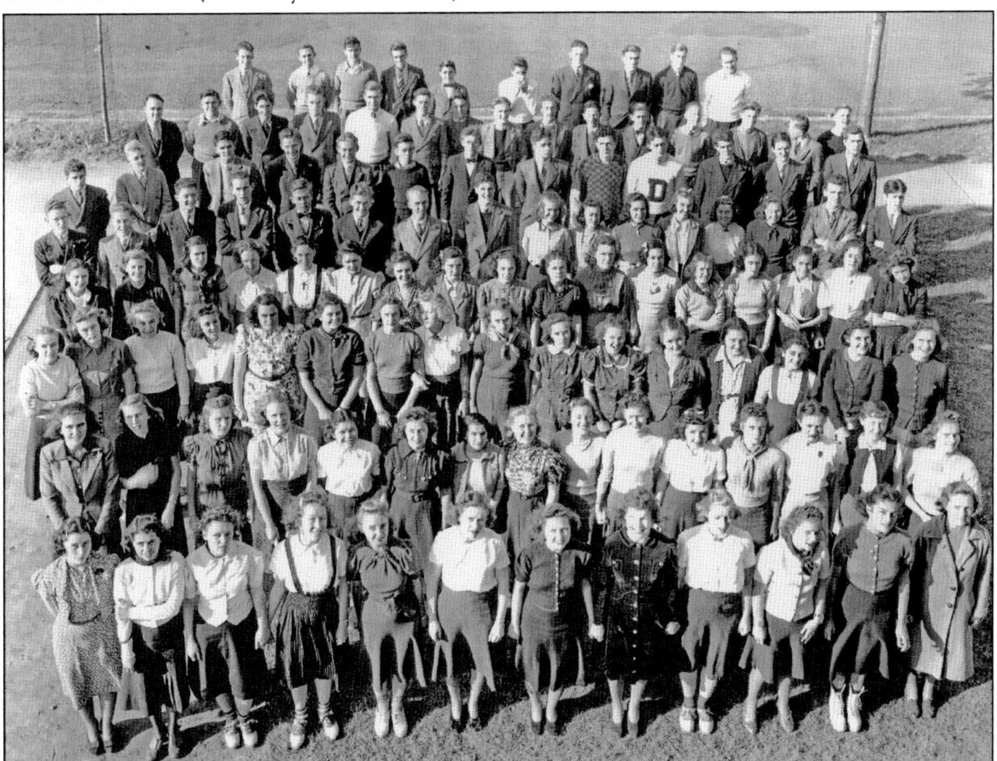

The graduation class of 1940 is pictured here. Besides Dunellen residents, pupils from Green Brook, Middlesex, and parts of Piscataway attended the high school on a tuition basis. Graduation ceremonies were always held at Washington Park, weather permitting. (Courtesy of Bea Salvin.)

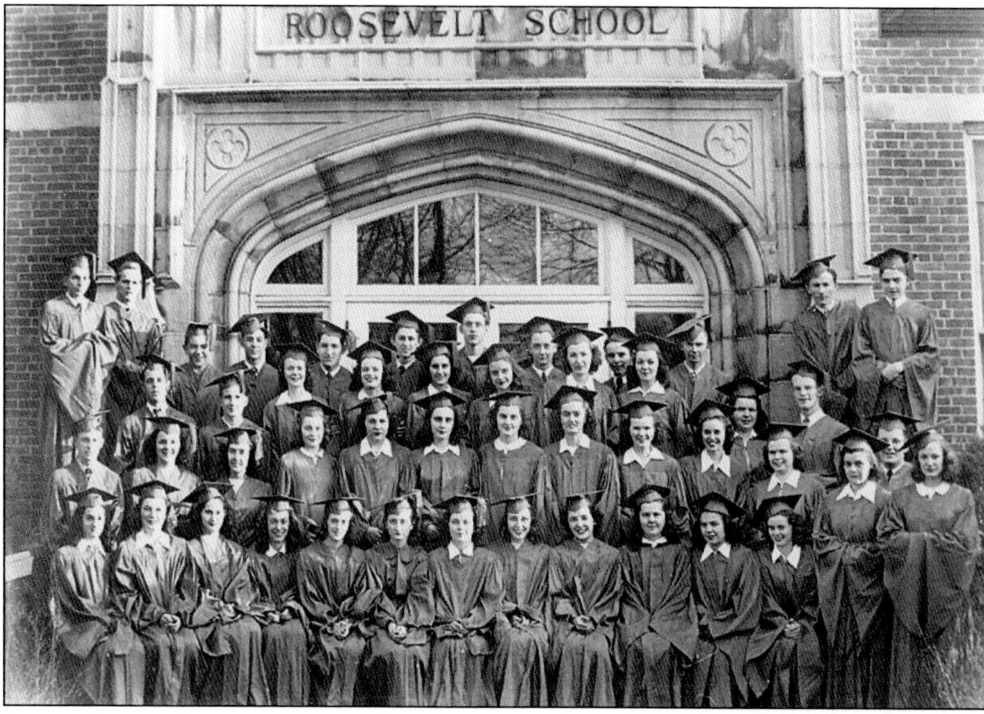


Here is the Dunellen High School graduating class of 1946. There are 30 girls and 17 boys. This picture was taken 10 months after the end of World War II. What a difference in the number of students in this class versus the class of 1940. The small town of Dunellen sent 757 men and women to the armed services from 1941 to 1945.

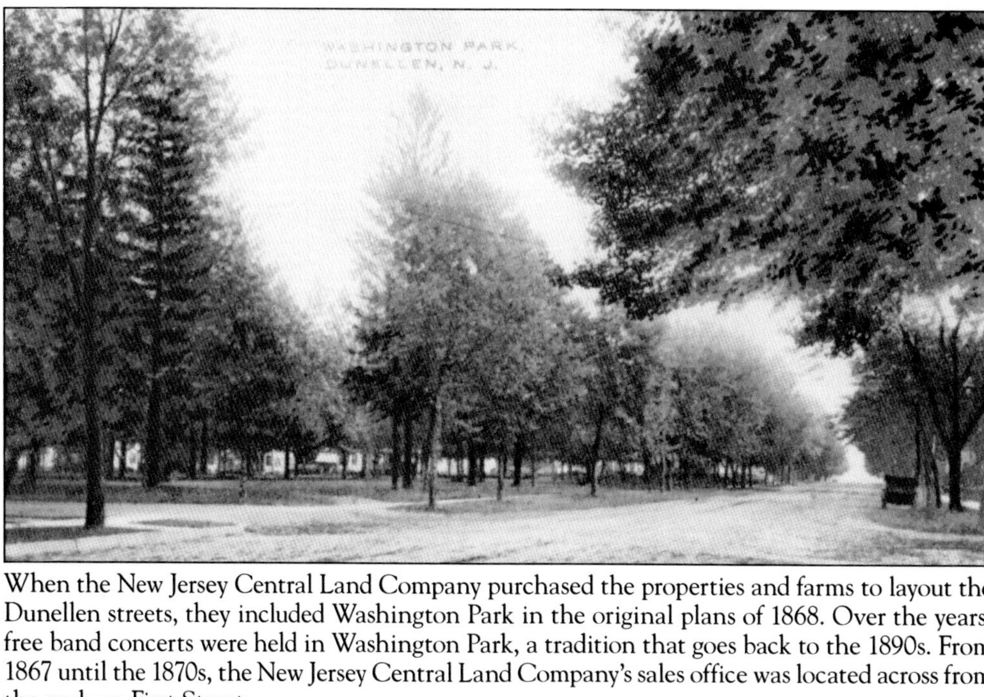


When the New Jersey Central Land Company purchased the properties and farms to layout the Dunellen streets, they included Washington Park in the original plans of 1868. Over the years, free band concerts were held in Washington Park, a tradition that goes back to the 1890s. From 1867 until the 1870s, the New Jersey Central Land Company's sales office was located across from the park on First Street.

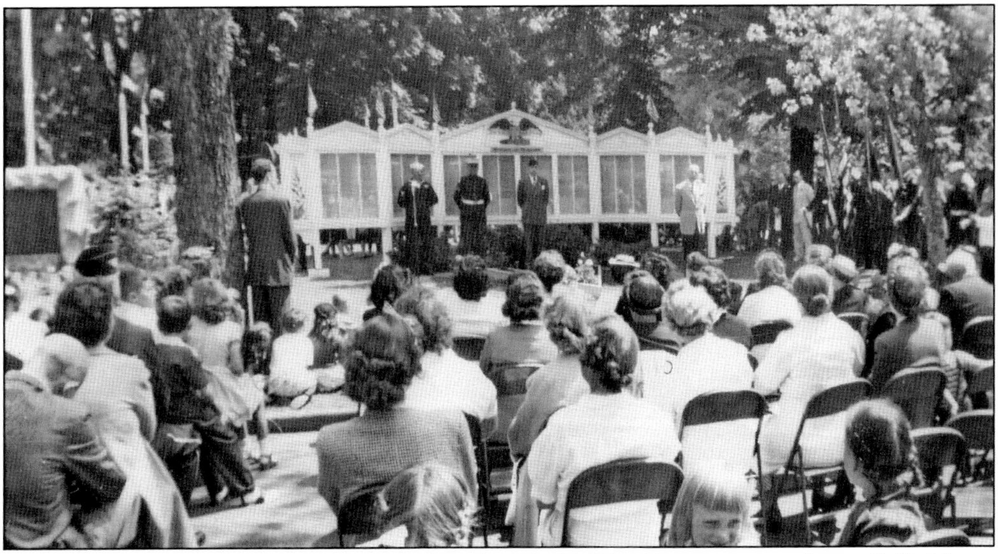

The park is seen here at a ceremony after the World War II victory parade in 1945. Mayor Joseph Morecraft is speaking on the right, and to his left stands a soldier, a Marine, and a sailor representing the US armed forces. The park has held ceremonies every Memorial Day to date. Dunellen High School graduation ceremonies are held here every June, weather permitting. (Courtesy of Schuyler family collection.)

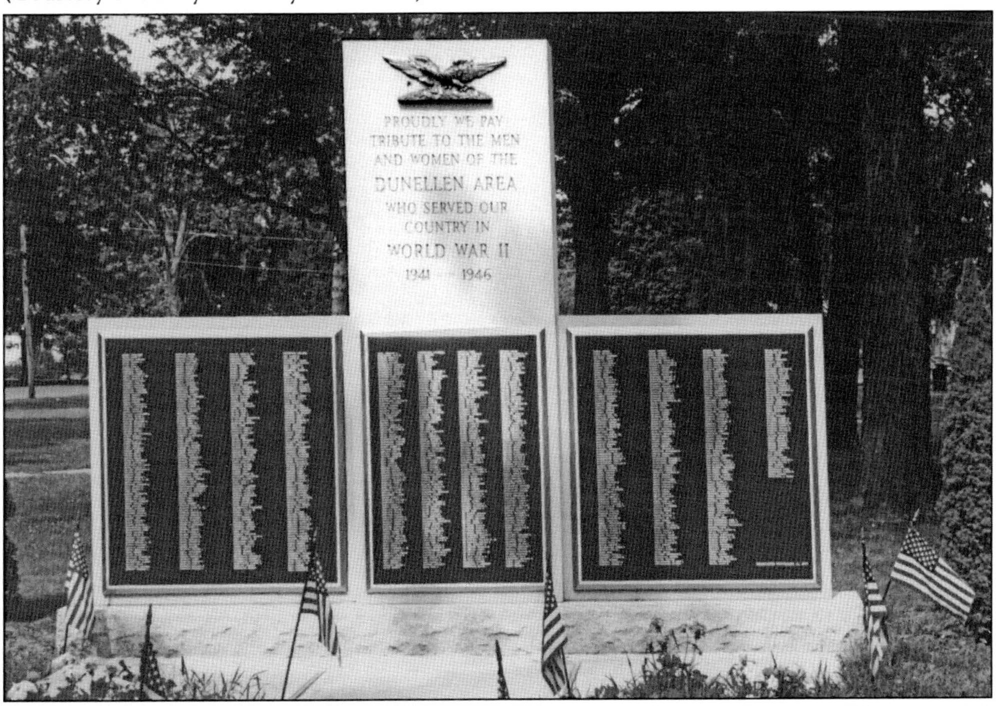


During World War II, Dunellen sent 757 men and women to the armed services. The memorial pictured displays the names of all those who served. This memorial was the work of the American Legion's Americanism officer Robert Salvin. It was dedicated on November 11, 1997. The park also contains memorials for World War I, the Korean War, the Vietnam War, and the fire department and rescue squad.

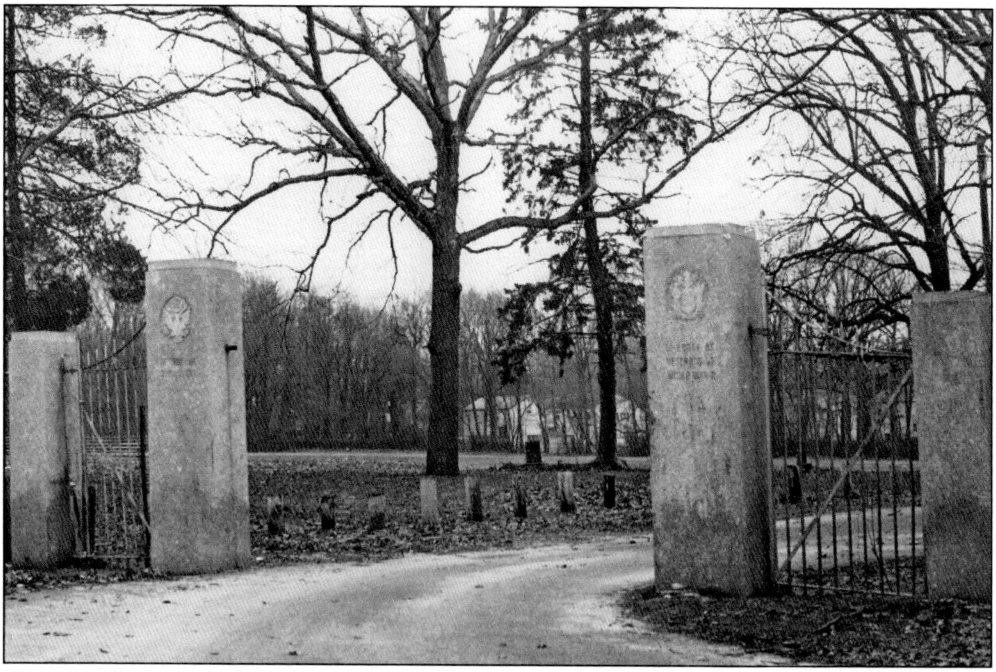

Columbia Park, a Works Progress Administration (WPA) project, was completed in 1938. It is the largest park in the borough and is used by Dunellen High School for football, baseball, and track. There are tennis courts and a large children's playground. The entrance gates shown here were installed in honor of the veterans of World War II in the late 1940s.

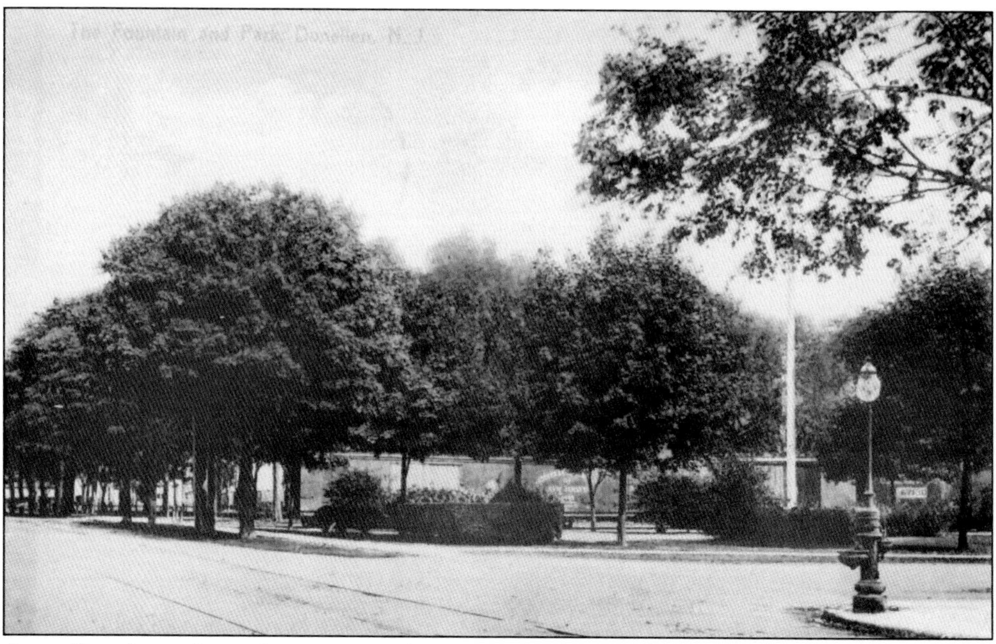

A small park was located on a triangular piece of property adjacent to the railroad station in 1909. North Avenue and its trolley tracks are in the foreground. Of note is the public drinking fountain on the right. Today, the five parks in Dunellen Borough are Columbia, Gavornik, McCoy, Morecraft, and Washington Parks. (Courtesy of John Triolo.)

# Seven

# MUNICIPAL SERVICES

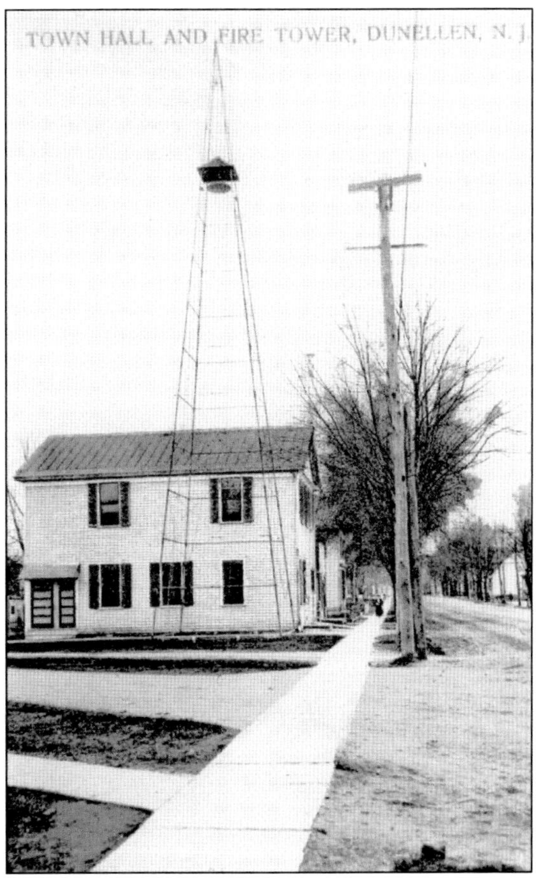


This is the borough hall and fire tower in 1903. The building was completed in January 1897 at a cost of $1,650. The first floor had an engine house, lockup, council room, and office for the borough justice, and the second floor had a hall and lodge room. The land purchased from the railroad at $400 was located at North and Prospect Avenues. A 60-foot tower was erected, and the fire department provided an 800-pound bell. This original bell is now located in Washington Park within the Firemen's Memorial. (Courtesy of John Triolo.)

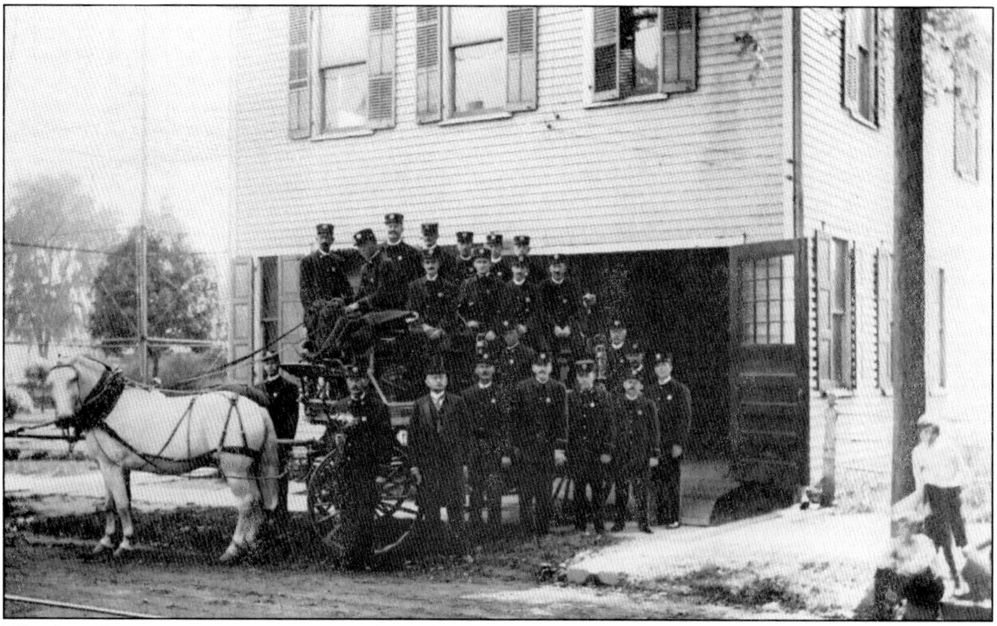

The first fire company was organized as a bucket brigade in 1877. This picture is of the Defender Fire Company in 1910; the wagon is a combination hook and ladder, hose carriage, chemical engine purchased in 1896 for $800. The wagon was pulled for the first eight years by manpower, and teams of horses were hired in 1906. The man in the top hat in the front row is Mayor William Sanford in one of the only known pictures of him. (Courtesy of Lawrence Anzavino.)

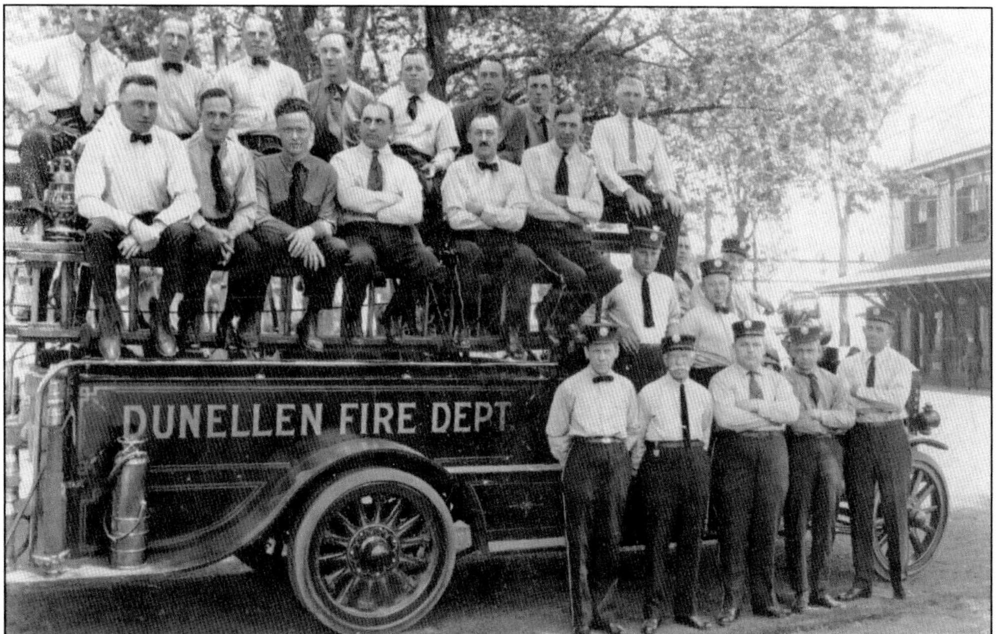


Dunellen's first motorized fire truck was delivered in 1917 by the Reo Motor Car Company at the cost of $3,300. Pictured here is the truck with fire company members. The department needed more room for equipment, and a building was erected on a lot to the rear and adjacent to the borough hall. It was completed in June 1924. (Courtesy of Lawrence Anzavino.)

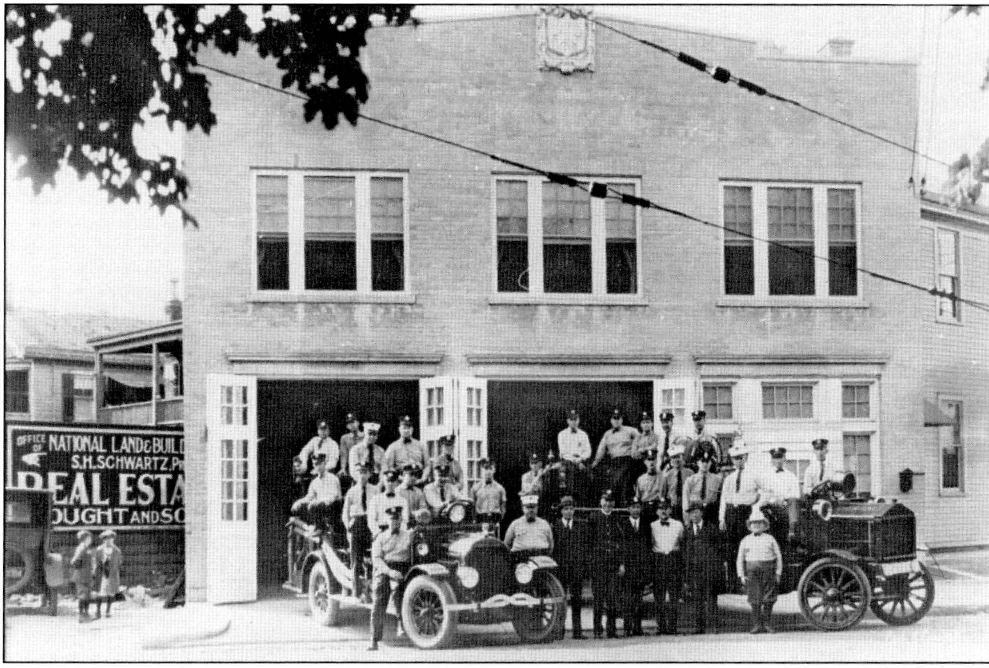

Pictured in front of the new station is the 1924 Defender Fire Department. The 21-year-old fire tower and bell were taken down to accommodate the new building. Residents on the south side of the railroad tracks were relieved to find out that another small building to house a fire truck was leased on Prospect Avenue. A slow-moving freight could hold up a fire truck waiting to cross the tracks for almost 10 minutes.

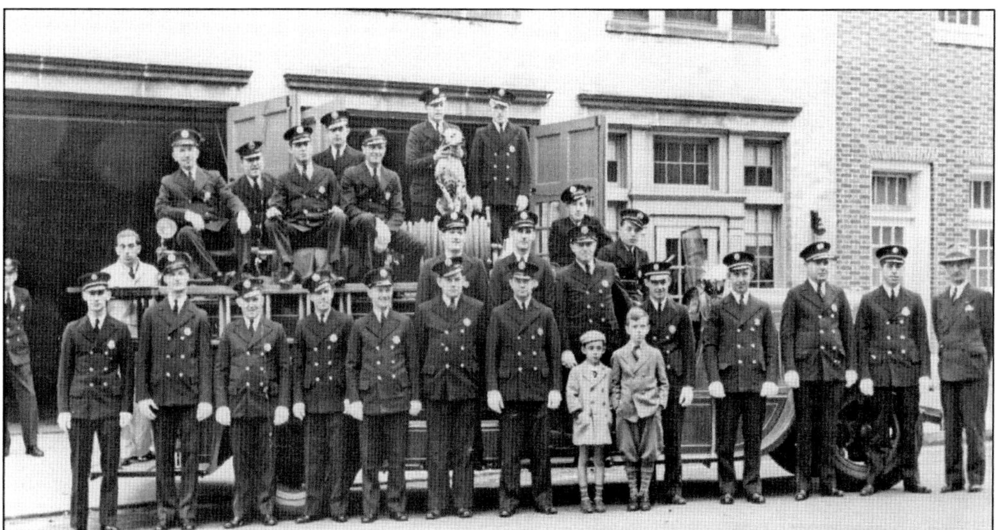

This is the Dunellen Fire Department in 1952. From left to right are (first row) E. Talada, J. Bublavek, W. Vliet, A. Bock, E. Mingle, W. Tully, C. Christianson, two unidentified boys, R. Haver, C. Haver, H. Goeller, C. Doyle, and Mayor Roff; (second row) P. Benson (in the doorway), W. Wyckoff, D. Luther, P. Fuchs, B. Handelman, and E. Kepplar; (third row) S. Heldt, C. Vliet, H. Day, C. Luch, S. Jarusewski, F. Schmidt (holding the dog), G. Vliet, and John Keppler. The department would have its new, expanded building on South Madison Avenue by 1963.

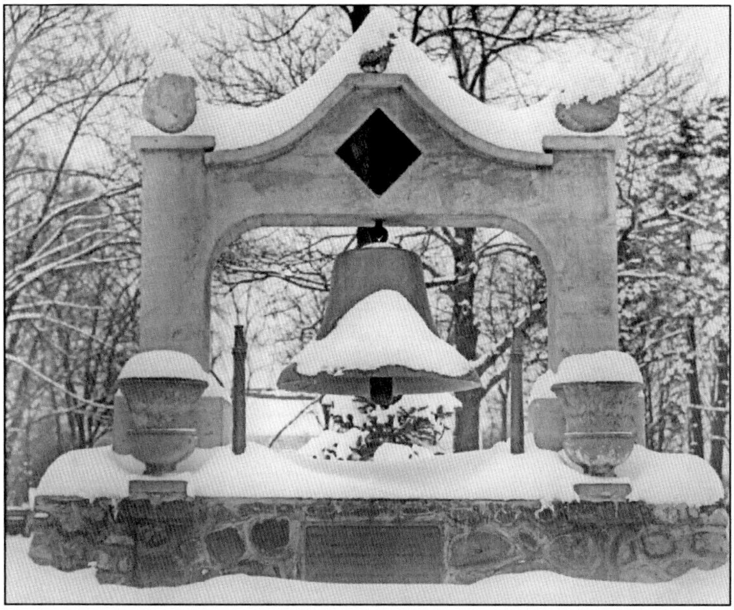

The original Fireman's Memorial in Washington Park was dedicated to all who served as firemen from 1897 to present day. The bell hanging from the arch is the original 800-pound alarm bell that was atop the tower next to the Municipal Building for 21 years. It was replaced June 2, 1916, by an electric whistle at the Municipal Building and tested by the night marshal everyday at 7:00 p.m.

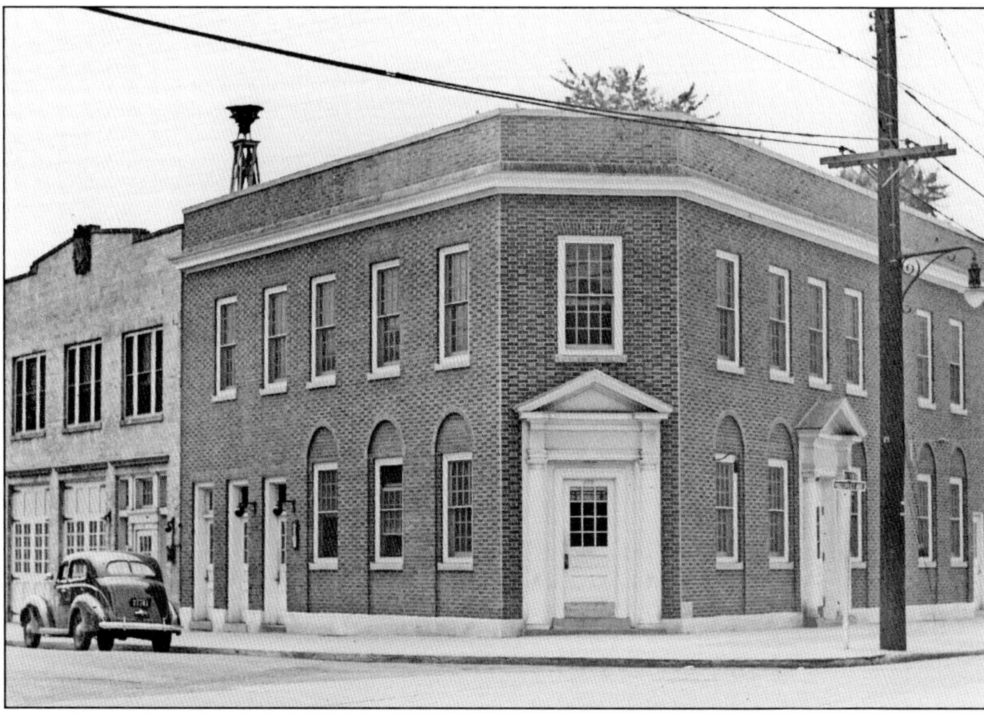

Pictured here is the current Municipal Building around 1940. In 1937, this brick, two-story building was constructed using federal Works Progress Administration (WPA) funds. It replaced the old wooden structure. The new building consisted of a police garage, police department, and fire department. On the second floor was the courtroom, recreation department, and the Dunellen Public Library. It is still in use today, but the library and fire department are located in their own buildings.

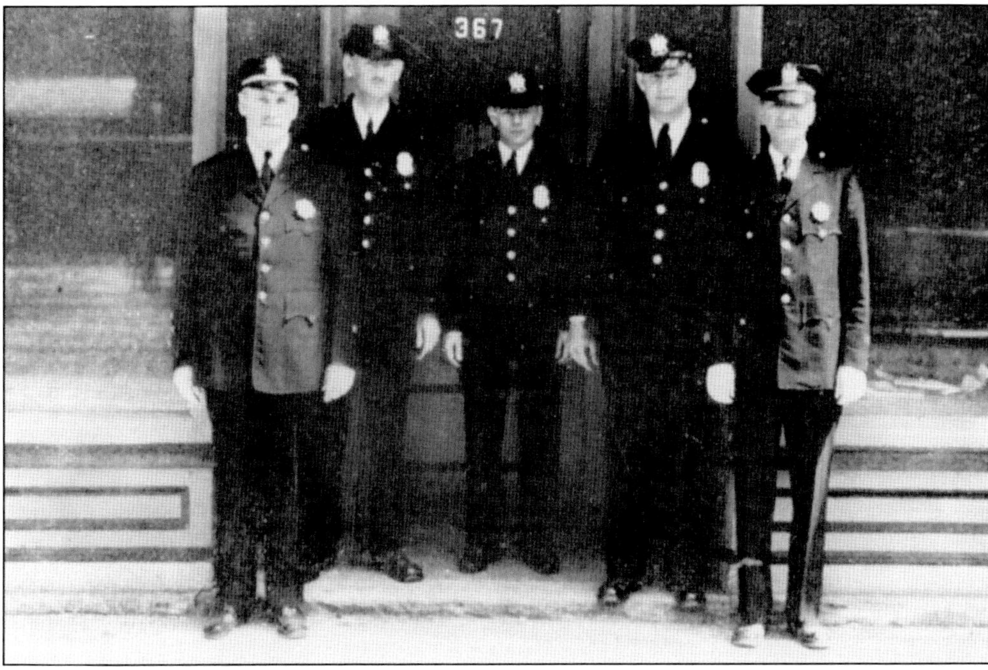


The Dunellen Police Department in 1937 includes, from left to right, Chief Patrick Tarpy, William Shields, Norman Schuyler, John Sobel, and Capt. John Yunker. From 1893 until 1924, the borough used a series of marshals to control the peace. The first police department in Dunellen was formed in 1924 with Owen Mohan as chief and patrolmen Patrick Tarpy and Samuel Strickland.

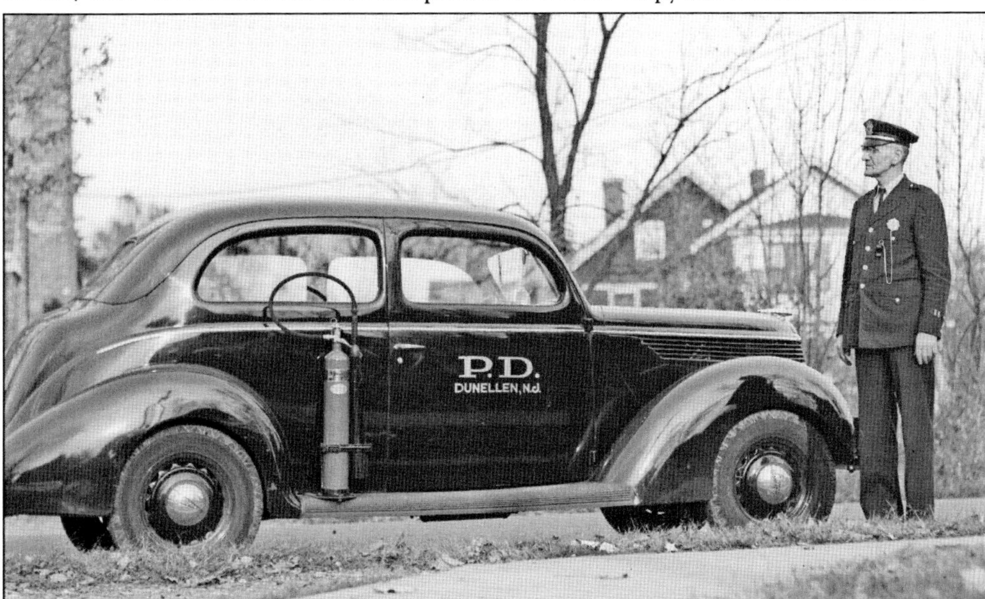


Capt. John Yunker is pictured with Dunellen's new 1940 patrol car. Yunker joined the force in 1925 with the expansion of the department to four officers and the chief. The first patrol car was an Overland, which cost $500. In 1925, officers had only two days off per month until the Law and Ordinance Committee gave each member of the force one day per week off. (Courtesy of Schuyler family collection.)

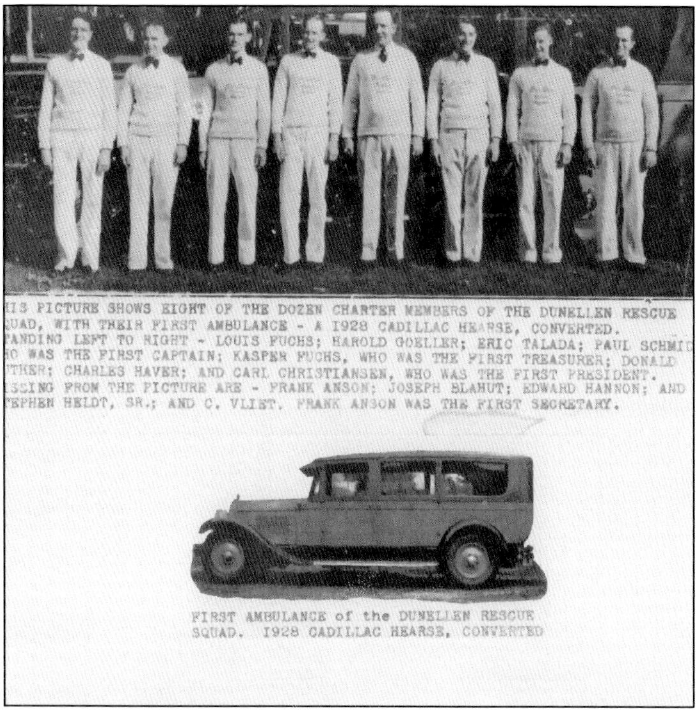


In 1932, thirteen men became interested in forming a first-aid squad. The charter members were Carl Christiansen, Francis Anson, Kasper Fuchs, Eric Talada, Paul Schmidt, Harold Goeller, Louis Fuchs, Charles Haver, Edward Hannon, Donald Luther, Joseph Blahut, Clifford Vliet, and Steven Heldt Sr. The squad's first ambulance was a converted 1928 Cadillac hearse. In 1934, the squad responded to 144 calls and covered 2,779 miles. At that time, the town had many industrial and manufacturing sites.

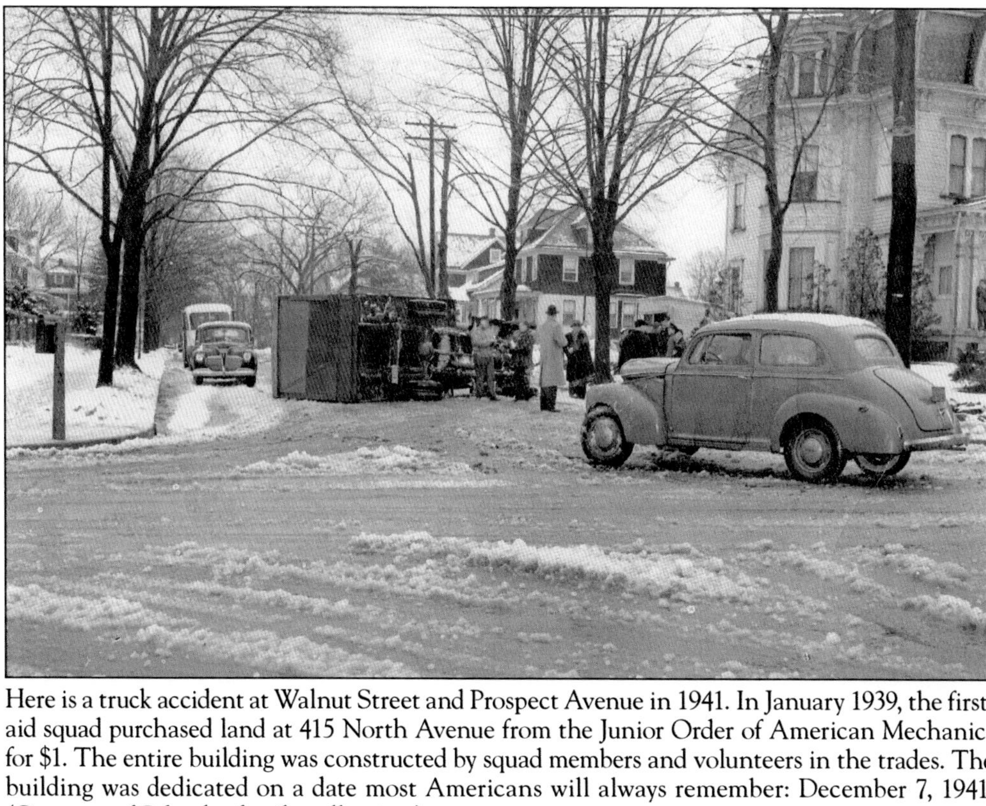

Here is a truck accident at Walnut Street and Prospect Avenue in 1941. In January 1939, the first-aid squad purchased land at 415 North Avenue from the Junior Order of American Mechanics for $1. The entire building was constructed by squad members and volunteers in the trades. The building was dedicated on a date most Americans will always remember: December 7, 1941. (Courtesy of Schuyler family collection.)

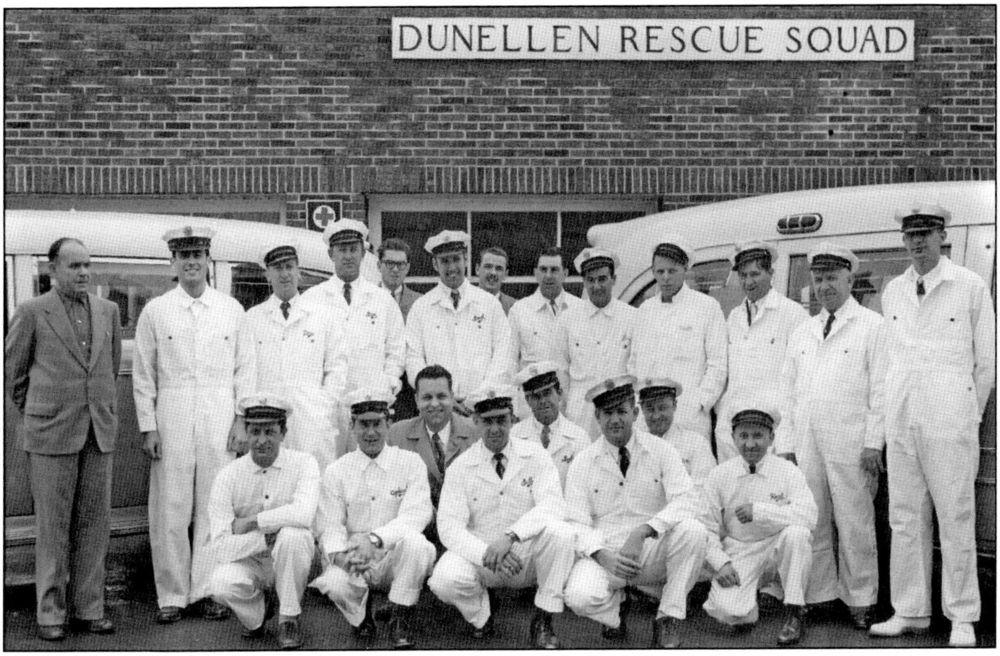


This 1958 picture has 21 members shown in front of the first-aid squad building. From left to right are (kneeling) Steve Heldt, Lee Arboreen, William Bogart, Bill Leary, Ogden Mills, Lawrence Anzavino, John Gibney, and Karl Anthony; (standing) Harold Goeller, Al Anzavino, Bob Karz, Ben Garnecki, unidentified, Dan Dugan, unidentified, Frank McCann, William Wyckoff, Lou DiFillipo, Nick Snyder, Steve "Pop" Heldt, and Bun Talada. A 1961 fire damaged the squad's recreation room, but it was repaired and a new addition was built in 1963.

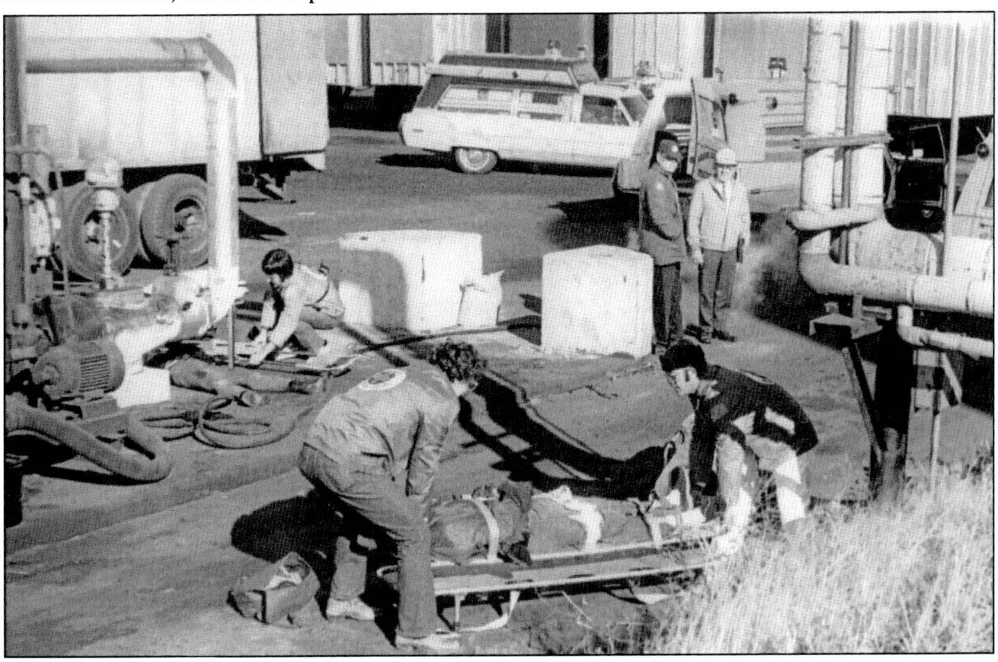

In this c. 1970 photograph, the Dunellen Rescue Squad responds to an industrial accident. In the background, two Cadillac ambulances can be seen.

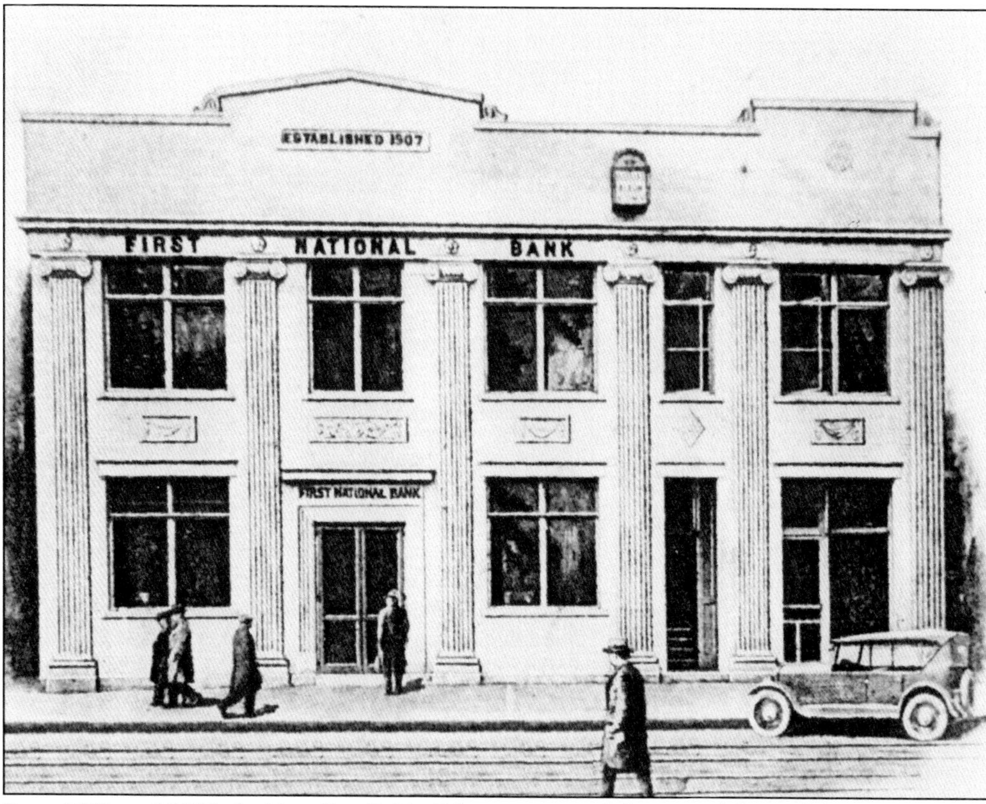


From 1922 until 1925, the Dunellen Public Library occupied the second floor of the First National Bank at 322 North Avenue. In 1925, the library then moved to the second floor of the Municipal Building, where it remained until 1974.

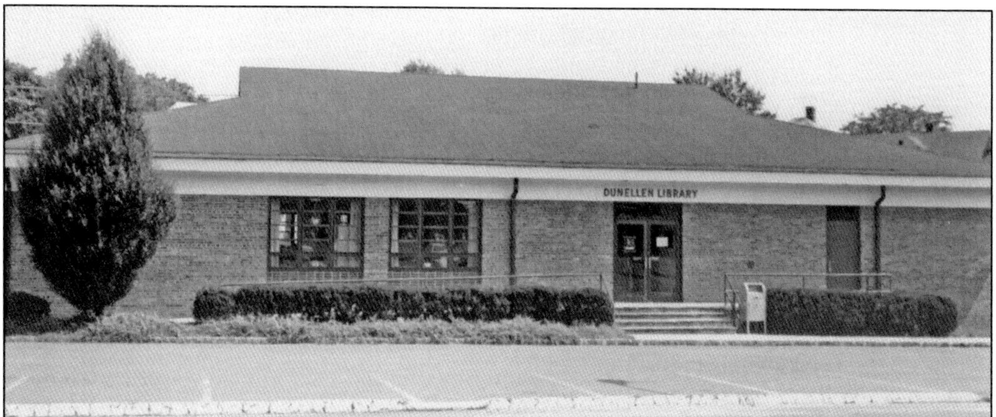


On June 15, 1970, the mayor and the borough council allocated a portion of the Art Color Printing Company parking lot on New Market Road as the site of the new library. The Arnold A. Schwartz Foundation granted $60,000 to the building fund. In 1972, state officials in Trenton and the Dunellen Library Board received a $53,000 federal grant. The Friends of the Library completed an outstanding fundraising campaign, and the goal of $227,250 was reached. The Arnold A. Schwartz Memorial Library, named in memory of the late head of the Art Color Printing Company, opened April 15, 1974.

# *Eight*

# Industry and Businesses

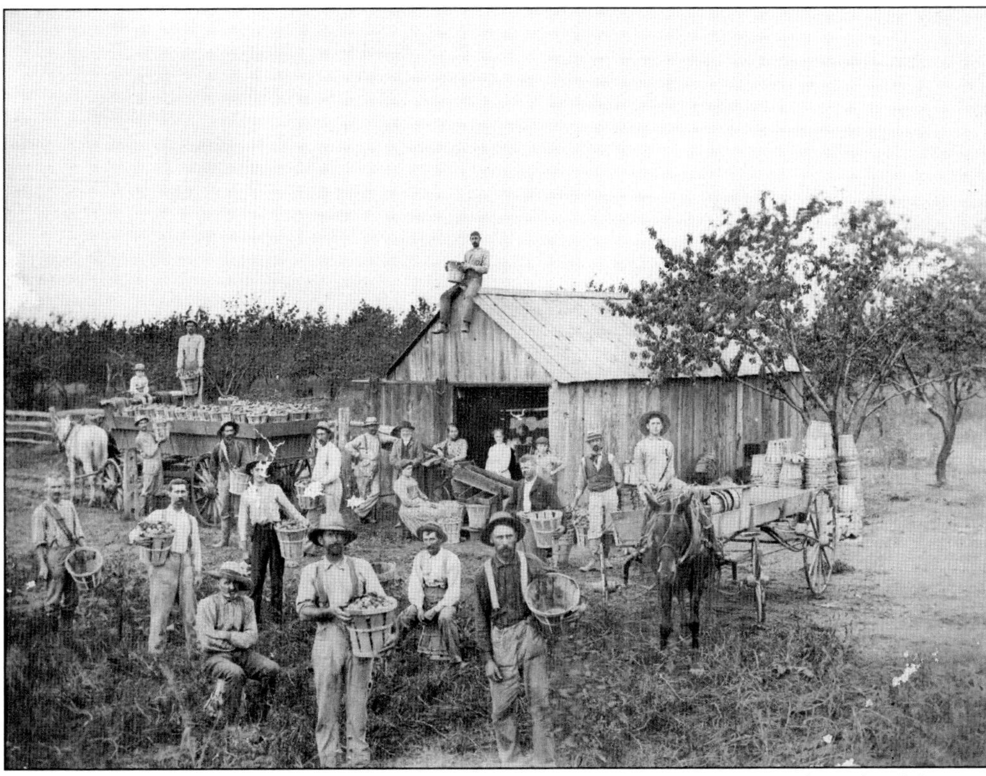

This is the Vail family harvesting peaches in 1898. Their farm encompassed much of the area that is now Columbia Park. When the Central New Jersey Land Improvement Company laid out the town of Dunellen in 1867, they stipulated no industries or factories could be established in Dunellen; it was to be a bedroom community to New York City. As the community grew, businesses and industries followed. (Courtesy of Lawrence Anzavino.)

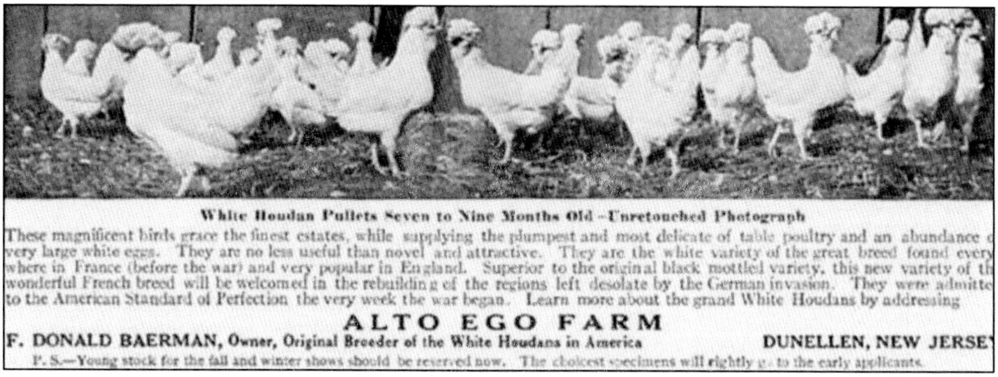


Another business in Dunellen in 1915 was the Alto Ego Farm. The chickens in the advertisement, white Houdans, were a breed developed by F.D. Baerman in Dunellen at the turn of the 20th century. In 1914, this breed became recognized by the American Poultry Association. In 1919, there were 75 poultry houses on his property at 736–752 Front Street, which extended the full block back to Dunellen Avenue.

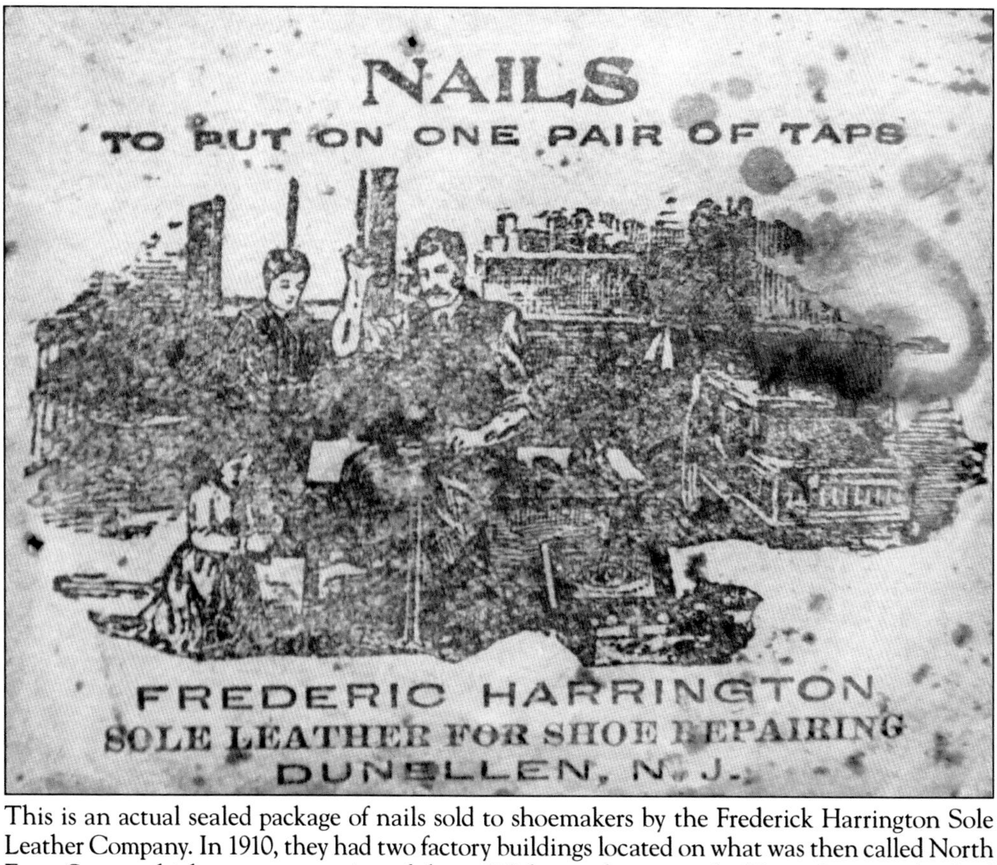


This is an actual sealed package of nails sold to shoemakers by the Frederick Harrington Sole Leather Company. In 1910, they had two factory buildings located on what was then called North Front Street, which was an extension of about 500 feet at the east end of Front Street and a dead end. (Courtesy of John Triolo.)

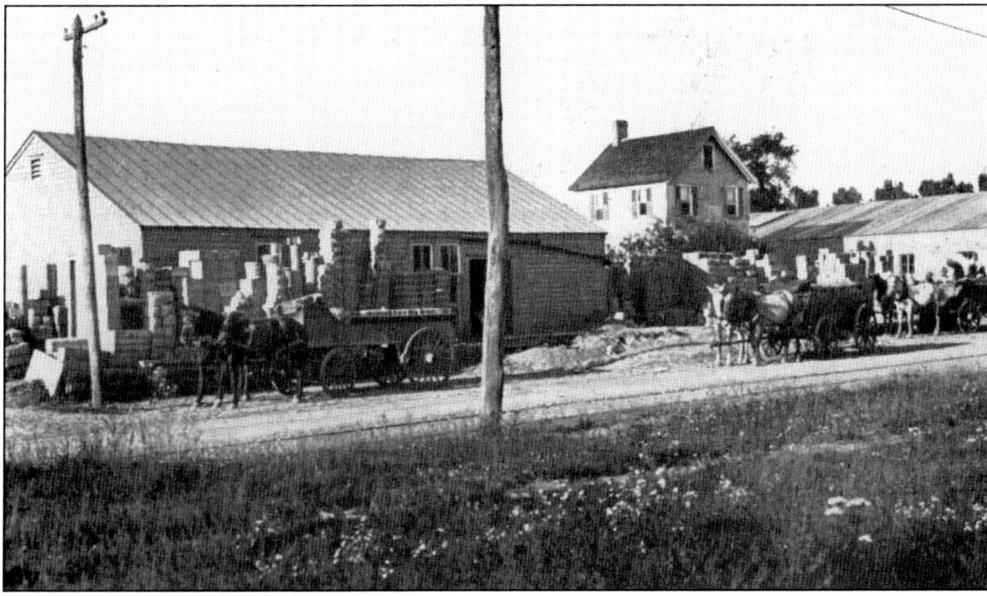

Much building was going on in Dunellen and surrounding areas. The Dunellen Cement Block Company, pictured here in 1911, was located at 281 South Washington Avenue. Teams of mules were used to pull wagons piled high with concrete blocks before the advent of trucks.

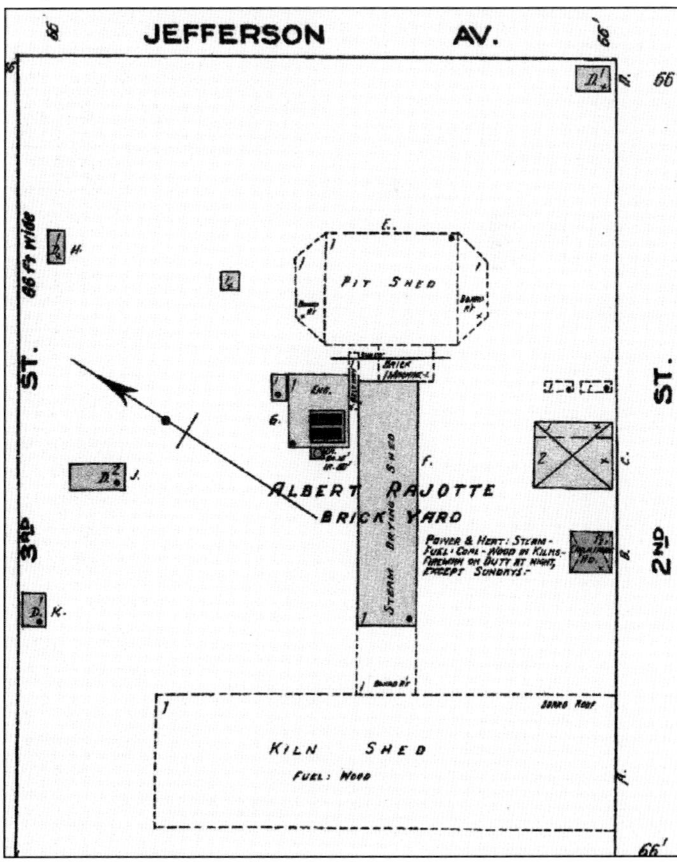


Here is a sketch of the Albert Rajotte Brickyard in 1910. It encompassed over 400 feet in length from Jefferson Avenue between Second and Third Streets. The company obtained its clay from a pit in nearby Green Brook. Even today, A. Rajotte bricks are dug up by residents in that area or found in the demolition of brick structures in Dunellen and surrounding towns.

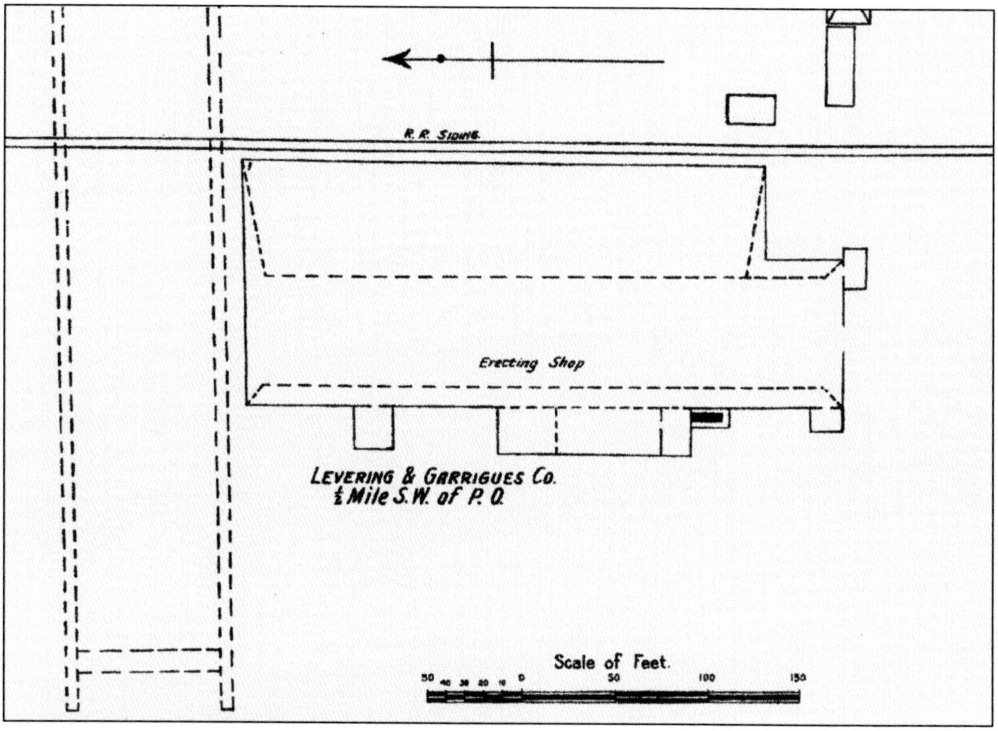


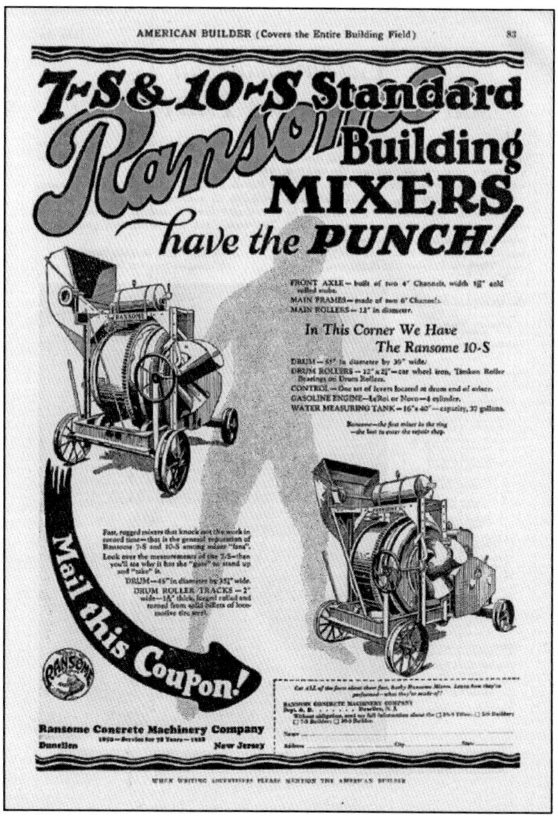


In 1902, Levering & Garrigues Ironworks was located at the edge of the borough off South Avenue. They fabricated iron and steel for construction projects. In 1911, the name was changed to Levgar Company. By 1915, it employed over 600 local residents. The company was sold to Buffalo Tank in 1939 and closed in November 1980 as a division of Bethlehem Steel.

The Ransome Concrete Machinery Company located just outside of Dunellen was world famous. The plant stretched from North Avenue between the railroad tracks to Rock Avenue in Plainfield. Ernest Ransome invented machinery to mix concrete at construction sites. Ransome machinery was used to construct buildings after the San Francisco earthquake, to form foundations of the George Washington Bridge, to build the Los Angeles aqueducts, and to assemble New York City's municipal docks. The plant closed in 1948.

R. Hoe & Company manufactured printing presses of all types. They purchased all the land, buildings, and equipment of the Hall Printing Press Company in 1924. The plant and facilities occupied 16 acres partially in Dunellen and in adjoining communities.

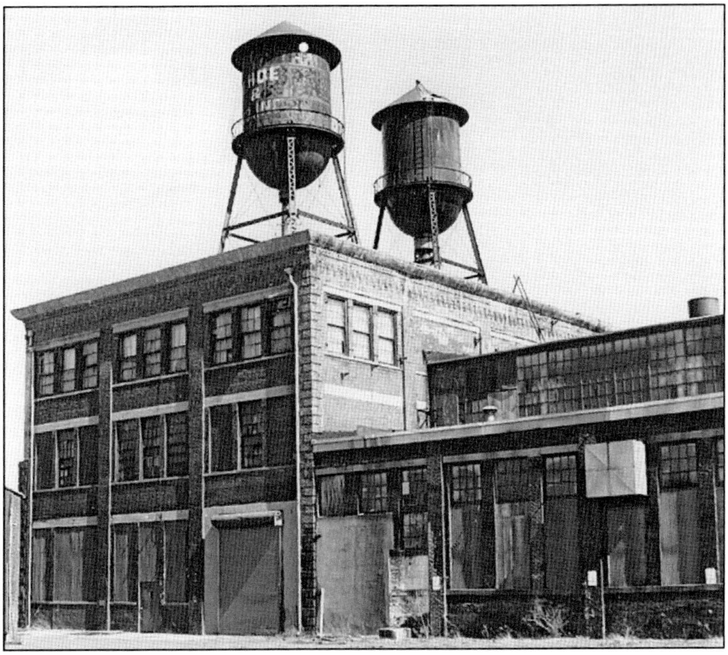

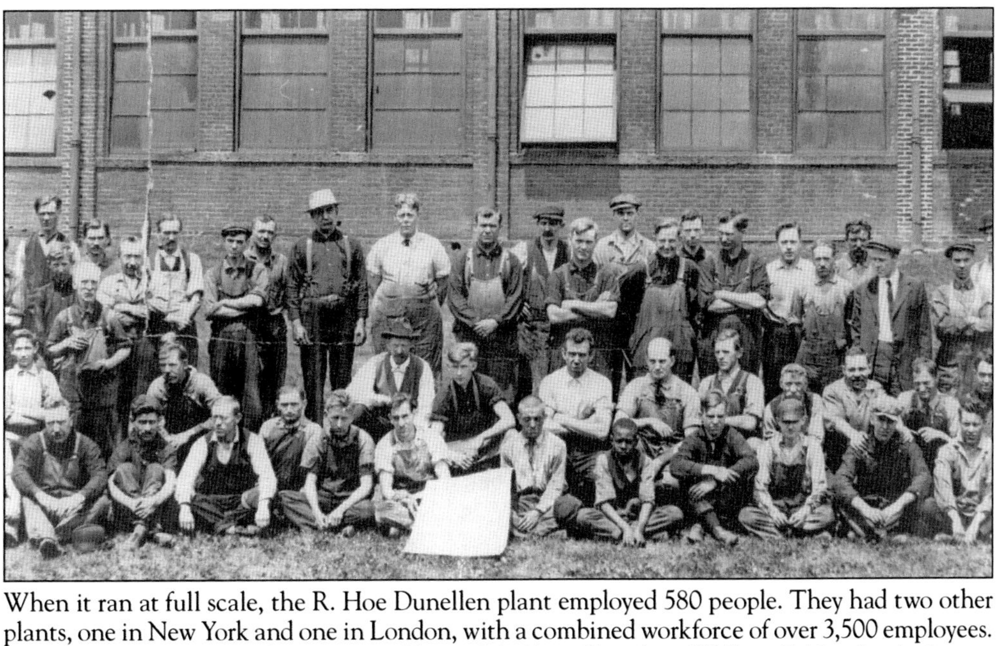

When it ran at full scale, the R. Hoe Dunellen plant employed 580 people. They had two other plants, one in New York and one in London, with a combined workforce of over 3,500 employees. In this undated photograph are men and boys of the Dunellen plant. William Eckhard, a draftsman at R. Hoe, invented a mercury switch for use on a press. The switch acquired many other uses, one being in thermostats for industries and homes.

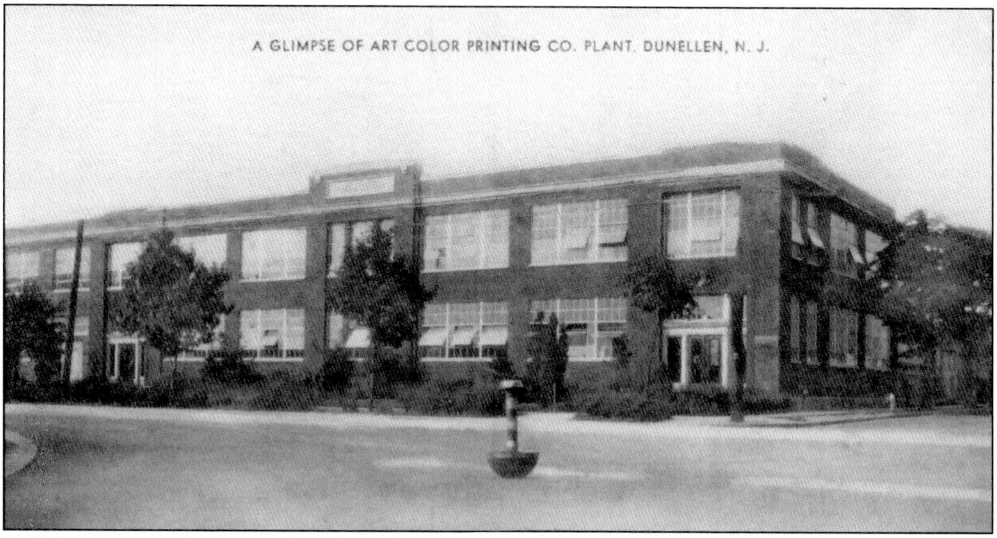


In February 1924, borough officials and the local Rotary Club were making efforts to convince the Art Color Printing Company to locate its plant in Dunellen. The company asked that Dunellen residents purchase $50,000 in stock. The quota was reached, and ground was broken for the new plant on July 24, 1924. The initial building was 140 feet wide and 780 feet long at a cost of $400,000, including machinery. It employed 350 people at that time. (Courtesy of John Triolo.)

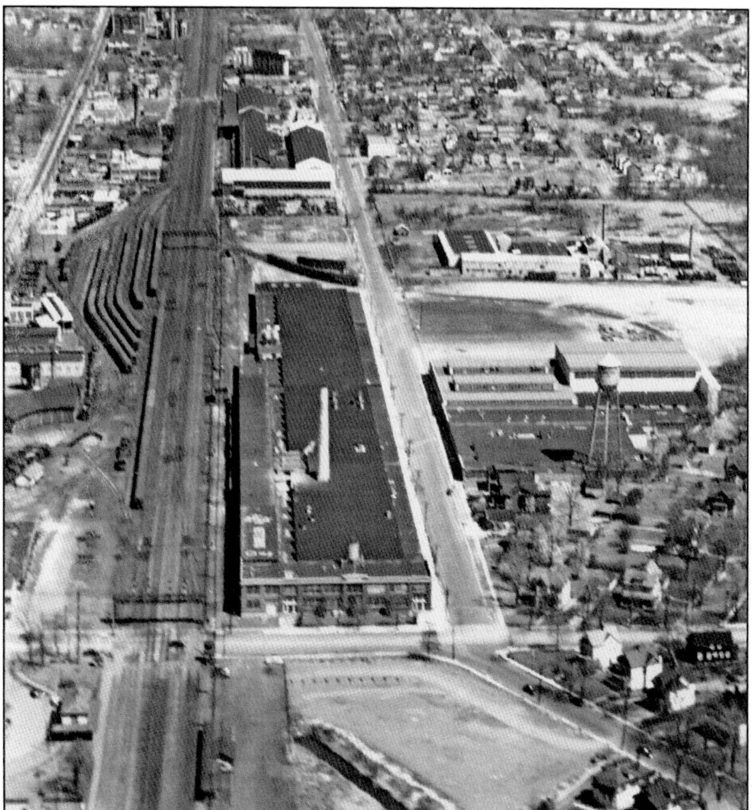

This is an aerial photograph of Art Color Printing Company in 1938. After the magazine output of the plant had exceeded all expectations, a 588-feet-long, 100-feet-wide extension was added to the east end. A year later, another building measuring 140 feet by 200 feet was added on the south side of South Avenue. In all, five additions were made to accommodate additional presses and paper storage.

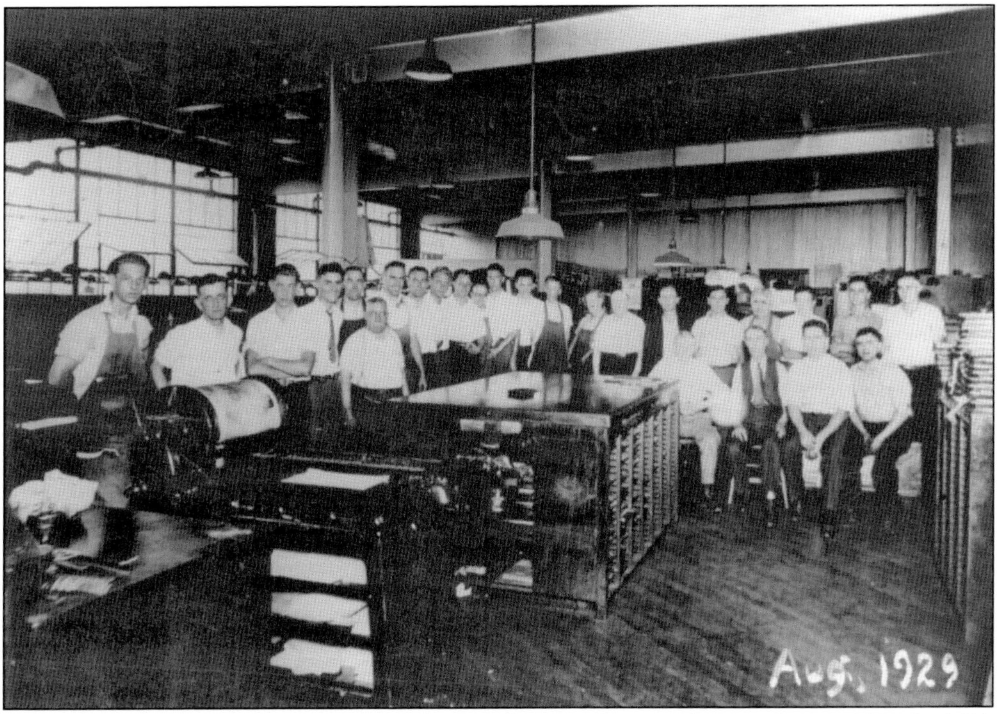


This Art Color Printing Company employees photograph was taken in August 1929. In 1931, the W.F. Hall Printing Company of Chicago purchased Art Color Printing Company for $2.7 million. The merger increased the number of employees at the Dunellen plant, and the combined facilities of Art Color Printing Company and W.F. Hall Printing Company made it the largest printing company in the world. The Dunellen plant produced 11 million copies of magazines per month.

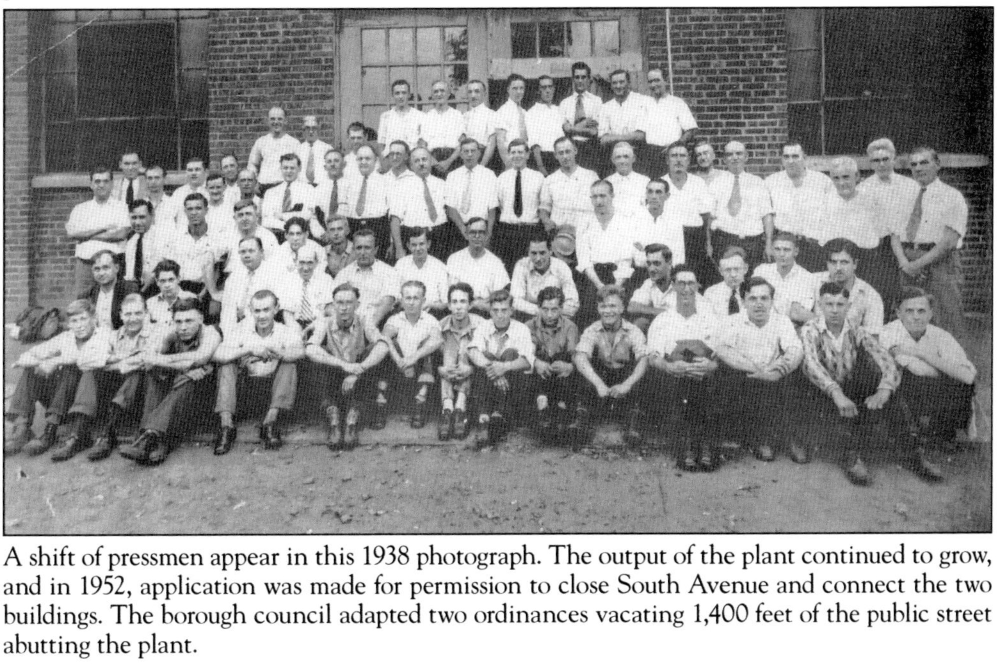

A shift of pressmen appear in this 1938 photograph. The output of the plant continued to grow, and in 1952, application was made for permission to close South Avenue and connect the two buildings. The borough council adapted two ordinances vacating 1,400 feet of the public street abutting the plant.

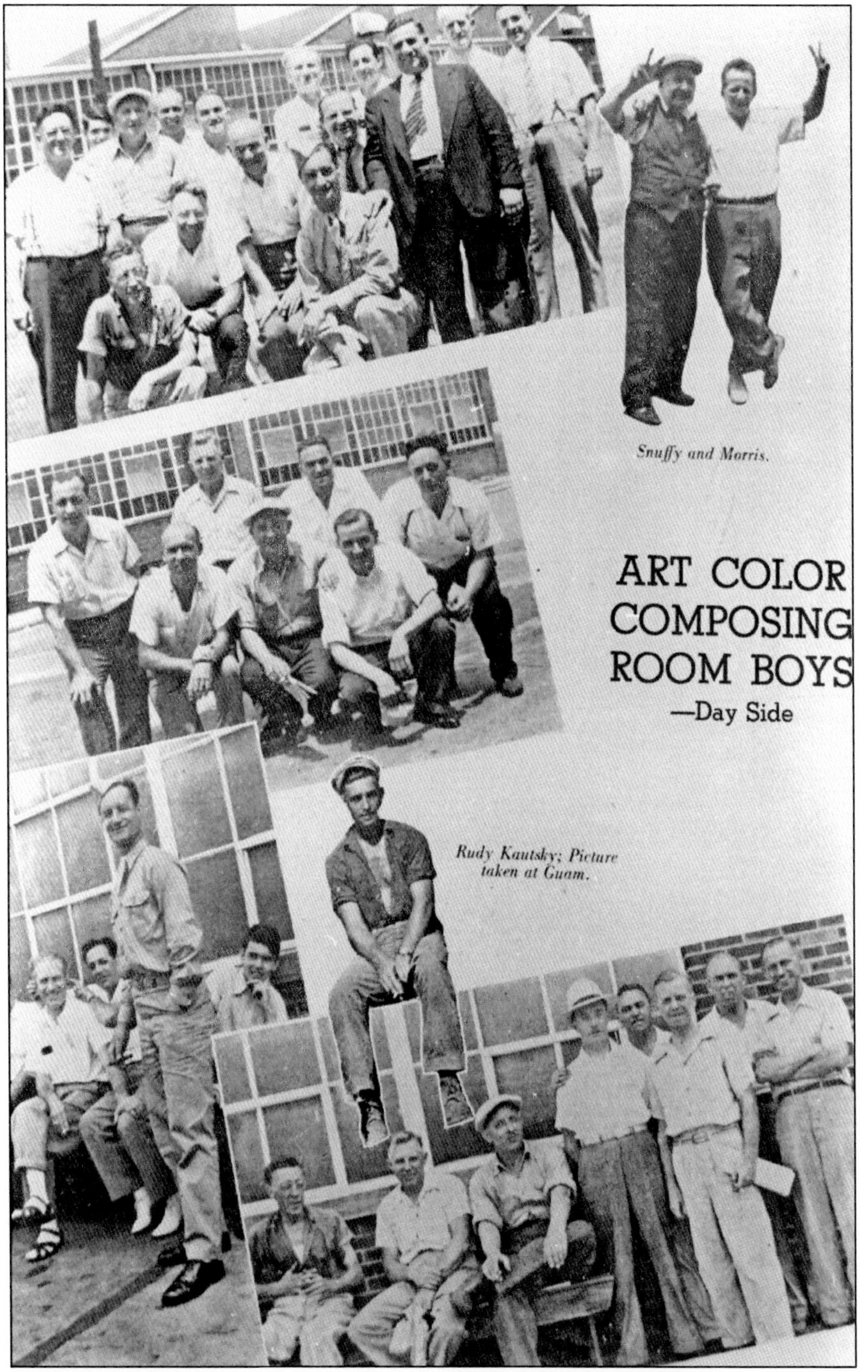


This is a page of the Art Color Printing Company newsletter in 1945 featuring the composing room boys. World War II was nearing its end, and sailor Rudy Kautsky (sitting in the center) and soldier John Bublovic (standing to the left of Kautsky) were back at the presses. Almost every major magazine and catalog was printed in Dunellen. The company employed fathers and sons for over four decades. The loss of the McFadden Publishers contract, along with other financial problems, closed the plant in 1968. Over 1,000 jobs were lost, and it impacted Dunellen heavily.

This picture of the *Weekly Call* printing shop at 318 Front Street was taken in 1895. George Day purchased the *Call* and built his residence at the front of the lot. The newspaper grew; by 1914, there were 610 homes and businesses in Dunellen. On October 17, 1935, after 43 years of publication, George W. Day sold the newspaper. After only eight months, the new owners sold the company to George W. Spayth.

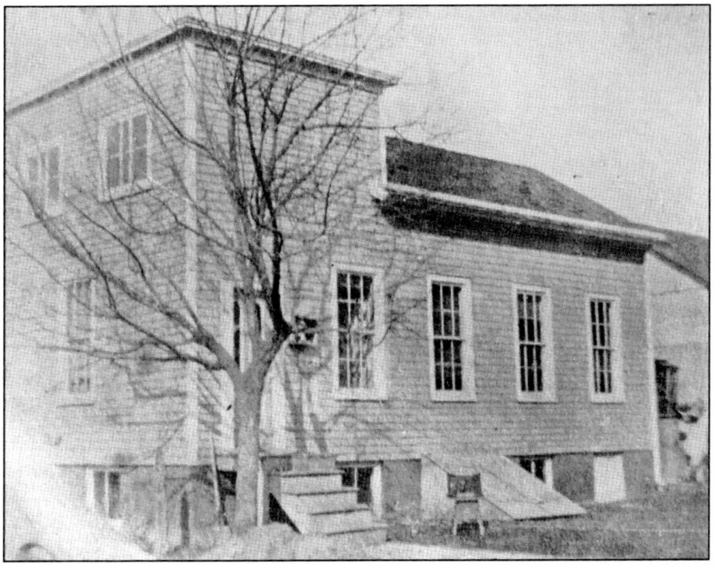

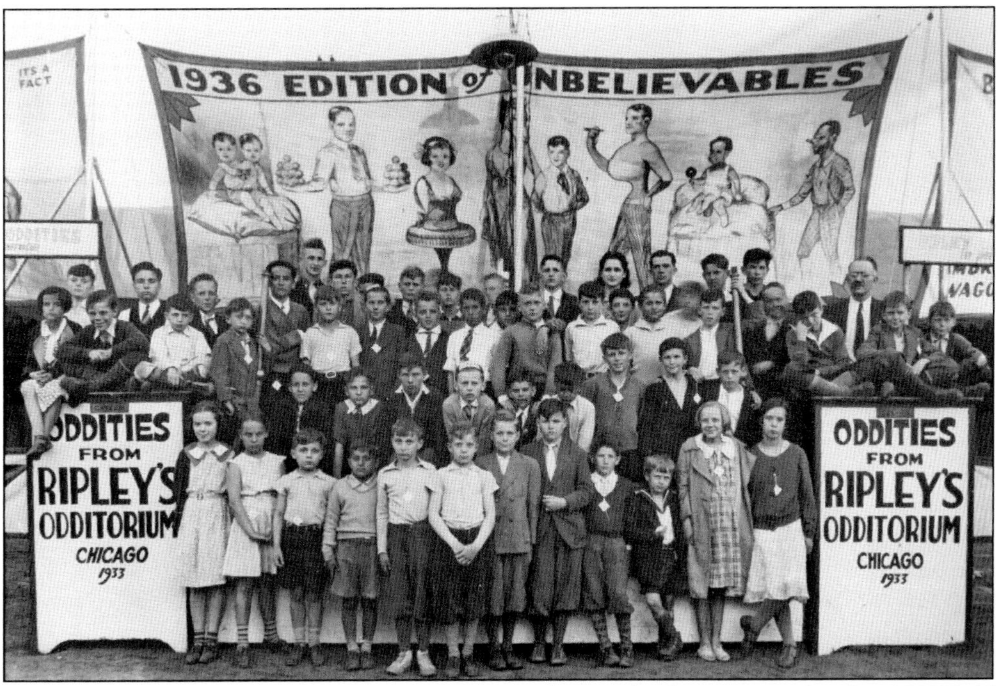


George W. Spayth (top row, right) and all of his paper boys and girls are pictured at the 1936 World of Mirth Carnival on the Arbor Firehouse grounds in New Market. Each year, Spayth would reward his carriers with an outing to the carnival, paying for their food, rides, and entertainment. He did this from 1933 until 1963. After 76 years, the *Weekly Call* ceased operation in 1968.

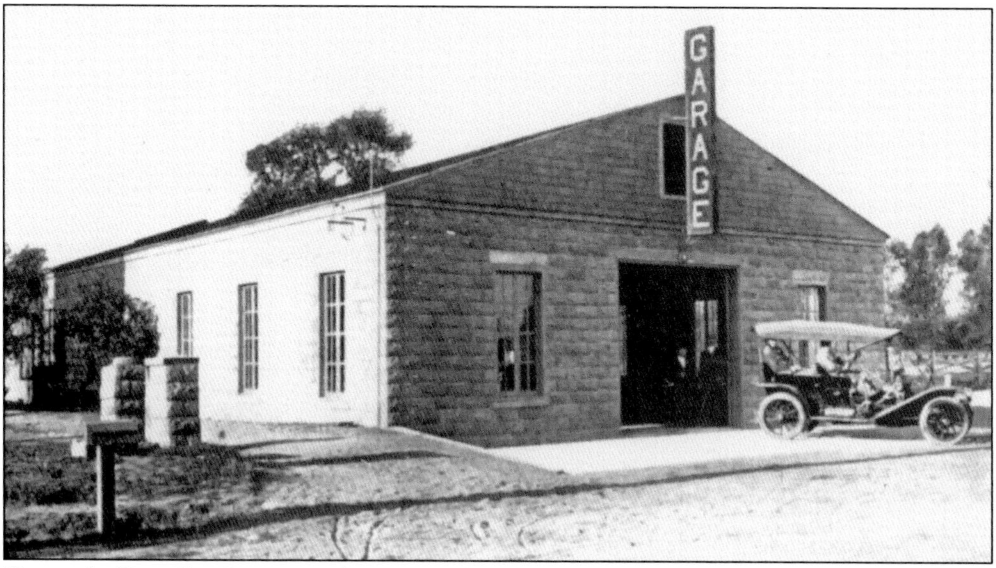


Here is the Dunellen Garage on the corner of Washington and North Avenues in 1915. Gasoline was 12¢ per gallon. The first horseless carriage in Dunellen was purchased by Dr. Nelson in 1903. The farmers were upset because the automobiles scared their horses. The county organized the Highway Protectors Association to regulate the speed of automobiles on the roads, and the borough put up three signs limiting the speed to 10 miles per hour.

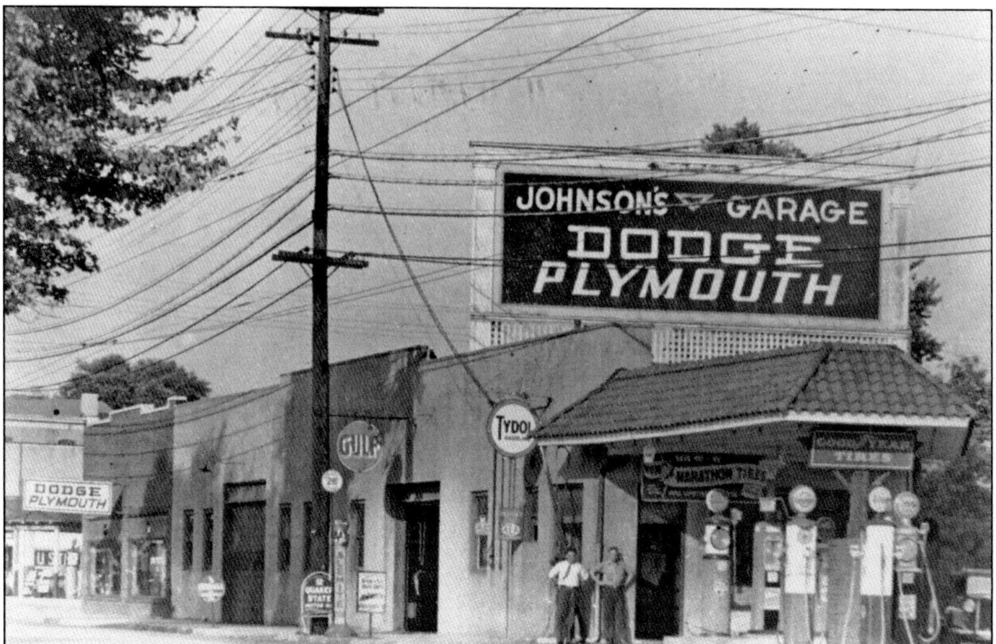


Johnson's Garage was located on the triangular property between North Avenue, Madison Avenue, and Bound Brook Road in this 1938 photograph. It was a full-service garage and car dealership for Dodge and Plymouth automobiles. Gasoline was 13¢ per gallon. At the time, residents could purchase a new Plymouth or Dodge for $700 to $910. At present, this building is still an automobile repair shop.

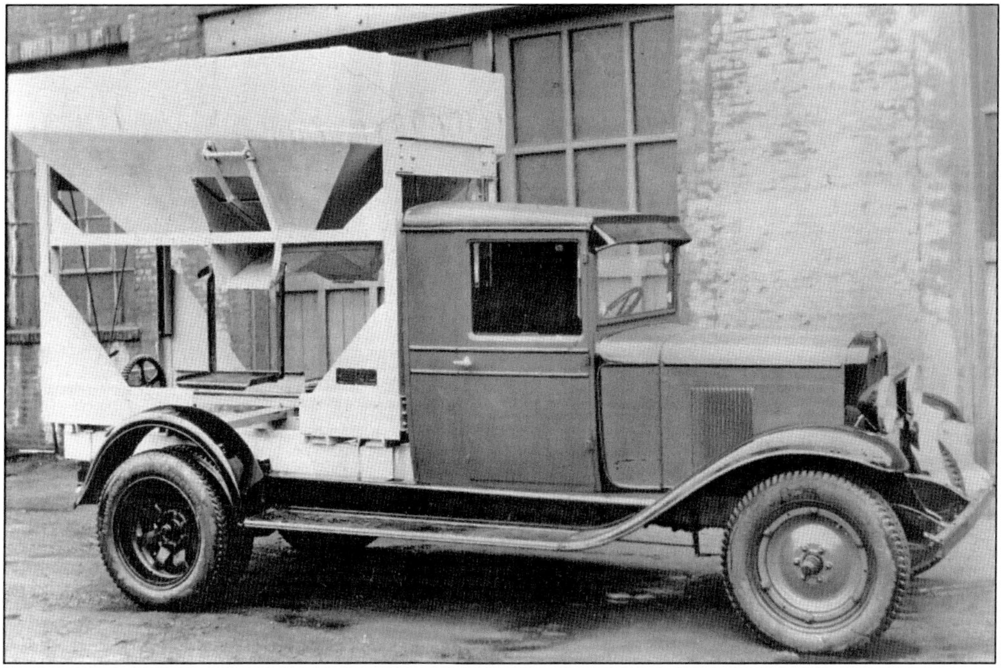

In 1930, almost all homes and businesses were heated with coal. Here is a picture of a truck used by the Morecraft Fuel Company to deliver coal. Buildings had coal chutes to transfer coal deliveries to their storage areas. Joseph Morecraft Jr., the owner, went on to become mayor from 1936 until 1946 and again from 1954 to 1958. He later became chairman of the New Jersey Turnpike Authority.

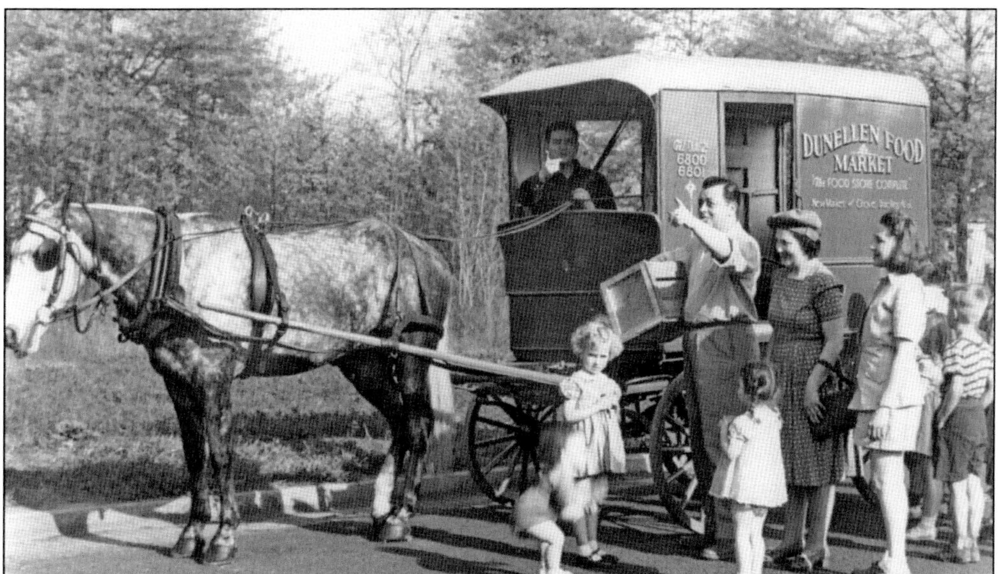


Not all deliveries were done by truck in the 1940s. This horse and wagon was used by the Dunellen Food Market, also known as Botwin's, in 1946. Their grocery was located on the northwest corner of New Market Road and Grove Street. In 1932, Botwin's had a contest in which one lucky shopper per month won a $20 gold piece.

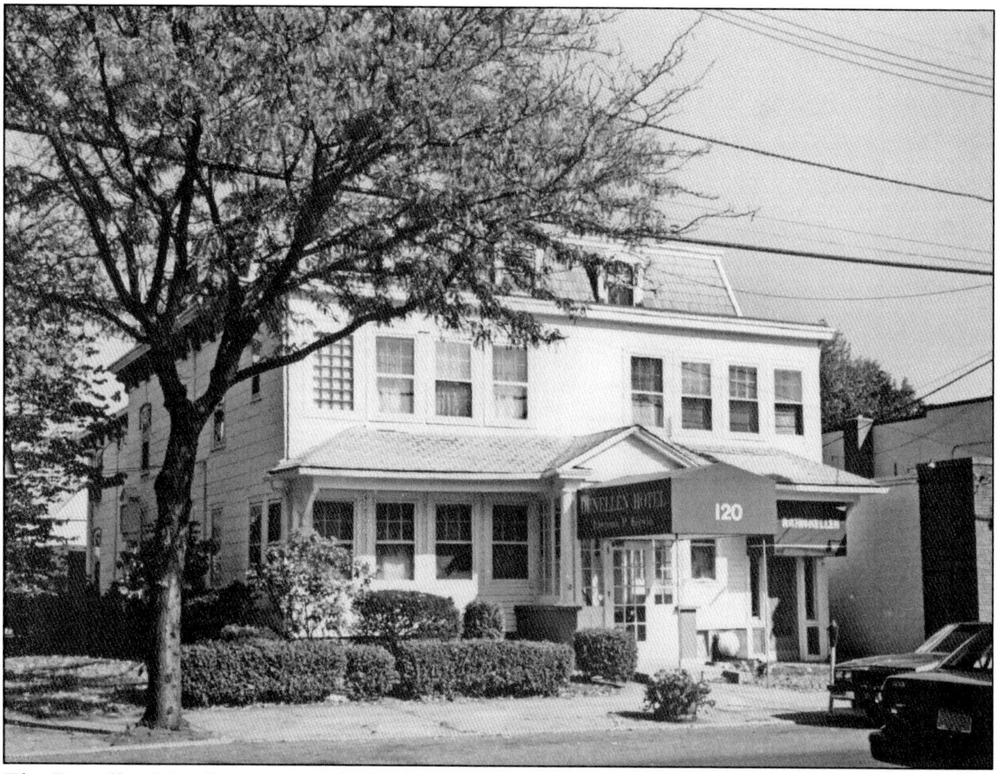


The Dunellen Hotel was originally built in 1869 as the residence of William Richardson. It was remodeled in 1925 by new owners Lawrence and Michael Kerwin, who changed the interior to a restaurant and hotel, first known as the Charlotte Inn and now the Dunellen Hotel. After an 1869 fire destroyed Mount Horeb Church, the original hand-hewn beams were purchased by Richardson, hauled to Dunellen by teams of oxen, reused in building his home, and are the ceiling beams of the present-day Rathskeller basement pub.

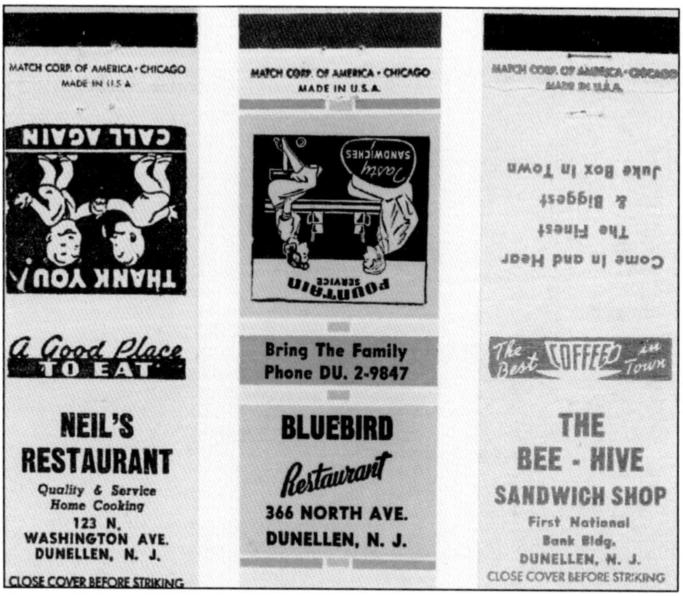


These are some examples of matchbook-cover advertising from other Dunellen businesses. As with any community, there are many businesses that have passed into oblivion over the years. These three were operating in the 1950s and 1960s. (Courtesy of John Triolo.)

# *Nine*

# MEMORABLE EVENTS

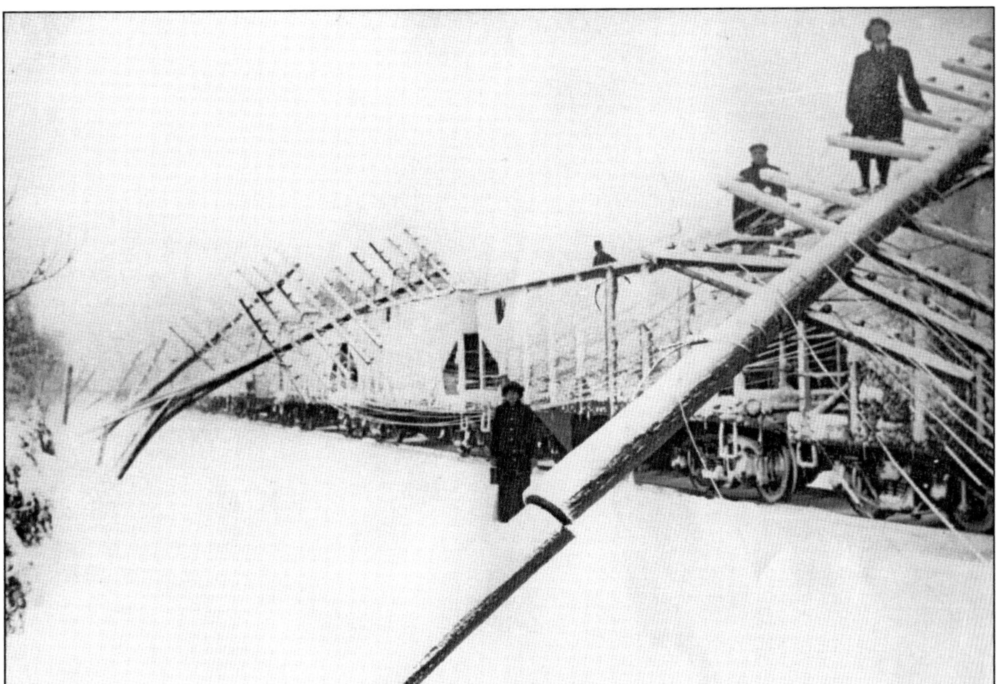

A snow-and-ice storm in 1914 cut telephone and telegraph communications along the New Jersey Central line, shown in this picture. A couple of decades earlier in 1895, there was a blizzard so severe that manpower was used to clear the tracks and keep the trains running. The railroad had 90 men housed and fed at the Park Hotel for three days to accomplish the track-clearing task.

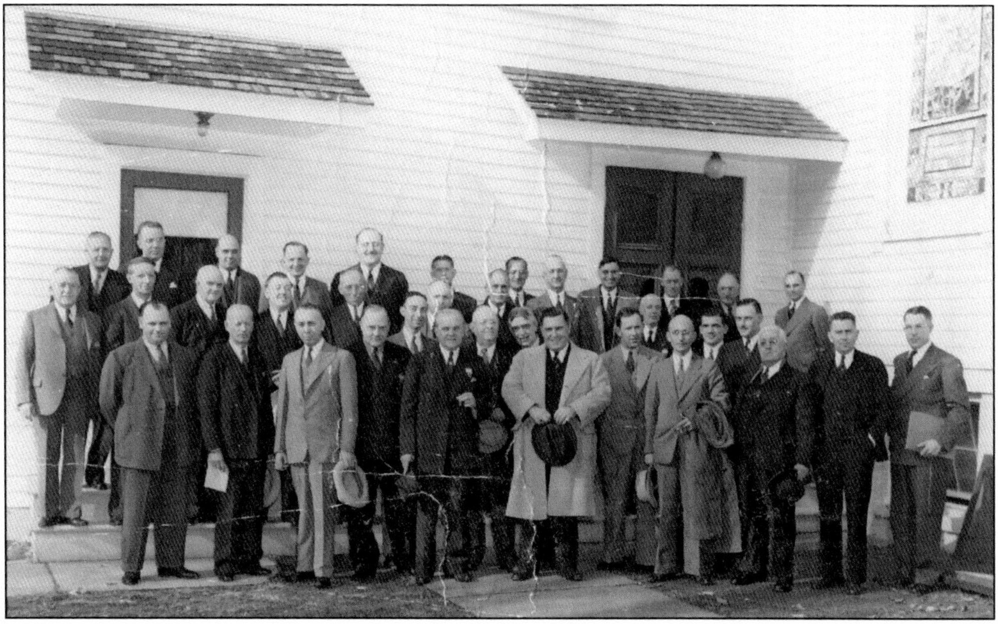

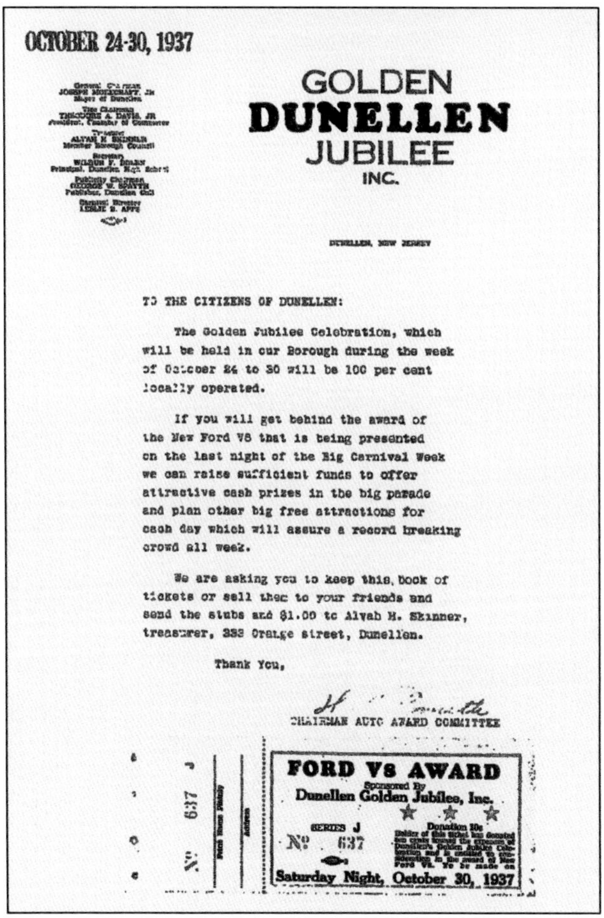

OCTOBER 24-30, 1937

GOLDEN
**DUNELLEN**
JUBILEE
INC.

General Chairman
JOSEPH MORECRAFT, JR
Mayor of Dunellen
Vice Chairman
THEODORE A. DAVIS, JR
President, Chamber of Commerce
Treasurer
ALVAH H. SKINNER
Member Borough Council
Secretary
WILBUR F. BOLEN
Principal, Dunellen High School
Publicity Chairman
GEORGE W. SPAYTH
Publisher, Dunellen Call
[illegible] Director
LESLIE S. APPE

DUNELLEN, NEW JERSEY

TO THE CITIZENS OF DUNELLEN:

The Golden Jubilee Celebration, which will be held in our Borough during the week of October 24 to 30 will be 100 per cent locally operated.

If you will get behind the award of the New Ford V8 that is being presented on the last night of the Big Carnival Week we can raise sufficient funds to offer attractive cash prizes in the big parade and plan other big free attractions for each day which will assure a record breaking crowd all week.

We are asking you to keep this book of tickets or sell them to your friends and send the stubs and $1.00 to Alvah H. Skinner, treasurer, 333 Orange street, Dunellen.

Thank You,

[signature]
CHAIRMAN AUTO AWARD COMMITTEE

Nº 637

**FORD V8 AWARD**
Sponsored By
Dunellen Golden Jubilee, Inc.
★ ★ ★
SERIES J
Nº 637
Donation 10c
Saturday Night, October 30, 1937

This 1937 picture taken alongside the First Presbyterian Church is of the Dunellen Golden Jubilee Committee. The members were composed of the mayor and council, businessmen, and civic leaders. Mayor Joseph Morecraft Jr. (first row, third from left) is wearing the light-colored suit. The gentleman on the first row, extreme right is Wilbur Bolen, principal of the high school. Bolen wrote the souvenir book for the 75th anniversary in 1962.

This letter and book of chances were sent to Dunellen residents prior to the 1937 Golden Jubilee Week. They were asked to buy or sell the tickets at 10¢ each and send $1 to treasurer Alvah Skinner. The drawing prize was a new Ford V8 automobile. The jubilee featured a carnival, live shows, a parade, and other activities during the week of October 24–30, 1937. (Courtesy of George Deene.)

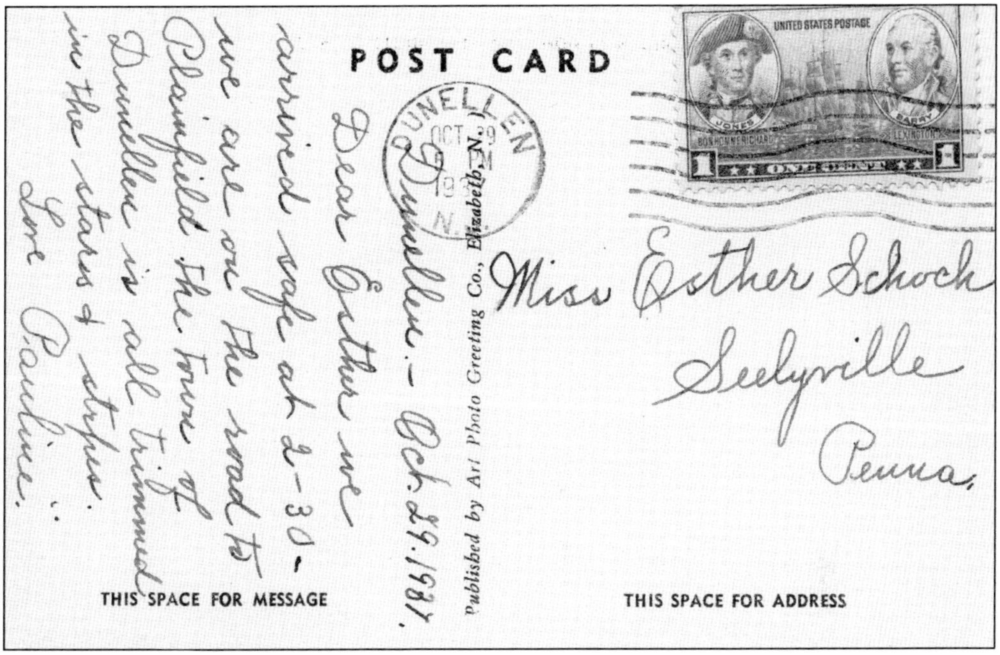


The postcard shown above is from the author's collection and, by chance, it was mailed during the Dunellen Golden Jubilee. The message reads: "Dunellen, October 29, 1937. Dear Esther, we arrived safe at 2:30—we are on the road to Plainfield. The town of Dunellen is all trimmed in the stars and stripes. Love, Pauline." (Courtesy of John Triolo.)

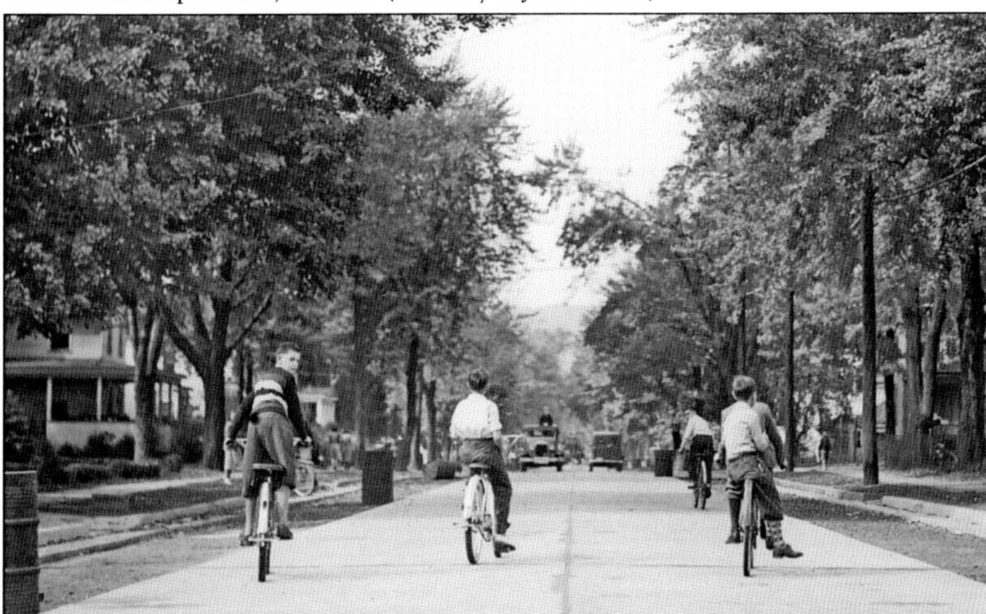

These five boys on four bicycles are waiting for the Dunellen Golden Jubilee parade as it heads toward them. They will probably follow it, as boys do. They are riding along on the new concrete roadway of Washington Avenue. Of note are the barrels on both sides, as the shoulders have not yet been poured. Federal WPA projects were all over town in 1937. (Courtesy of Schuyler family collection.)

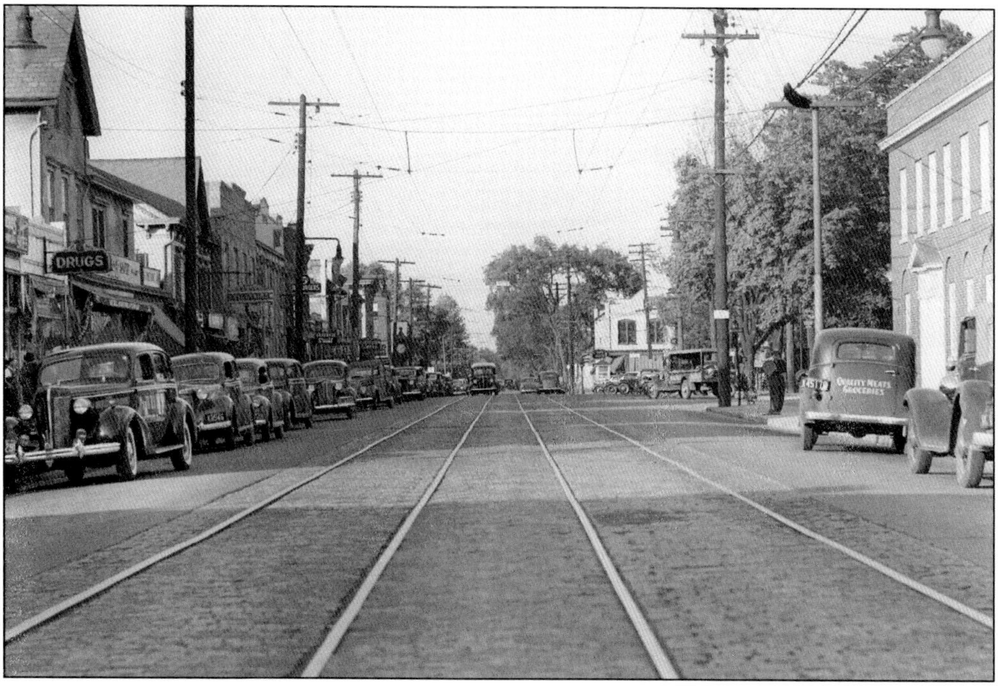


This 1937 picture of the North Avenue business district facing east shows the cobblestone road. The double set of trolley tracks were to be removed in yet another WPA project. These tracks extended from the borders of Middlesex and Plainfield. (Courtesy of Schuyler family collection.)

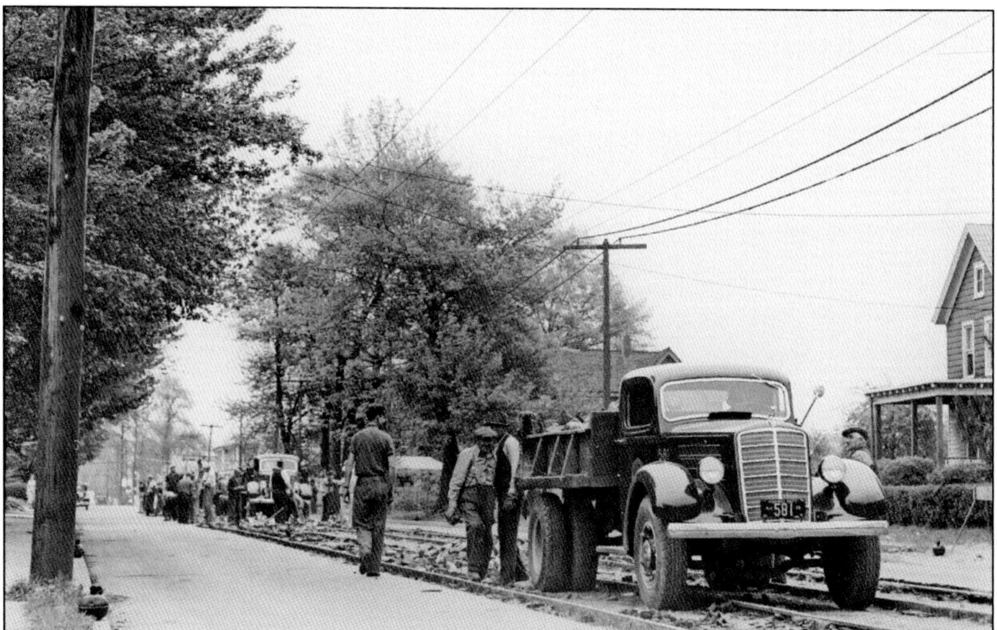

Here, a construction crew is tearing up the old roadway and trolley tracks. Concrete roadways were poured to replace the old. All the tracks were scrapped. According to town lore, the tracks were taken up to aid the war effort after December 7, 1941. This was not so. The work was done in 1938 as part of a WPA project.

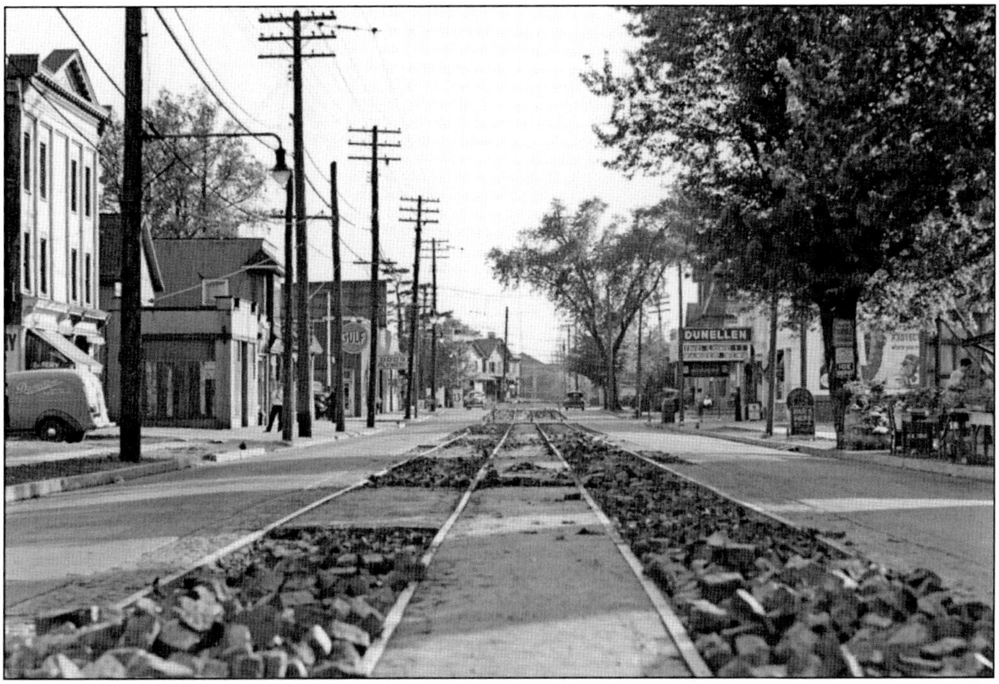


Dunellen says good-bye to cobblestoned North Avenue. In the background on the right is the Dunellen Theater. On the marquee, the *Lone Ranger* is the Saturday matinee. The banner hanging beneath the marquee is for the 1938 feature film *The Kid Comes Back*. Below, the street is ready for pouring concrete. (Courtesy of Schuyler family collection.)

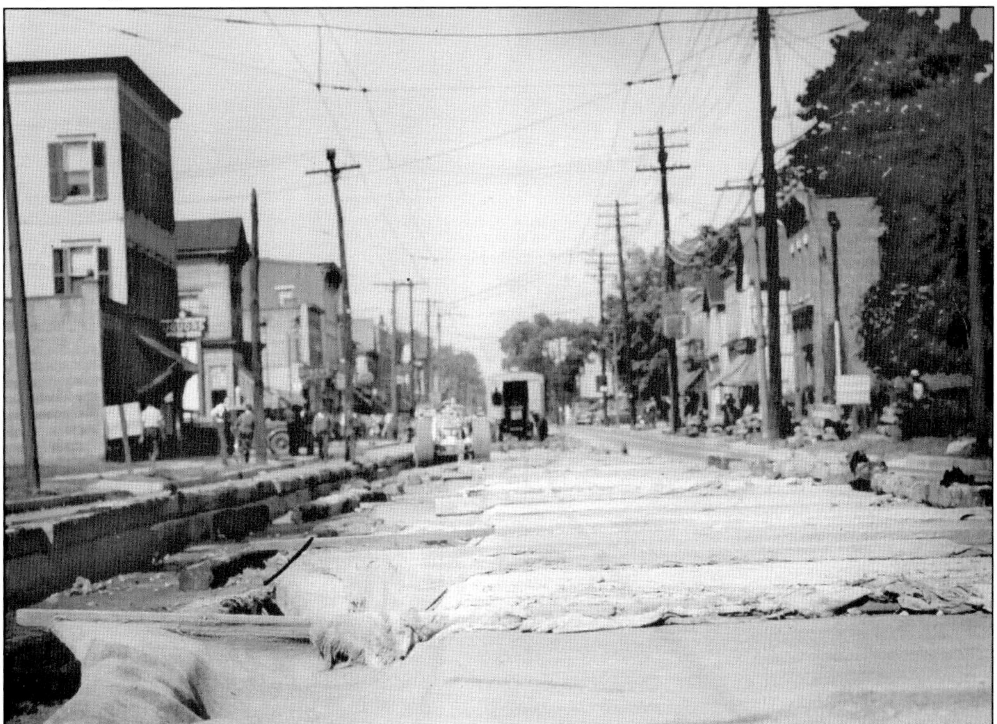

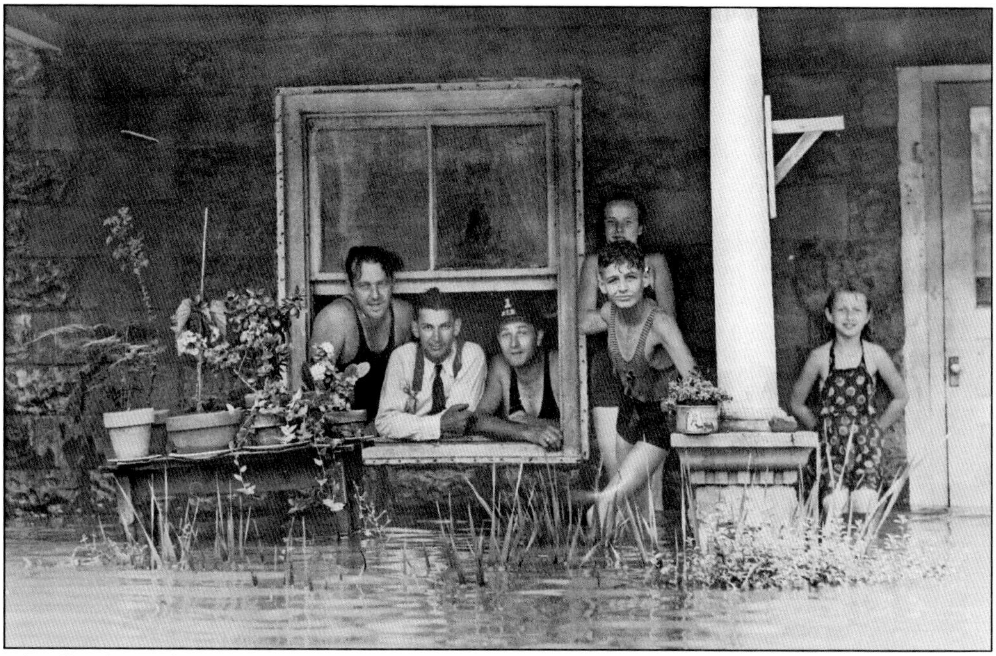

This flood on July 14, 1938, was the result of a prolonged period of thunderstorms in the Raritan River Basin, causing flooding in many sections of Dunellen and other area towns. Above, a few of the people living here at 240 Orange Street can still smile for the camera. Below, when the adults are away, the children will play. (Courtesy of Schuyler family collection.)

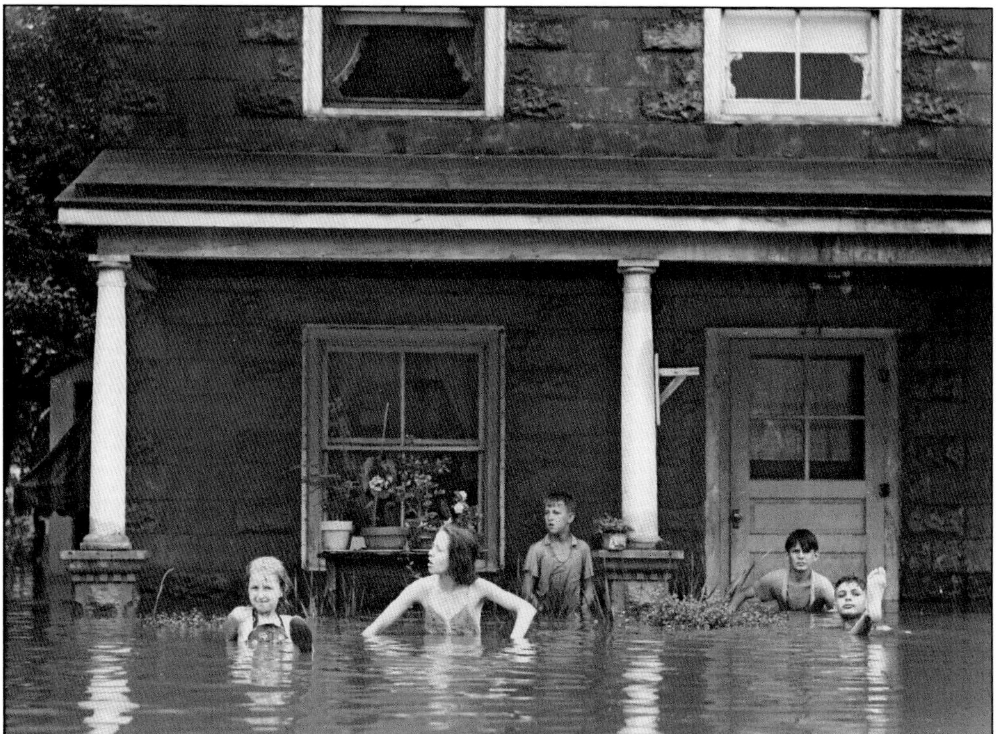

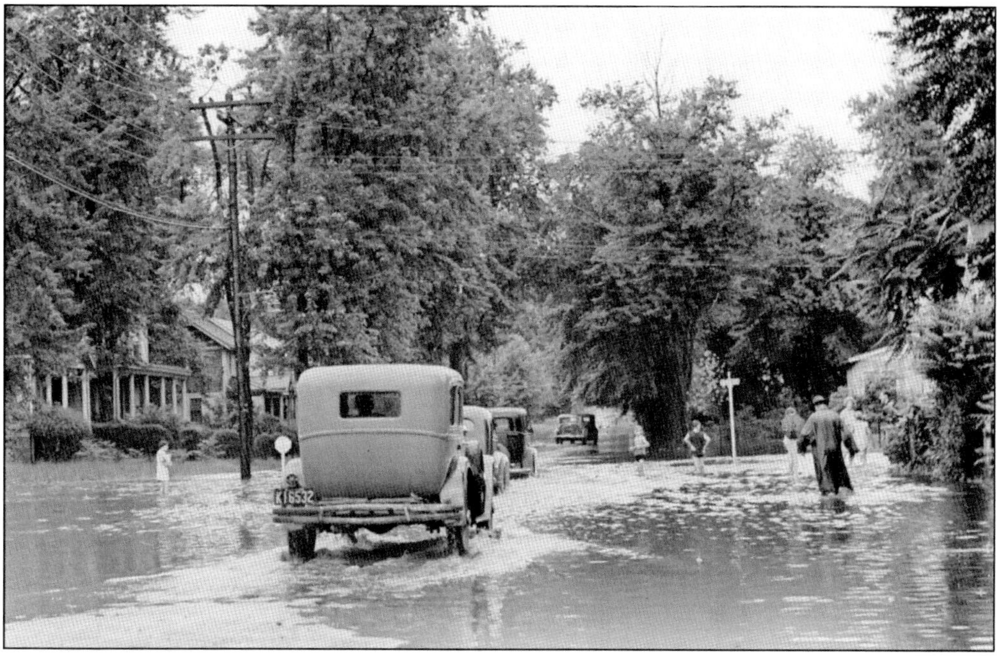

This is the scene at the intersection of Grove Street and Prospect Avenue. Cars slowly drive through, a man wades, and children play. The storm flooded sections of North and South Avenues, Bound Brook Road, Mountain View Terrace, and Orange, Columbia, and Pulaski Streets as well as the west end of Dunellen Avenue. (Courtesy of Schuyler family collection.)

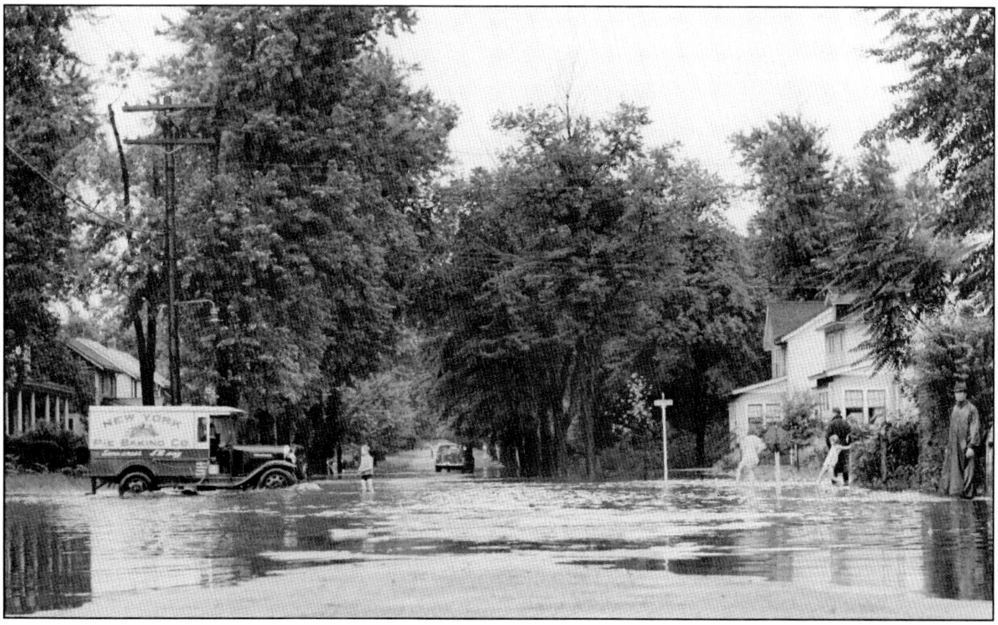


Grove Street looking east at its intersection with Prospect Avenue shows a New York Pie Baking Company truck trying to cross the intersection. The water is up to his running boards. Children are playing, and adults are looking on. The little girl on the right is leaning on a small bridge abutment of the Bonagut Brook. The brook, which is piped underground, still creates flooding to this day. (Courtesy of Schuyler family collection.)

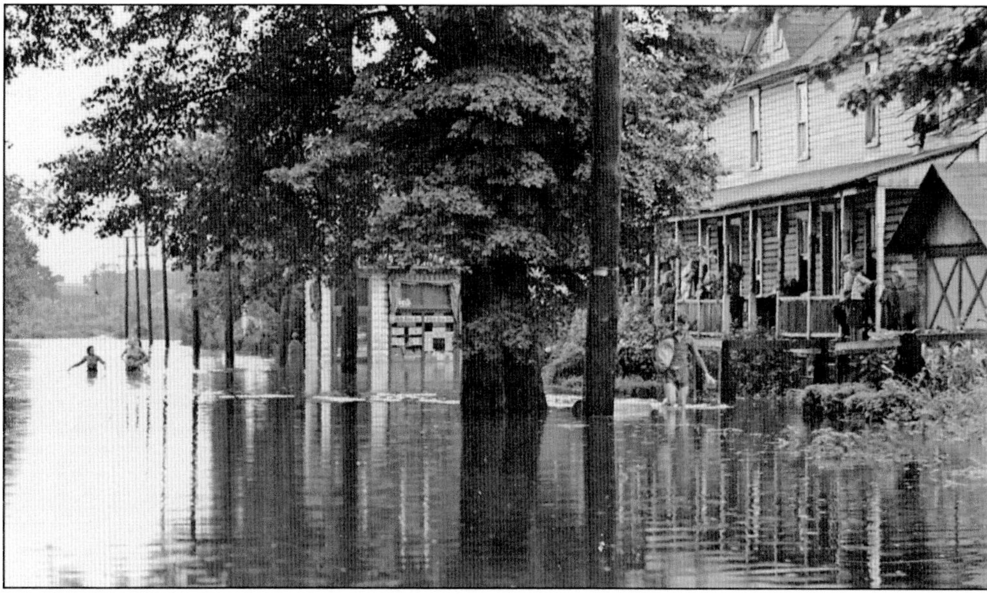

This picture was taken looking south from where the railroad embankment now stands on Pulaski Street. The house on the right has adults and children looking from the porch. A boy carries a bag of groceries from the store across the street. The store, a grocery and butcher shop, was owned by Joseph and Helen Boniakowski and built in 1916. The house at 140–150 Pulaski Street still stands today. (Courtesy of Schuyler family collection.)

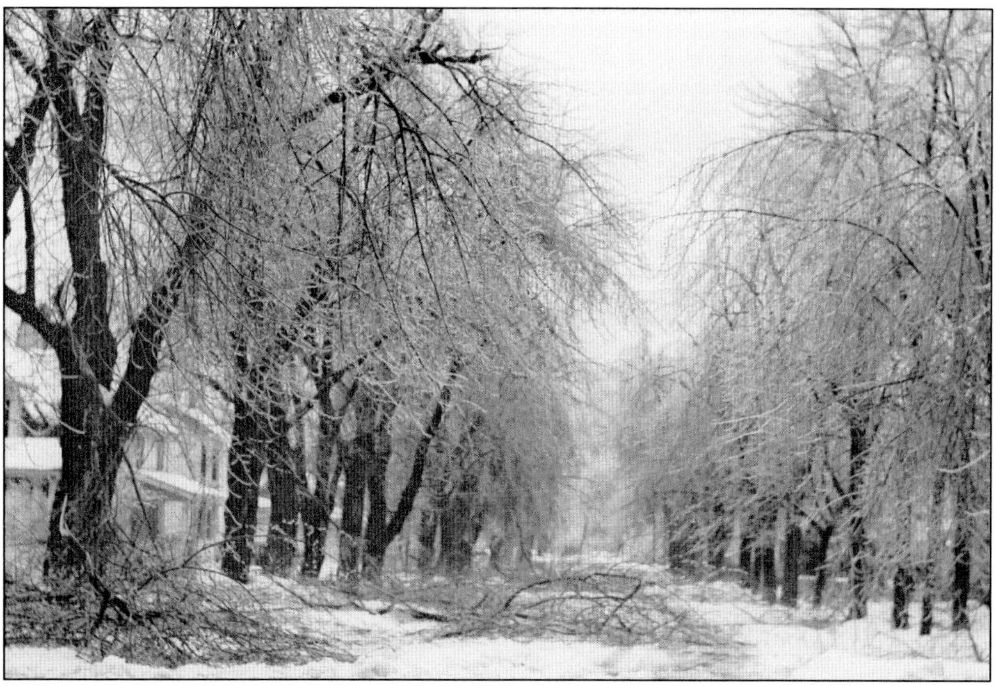

On November 27, 1938, the Sunday after Thanksgiving, 11 inches of snow fell. The snowfall is still the record for November. Besides the snow, ice brought down many trees and power lines throughout the town. Snow removal in those days was performed using a road grader and manpower. (Courtesy of Schuyler family collection.)

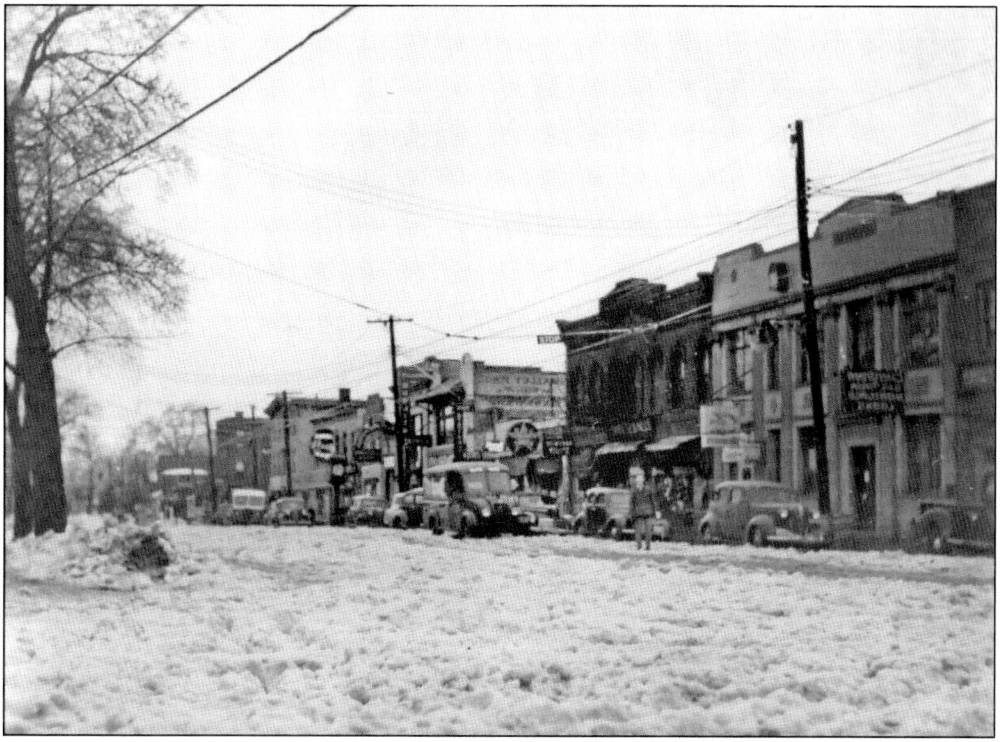

Above, on Monday, November 28, 1938, it was business as usual at the bank. The picture below, taken on December 2, 1938, shows part of the downtown after the storm cleanup. Shown here on North Avenue facing west near the intersection of Washington Avenue are considerable sized piles of snow. The Dunellen Café, Gregory's Diner, and Cashin's Hardware Store are visible on the right. Tom's Tavern is on the corner across the street where the Town Pharmacy building now stands. (Courtesy of Schuyler family collection.)

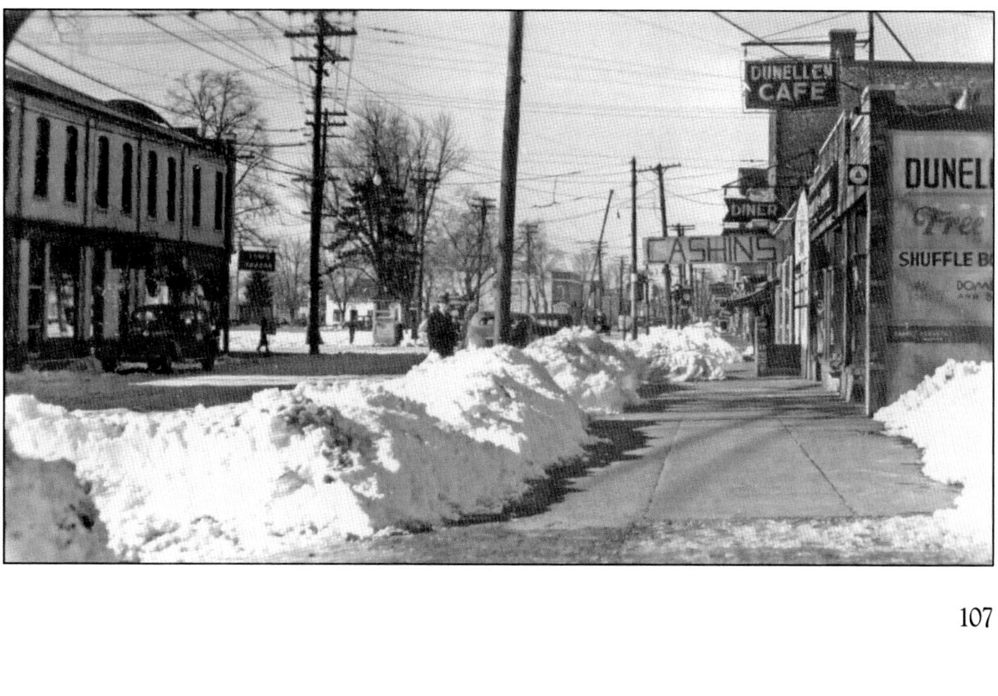

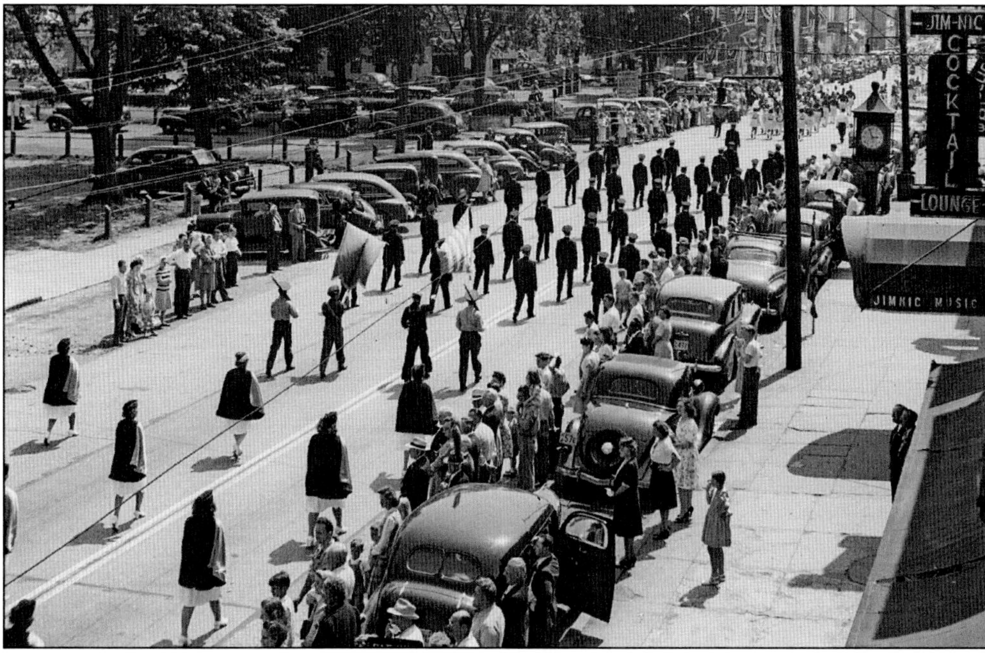


The Dunellen World War II Victory Parade was held on Memorial Day, May 30, 1946. In this picture, the Dunellen High School band, followed by marchers, heads west on North Avenue. To the left is the train station parking lot where the present post office and bank stand today. (Courtesy of Schuyler family collection.)

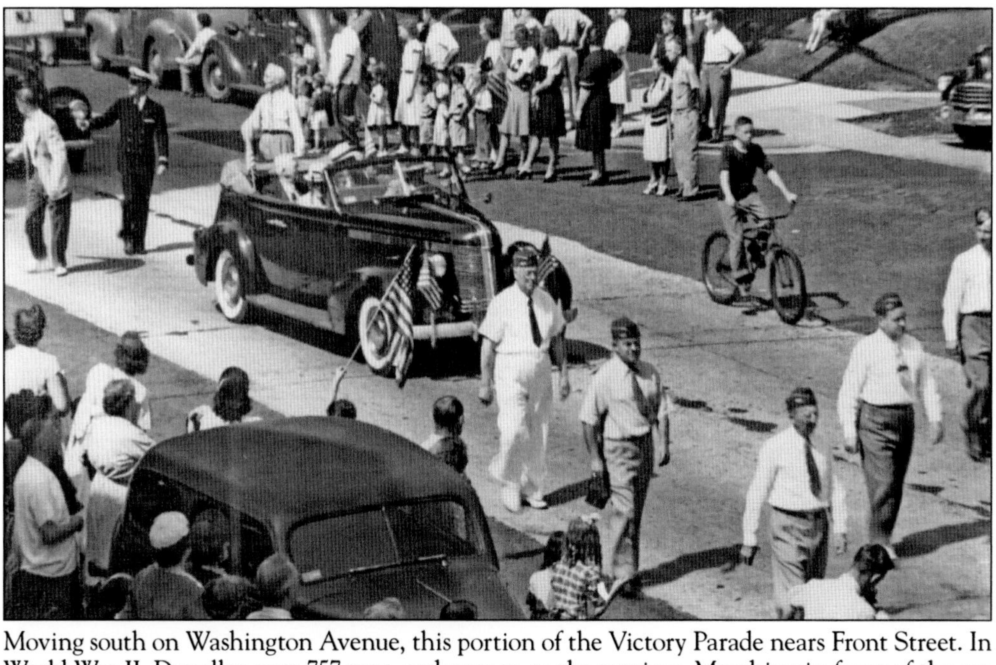

Moving south on Washington Avenue, this portion of the Victory Parade nears Front Street. In World War II, Dunellen sent 757 men and women to the services. Marching in front of the car are some of the past commanders of American Legion Post No. 119. Dunellen was also home of 27 Civil War veterans, with the last surviving being John W. Moynihan, who died in 1935. (Courtesy of Schuyler family collection.)

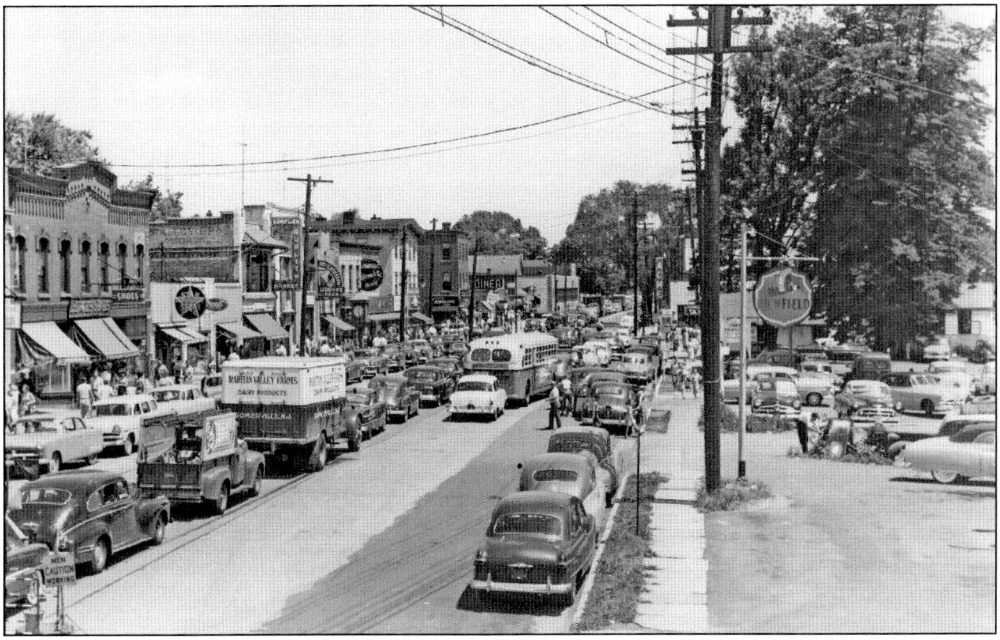

Traffic is bumper-to-bumper in the North Avenue business district on Saturday, July 19, 1953. The Jehovah's Witness World Convention was being held at Yankee Stadium the following week. A farmer in Piscataway leased 40 acres of farmland to them where a "trailer city" was constructed with eight miles of pipeline, 41 miles of wiring on 400 poles, and 78 buildings to support and house 50,000 people. And they all came to Dunellen to shop for necessities. (Courtesy of Schuyler family collection.)

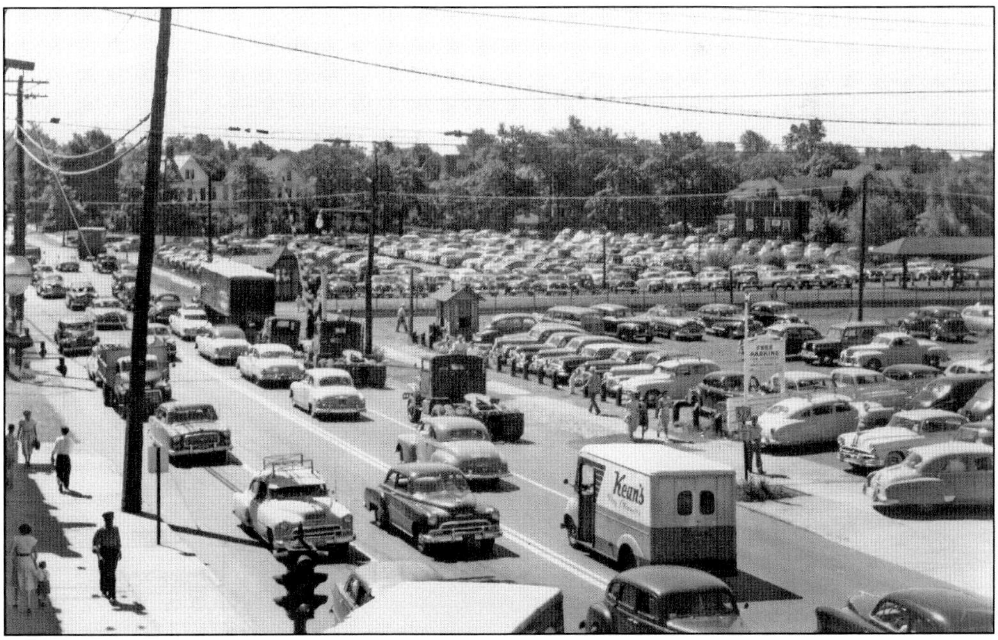

Besides bumper-to-bumper traffic, all the parking lots were filled to capacity. The local merchants were very happy in these days before shopping malls and big box stores. (Courtesy of Schuyler family collection.)

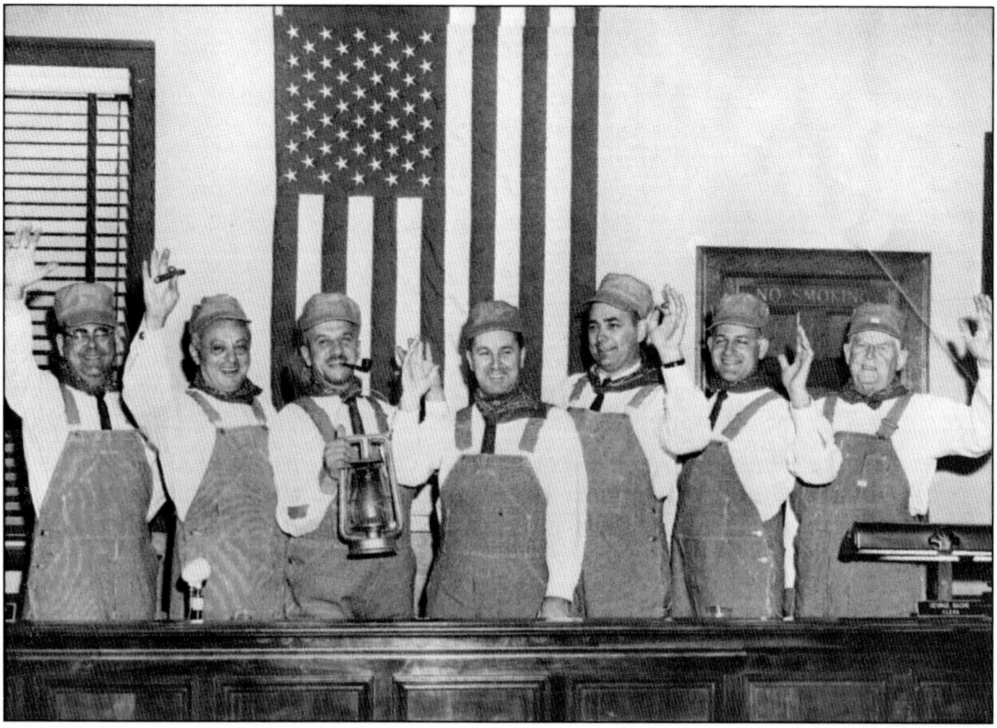


Dunellen's Diamond Jubilee celebration was held from May 26 to June 2, 1962. Dunellen's government is shown from left to right as follows: Councilman Norman Gray, Borough Attorney Henry Handelman, Councilman John Golday, Mayor Bernard Rodgers, Councilmen James Durhan and Lawrence Anzavino, and Borough Clerk George Bache. An executive committee of 16 residents and 88 people worked on 39 subcommittees along with hundreds of volunteers and Steve Gazi as parade chairman.

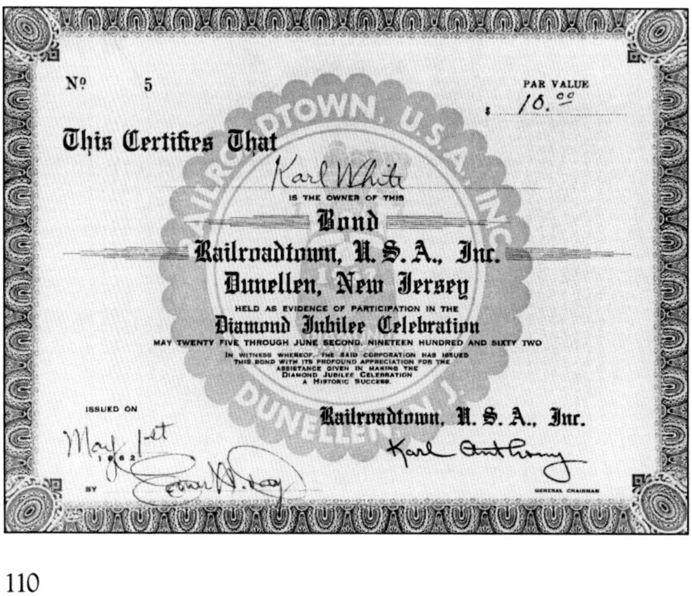


The pictured $10 bonds were sold to raise funds for this weeklong event. Donations of merchandise and monies were solicited from businesses and all the vendors to the businesses. Raffles were held, and tickets were sold to the pageants. Souvenirs, such as glasses, plates, and tokens, were also sold to pay for plays, fireworks, prize drawings, and more. Dunellen went all out for this Diamond Jubilee celebration.

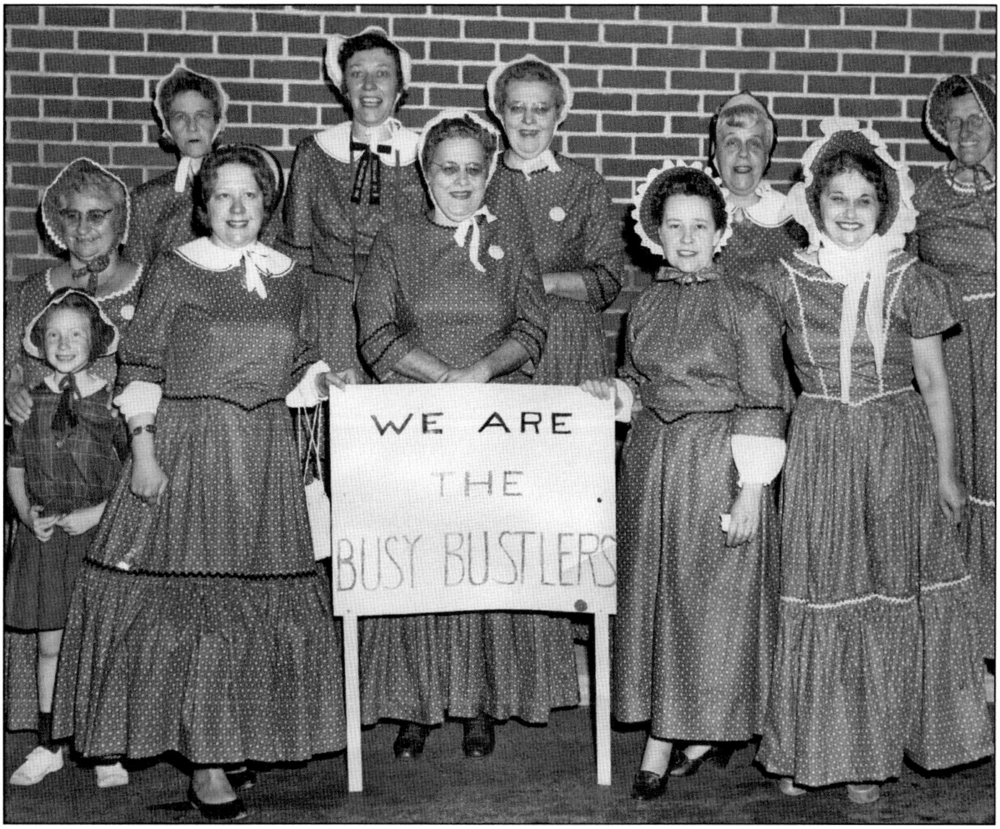


For the Diamond Jubilee of Railroad Town, USA, the ladies of the town revived the costumes of their grandmothers to help get Dunellen into the proper spirit. There were 15 chapters of the Jubilee Belles. Shown here from left to right, the Busy Bustlers are (first row) Debbie Smith, Ethel Garretson, Marion Zink, Margaret Hanyen, and Claire Burdick; (second row) Hazel Smith, Alice Trewin, Elva Coddington, Mildred Zink, Dorothy Garretson, and Emily Fitten.

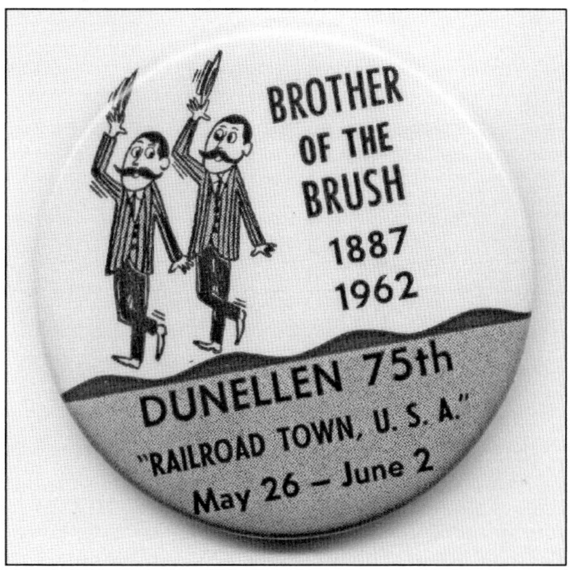


The men of Dunellen turned back the clock 75 years by growing beards, sideburns, mustaches, and other facial foliage. There were 10 chapters of the Brothers of the Brush with names such as the Fuzzy Wuzzies, Walnut Beardos, Hairy Mailmen, and Stransky's Kielbassa Benders. A good time was had by all in the months leading up to the celebration. (Courtesy of John Triolo.)

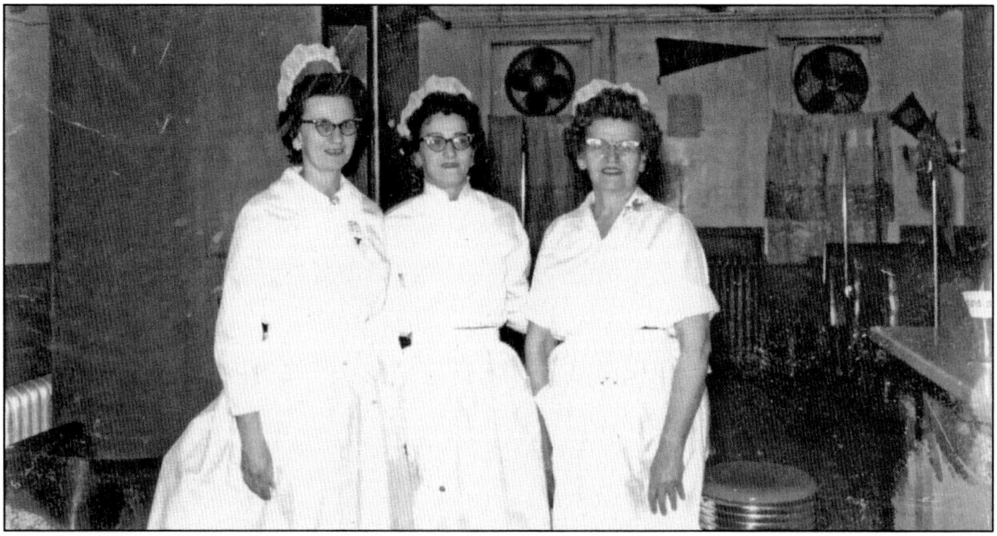

Standing from left to right in this photograph are Jubilee Belles Loretta Pasko, Mary Eskesen, and Mrs. Van Horn in their costumes. The picture was taken inside the Bluebird Luncheonette, owned and operated by Mary Eskesen. The "Bird" was the favorite watering hole for Dunellen High School students after school and after basketball and football games. Eskesen also founded the Dunellen Teen Canteen for the adolescents in Dunellen. (Courtesy of Loretta Pasko.)

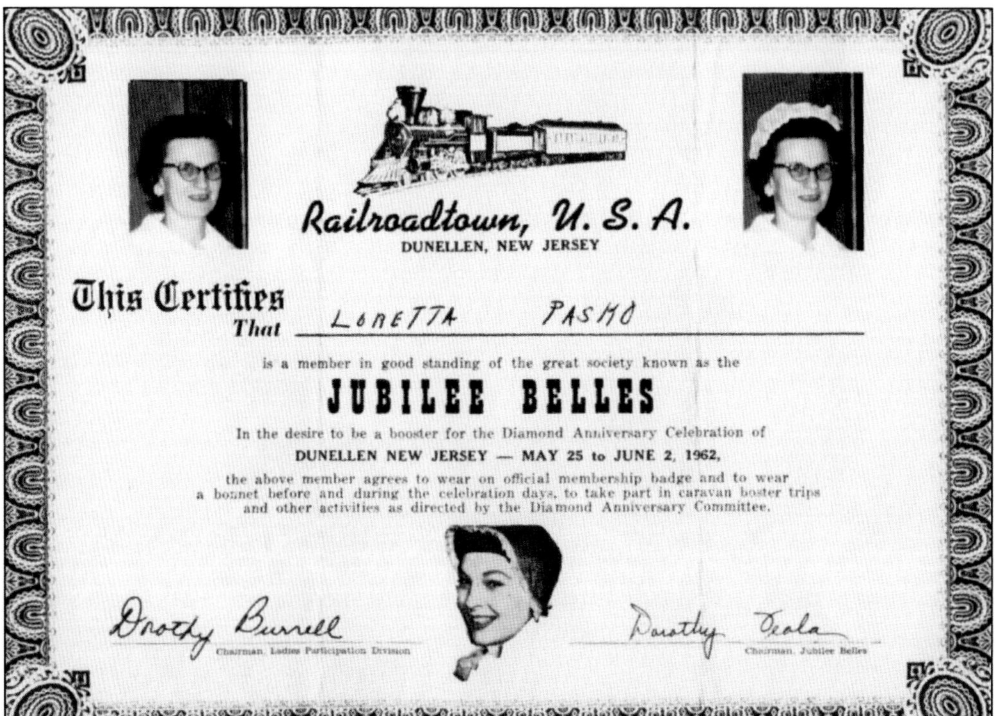

Railroadtown, U. S. A.

DUNELLEN, NEW JERSEY

This Certifies That Loretta Pasko

is a member in good standing of the great society known as the

JUBILEE BELLES

In the desire to be a booster for the Diamond Anniversary Celebration of

DUNELLEN NEW JERSEY — MAY 25 to JUNE 2, 1962,

the above member agrees to wear on official membership badge and to wear a bonnet before and during the celebration days, to take part in caravan boster trips and other activities as directed by the Diamond Anniversary Committee.

Chairman, Ladies Participation Division

Chairman, Jubilee Belles

Certificates of membership in the Jubilee Belles were issued for all members in all chapters. The ladies were required to wear their bonnets and badges when in town. All members worked on fundraisers to fuel the celebration. This certificate belongs to Loretta Pasko. (Courtesy of Loretta Pasko.)

The Railroad Town, USA, pageant program was presented every night except Sunday in Columbia Park. The play *Jubilee Junction* was presented each night. It had two acts with 10 episodes and followed Dunellen's history. In one episode, famous Dunellen residents Sir Thomas Lipton and Bob Fitzsimmons were played by high school students Raymond Bukowski and Dennis Gazi. Miss Railroad Town 1962 was joined on stage by Miss Dunellen of 1937 and 1949.

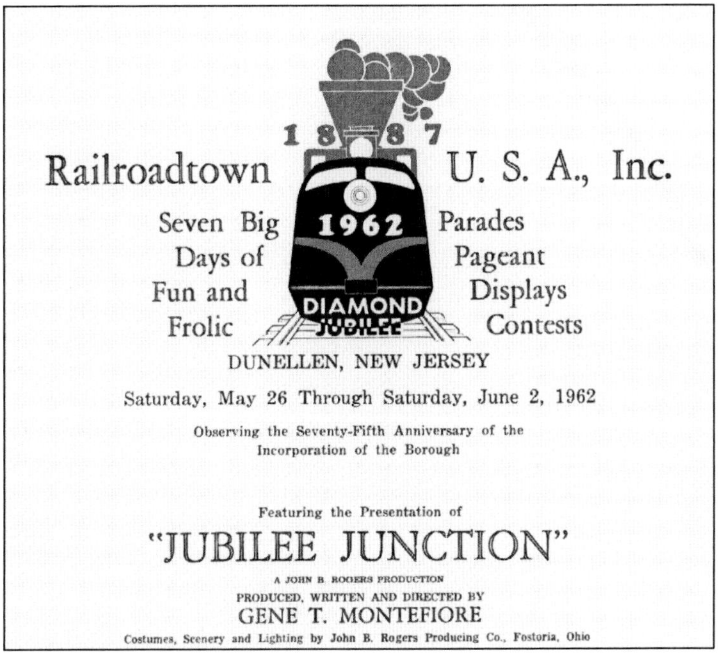


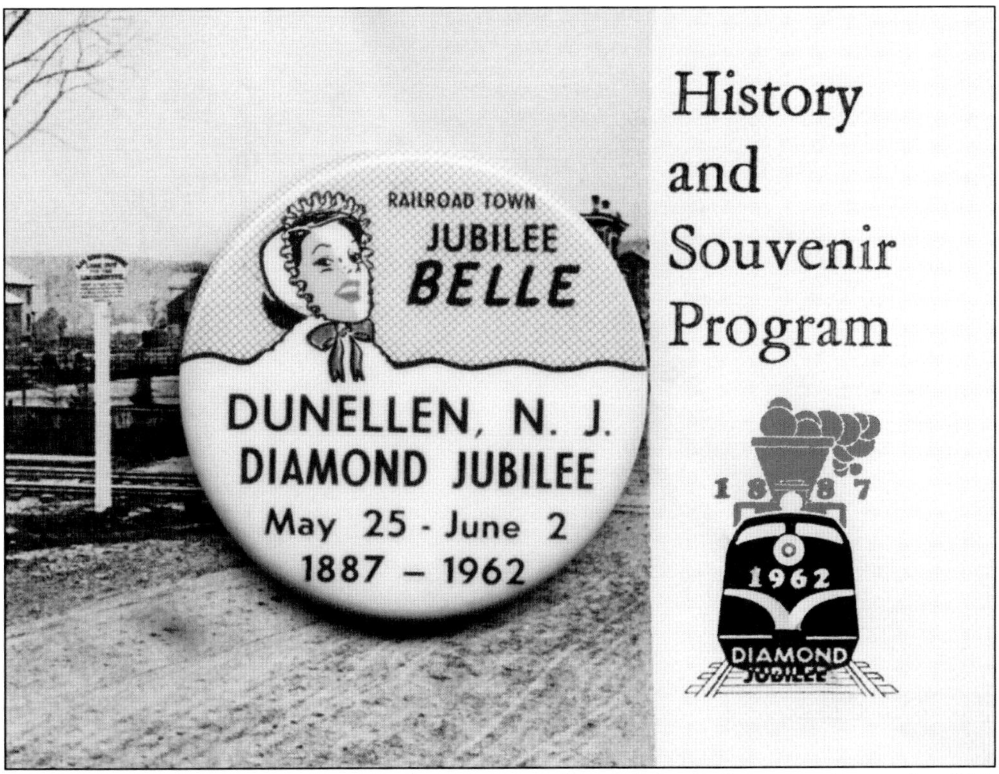


Here is an example of the pin back that the Dunellen Jubilee Belles wore during the 75th Anniversary celebration. The starting date on the ladies button is one day earlier than that of their male counterparts. The authors can only guess that they had more work to do than the men did! (Courtesy of John Triolo.)

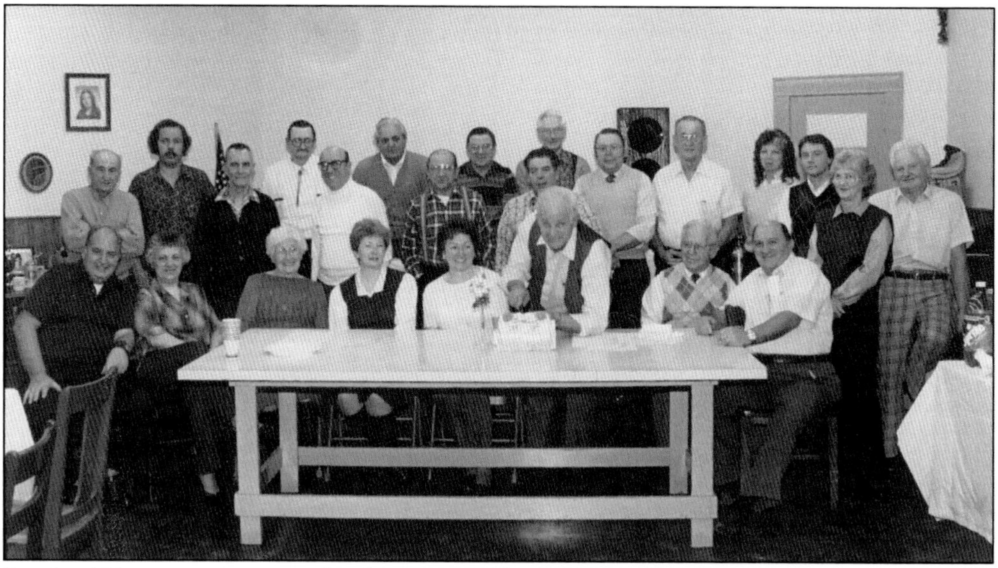

For the 100-year anniversary, the theme was Volunteertown, USA. This is the first committee meeting on February 23, 1986. Pictured from left to right are (seated) Clem Santy, K. Gangemi, Kathleen Callahan, Jeri O'Hehir, Betty Schneider, Larry Anzavino, Charles Nagy, and W. Smith; (second row) Wesley Ott, Henry Hodulik, A. Bonjione, Joe DeBiase, John Gibney, Bertha Ahr, and Henry Ahr; (third row) Jack Cassidy, Tom DeNapoli, George Weiss, Robert Brower, M. Autio, Paul Donne, and Carol Barrett.

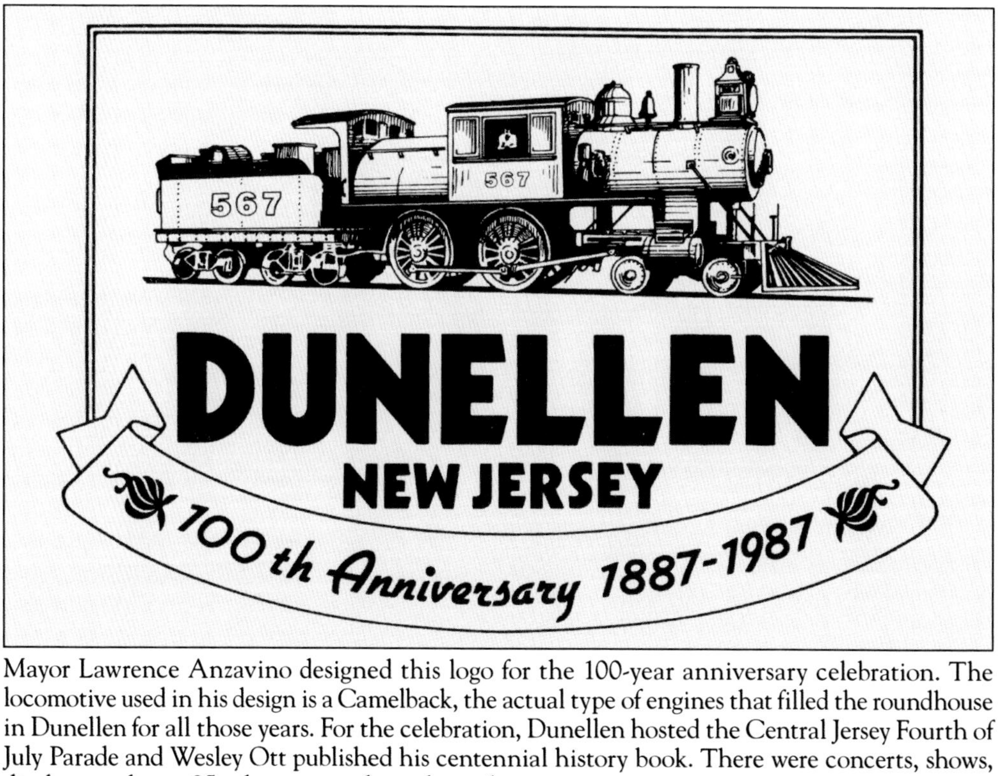


Mayor Lawrence Anzavino designed this logo for the 100-year anniversary celebration. The locomotive used in his design is a Camelback, the actual type of engines that filled the roundhouse in Dunellen for all those years. For the celebration, Dunellen hosted the Central Jersey Fourth of July Parade and Wesley Ott published his centennial history book. There were concerts, shows, displays, and over 25 other events throughout the year.

# *Ten*

# LITTLE-KNOWN FACTS

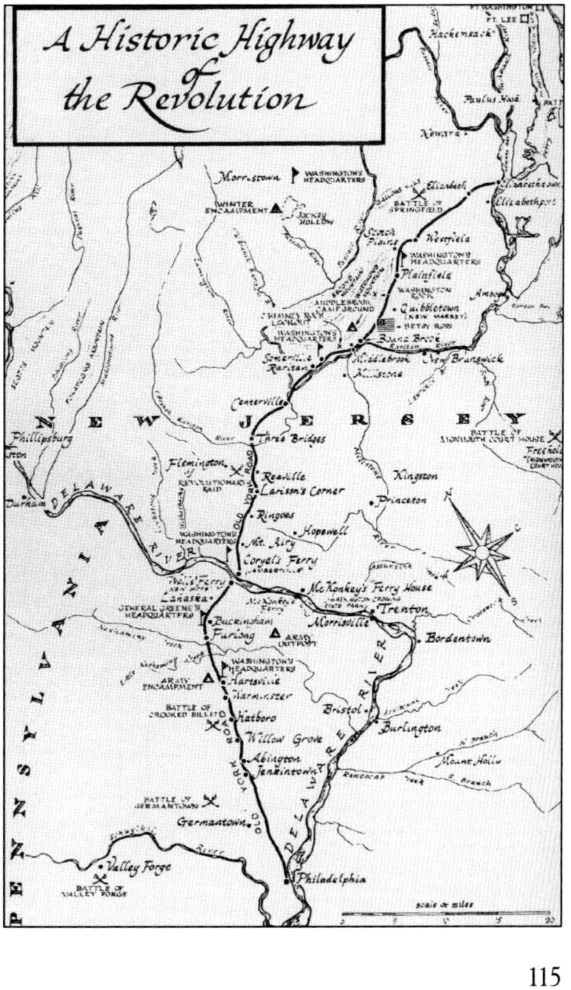


The Old York Road was the stagecoach route starting in Philadelphia and ending with a ferry from Elizabeth to New York City during and after the Revolutionary War. Along the way, it passed through Dunellen. From 1785 until 1790, New York City was the capital of the United States. In 1789, George Washington was inaugurated there. Readers can imagine who might have traveled through Dunellen during those years.

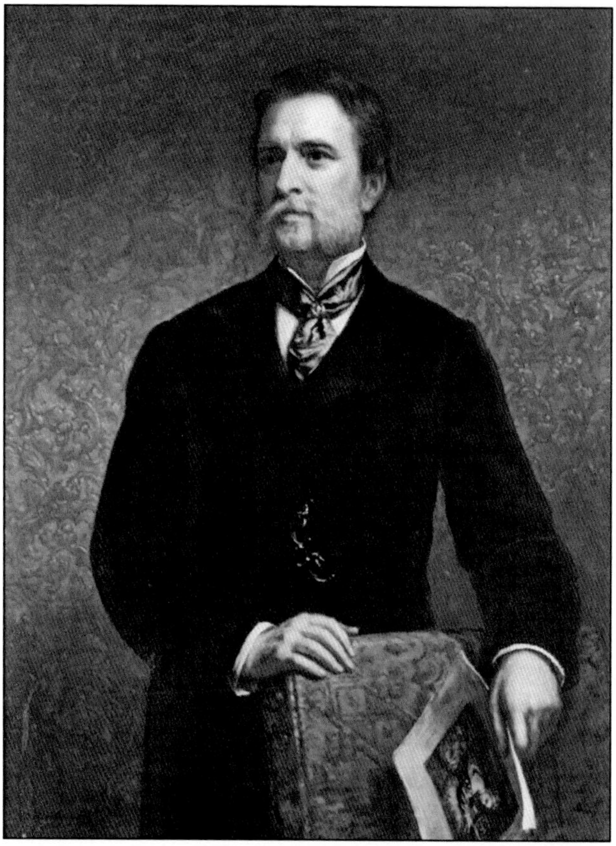

What does Dunellen have in common with the Metropolitan Museum of Art? The answer is John Taylor Johnson, the president of the Central Railroad of New Jersey who established the town of Dunellen in 1867. In 1870, he was the founding president of the Metropolitan Museum of Art and donated art, including 174 paintings (mostly Dutch Masters) and one Egyptian sarcophagus, filling the small town house on Fifth Avenue.

Christian Schepflin of Dunellen discovered lawn bowling while visiting Scotland in 1876. Upon his return, he laid out a bowling green near his home at the corner of Prospect Avenue and Grove Street. His neighbors became enthusiastic about the sport, and it quickly spread to nearby Philadelphia and into metropolitan New York. The Dunellen team was undefeated in league play until May 25, 1889.

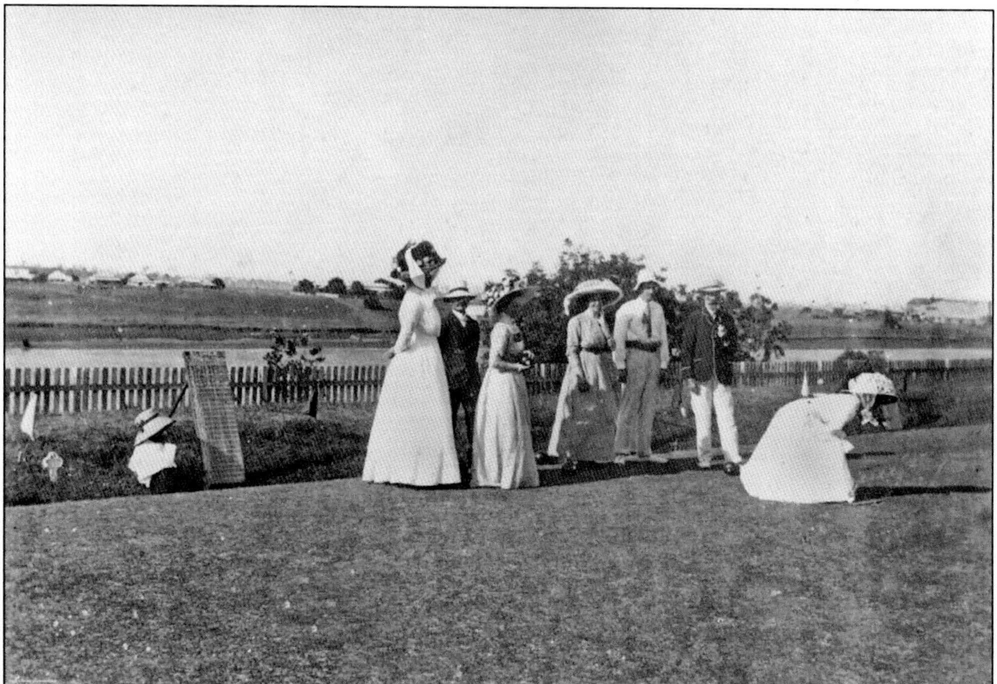

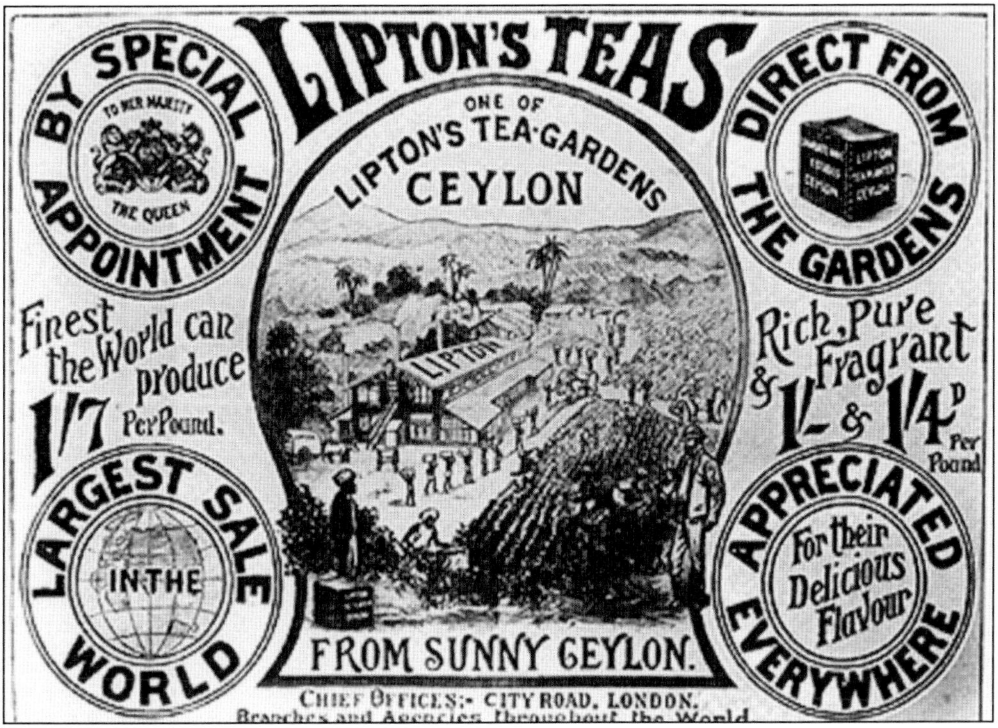


Sir Thomas Lipton is probably the most famous resident of Dunellen, although he only resided here for five months. He came to Dunellen when he was 15 years old and worked on Mrs. Newhall's farm on New Market Road. Lipton saved $150, returned to Scotland, and opened a store with this nest egg. He prospered and founded the Lipton Tea Company. This is an early advertisement.

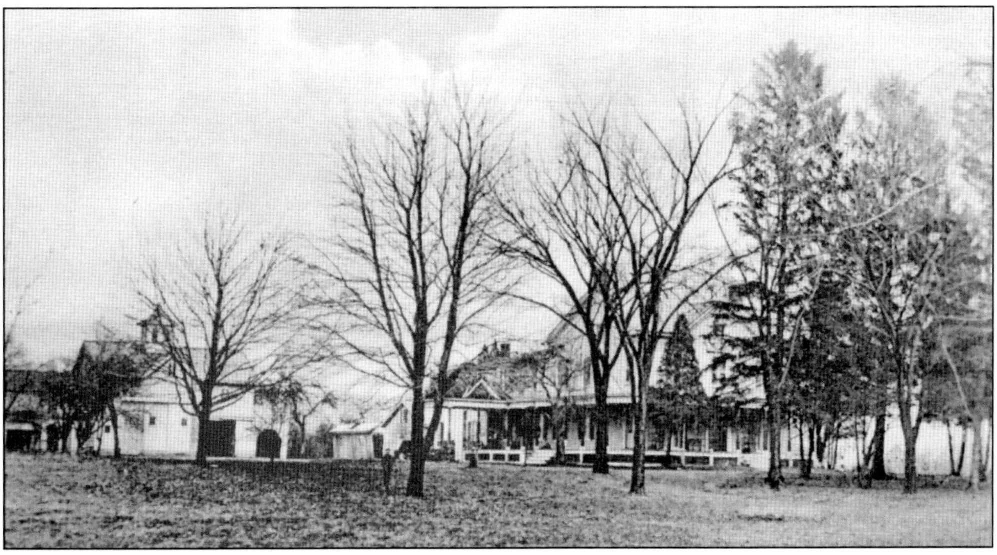

Heavyweight fighter Bob Fitzsimmons became world champion in 1897 when he defeated "Gentleman Jim" Corbett. Fitzsimmons was past his peak fighting days when he settled near Warrenville Road, just outside Dunellen's border. He was the vice president of the Dunellen Field Club in 1909. Fitzsimmons was often seen doing his roadwork in Dunellen and walking his pet lion along North Avenue. (Courtesy of John Triolo.)

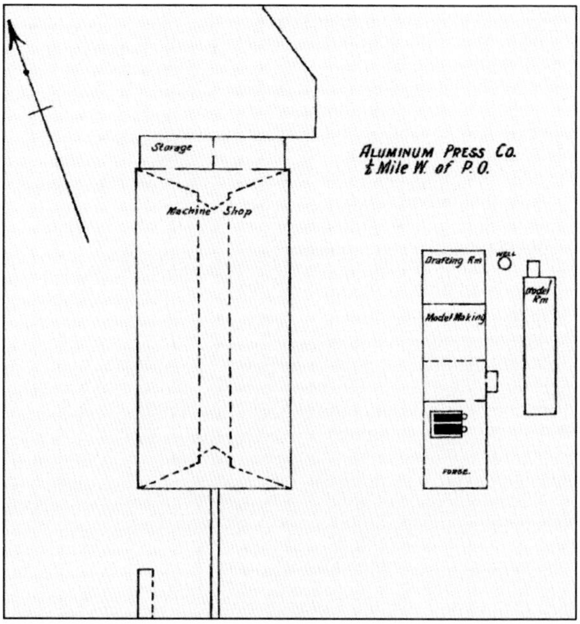


The Aluminum Press Company on Bound Brook Road is pictured in 1910. Margaret Bourke-White, the preeminent female photographer of the 20th century, was brought here by her father and witnessed molten metal being poured at the plant. In her autobiography she said, "One day in a plant in Dunellen . . . I saw a foundry for the first time. . . . This memory was so vivid and so alive that it shaped the whole course of my career." She went on to photograph the first cover of *Life* magazine and was the only female combat photographer in World War II.

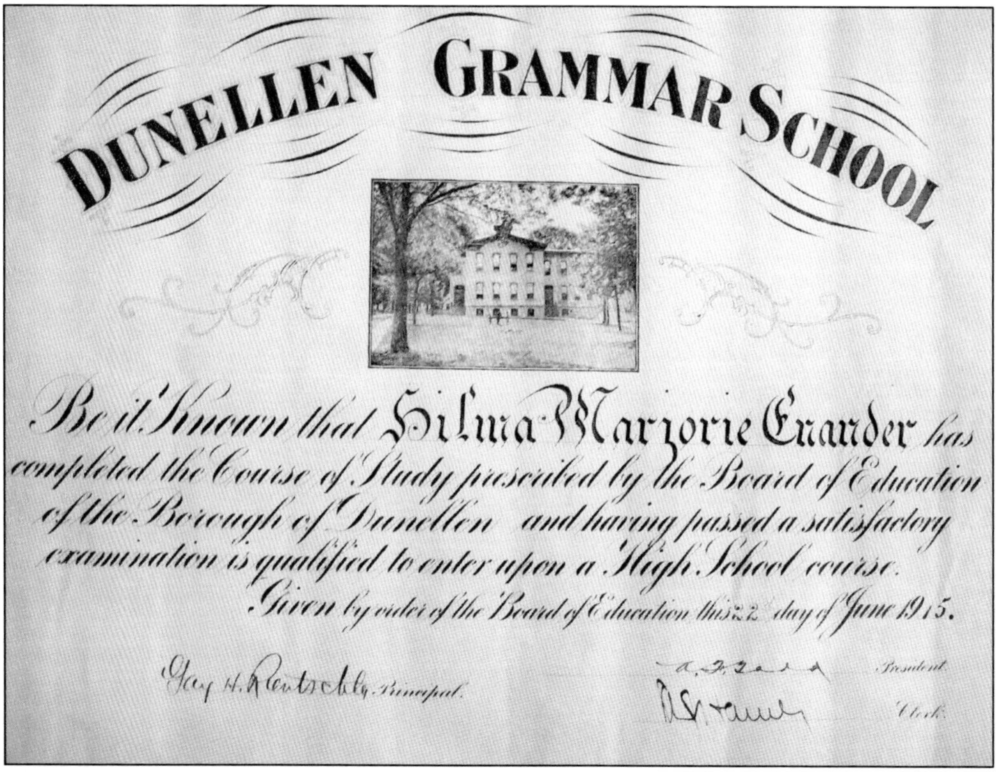

DUNELLEN GRAMMAR SCHOOL

Be it Known that Hilma Marjorie Erander has completed the Course of Study prescribed by the Board of Education of the Borough of Dunellen and having passed a satisfactory examination is qualified to enter upon a High School course.

Given by order of the Board of Education this 22 day of June 1915.

Principal. President. Clerk.

This Dunellen Grammar School diploma is for an eighth grader graduating in 1915. At that time, all girls were required to make their own graduation dresses. The board of education's rule at that time was that if a girl arrived at her graduation in a "store bought" dress, her diploma would be withheld. One child's mother contacted them and said, "No." After a meeting between the board and the parent, the practice was abolished.

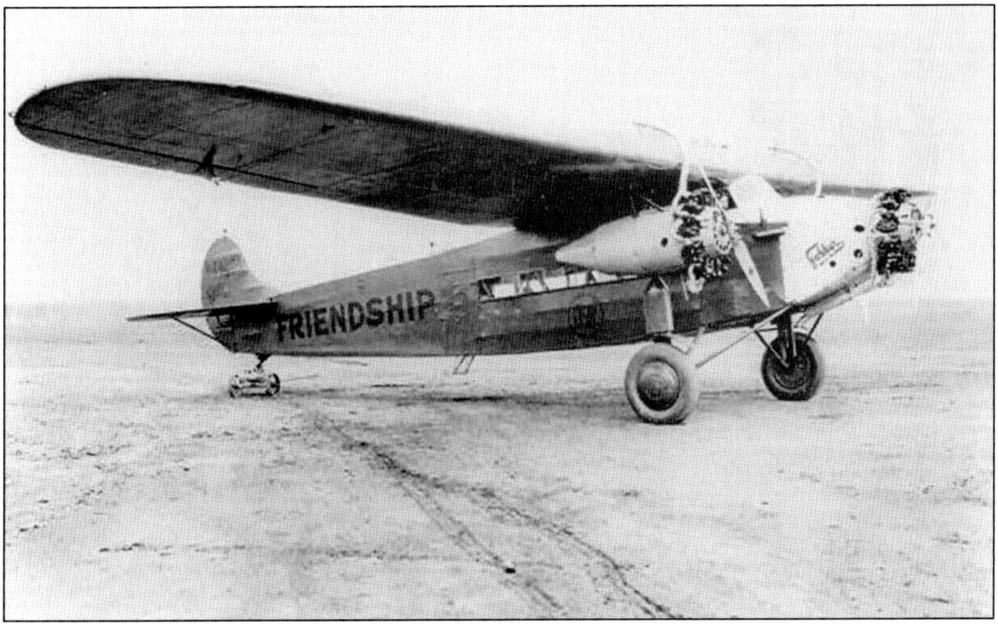


Louis Gordon, another Dunellen resident, was a pilot and mechanic on Amelia Earhart's 1928 transatlantic flight. The *Friendship*, a Fokker F-VIII trimotor seaplane, was flown from Newfoundland to Wales by Wilmer Stultz and Lou Gordon with Amelia Earhart. She soloed the Atlantic two years later.

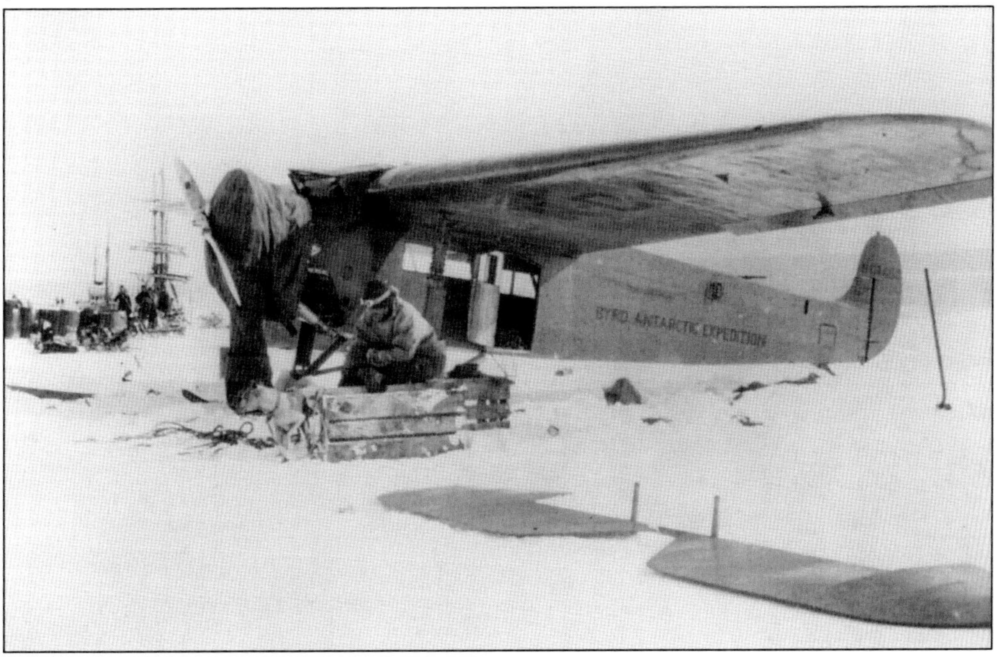


This Fokker Universal is being assembled by members of an Antarctic expedition. The plane was used by Comdr. Richard Byrd on his 1928–1930 Antarctic expedition to reach the South Pole. On that journey were Dunellen residents Henry T. Harrison Jr. and William Haines, serving as the expedition's weathermen. They reported, "The lowest temperature recorded at Little America was -72.2°F on July 28." Both had worked at Hadley Airport.

## 250 Residential and Business Lots at Public Auction, Friday

**Buy some of these DUNELLEN, N. J., lots for your all year home— or buy some for business purposes or for speculation or investment**

- - - -

**Remember every lot must be sold to the highest bidder regardless of cost, value or price.**

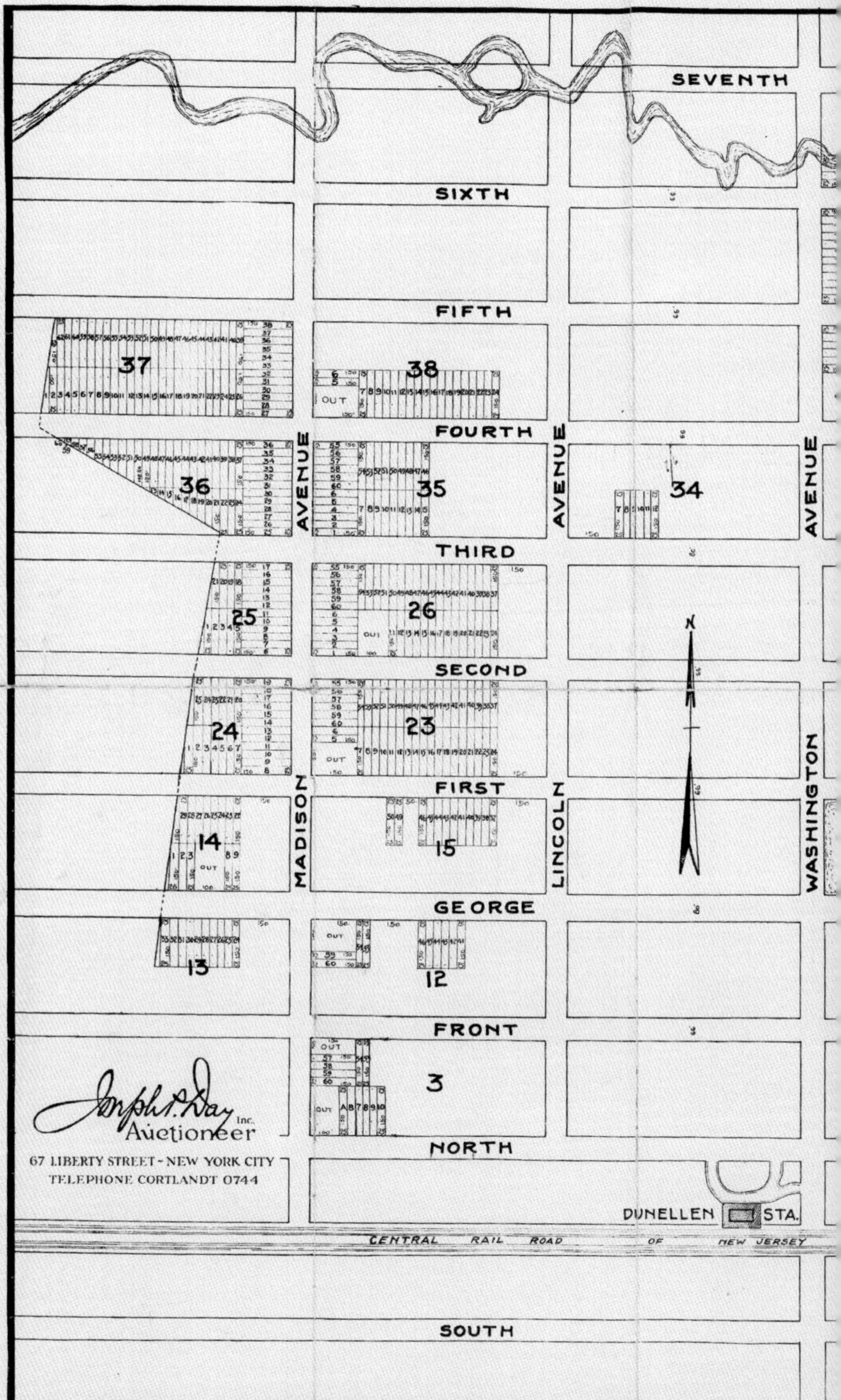

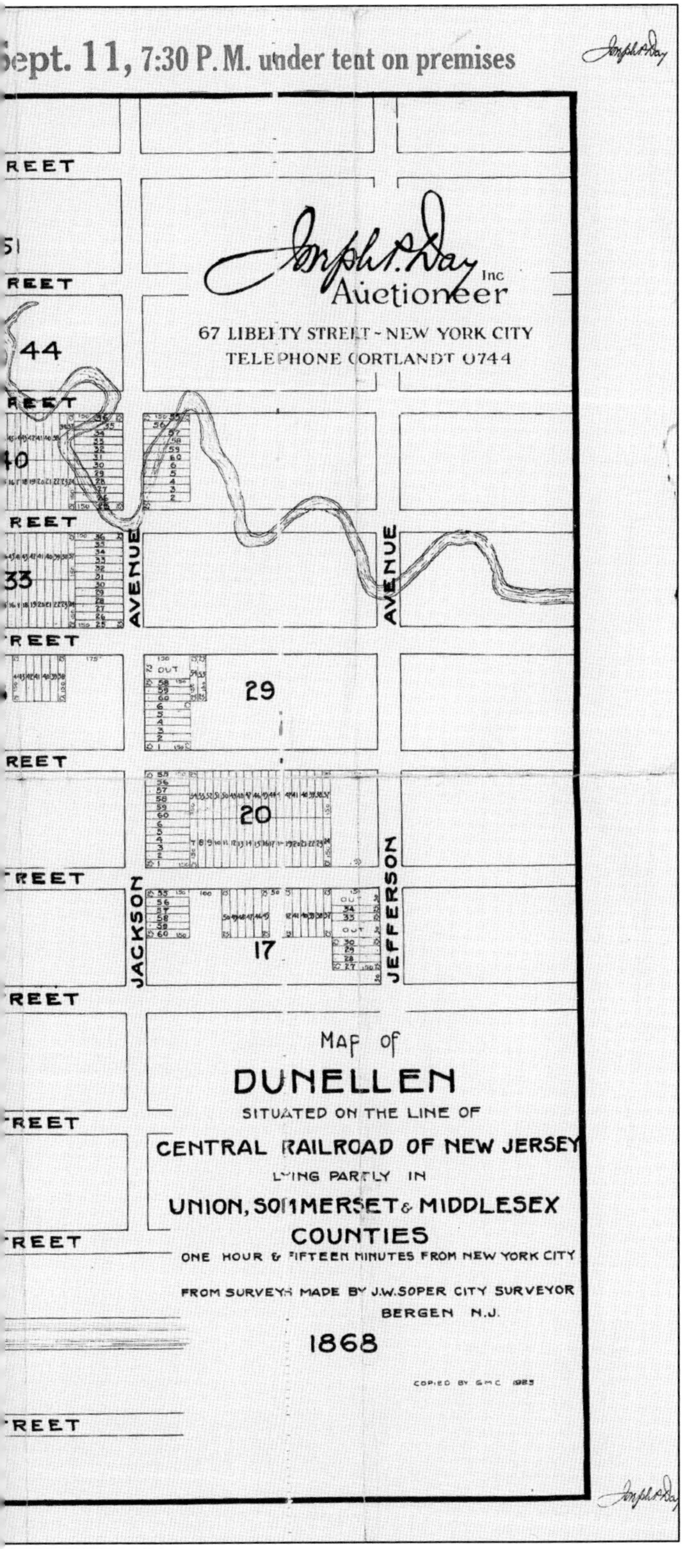


This 1925 real estate auction map of Dunellen was prepared by auctioneer Joseph P. Day. On the night of September 11, 1925, and into the next morning, Joseph Day sold 250 residential and business lots in Dunellen. Over a period of 50 years, Day sold about one-third of the Bronx, one-third of Queens, a generous slice of Brooklyn, and vast properties in Westchester and north New Jersey. He also developed San Clemente, California, a project including 300 buildings and 1,000 residences.

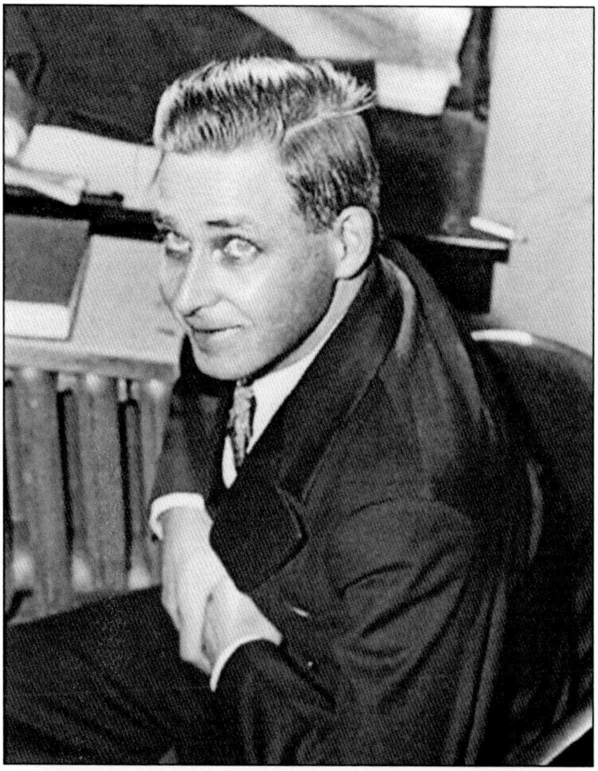

Elvert Carlstrom, a Dunellen link to the famous Lindbergh kidnapping trial, was the caretaker of a house in Dunellen at 418 Jackson Avenue. Carlstrom appeared as an alibi witness for Bruno Haupman for the fateful night of March 11, 1932. He said he had gone from Dunellen to the Bronx and claimed to have seen Haupman at Fredericksen's Bakery-Restaurant. Arthur Larsen and Oscar Christensen refuted this and testified that Carlstrom was with them that night in Dunellen.

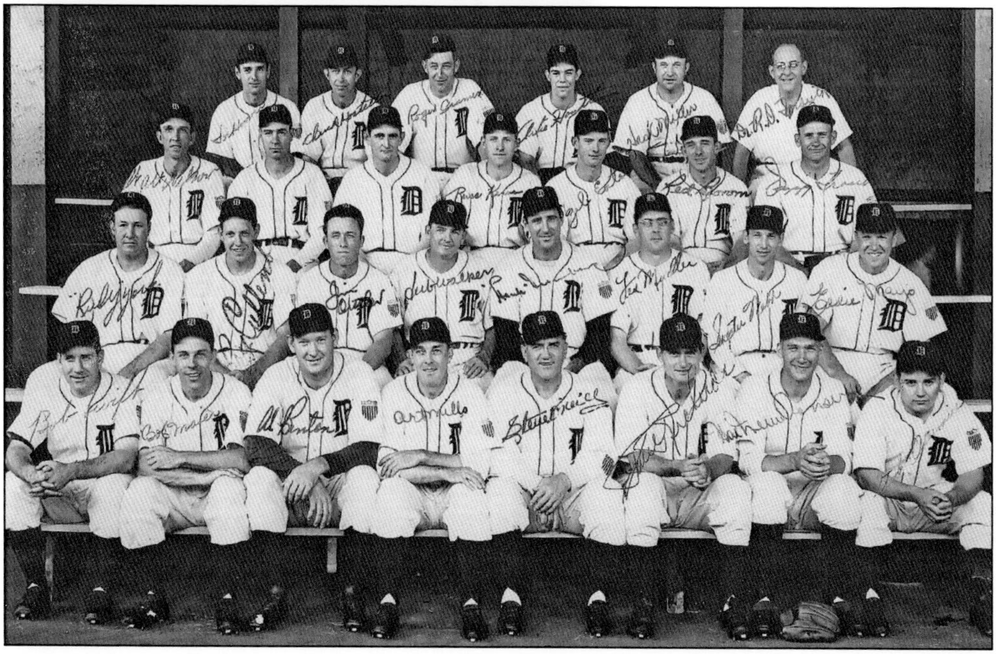

Pictured above is the Detroit Tigers baseball team during their 1945 World Series Championship season. In the first row, second from left, is Dunellen resident Robert Maier. Born in Dunellen in 1915, he played only one season in the major leagues, but he spent that season on a championship team and played 132 games.

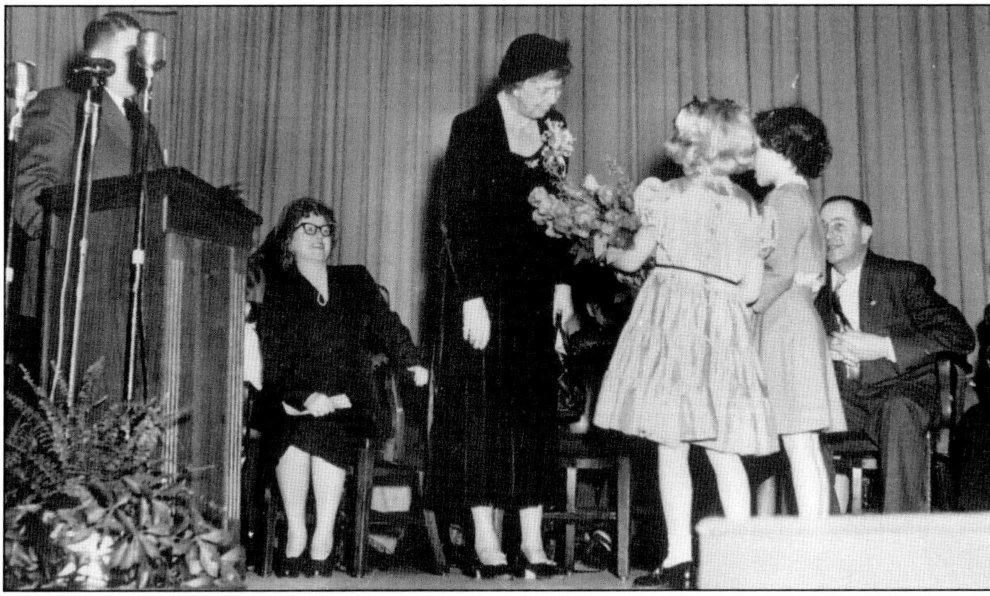

Eleanor Roosevelt visited Dunellen High School on January 24, 1951, for United Nations Day. Here, two unidentified girls are presenting the ex–first lady with a bouquet of flowers. Regina Krasnansky, a high school senior, was Roosevelt's aide for her visit to Dunellen that day.

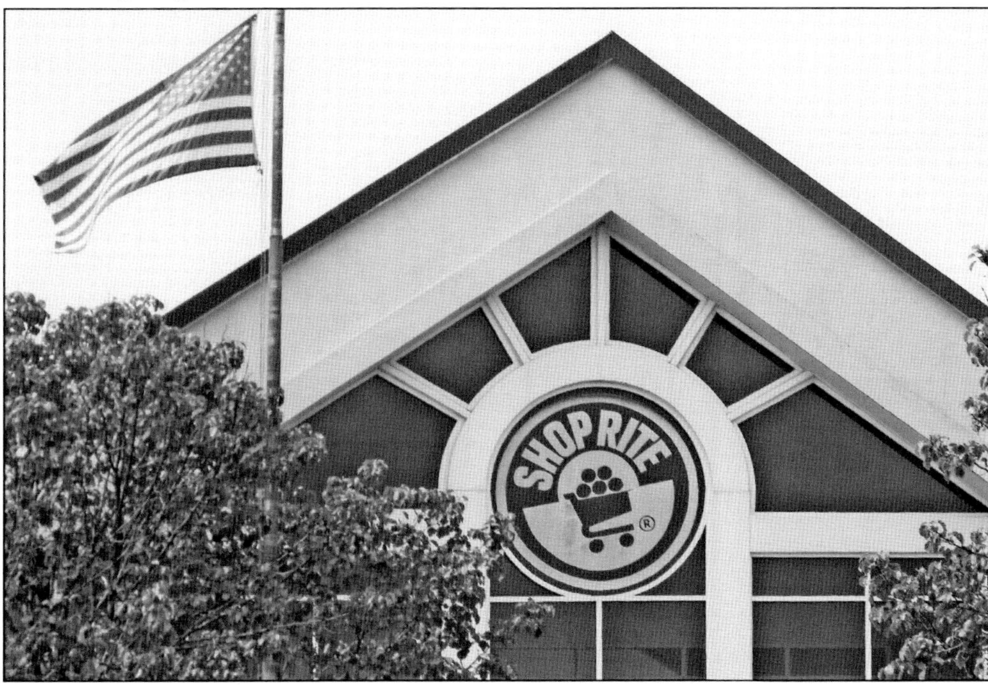


Luther Henry was a longtime Dunellen resident who owned a grocery store. In 1946, seven independent grocery store owners formed a food-buying cooperative called Wakefern Foods Corporation. They all traded under their own grocery store names, but all of them began doing business under the ShopRite banner in 1951. Today, ShopRite has grown into the largest retailer-owned cooperative in the United States and largest employer in New Jersey. (Courtesy of John Triolo.)

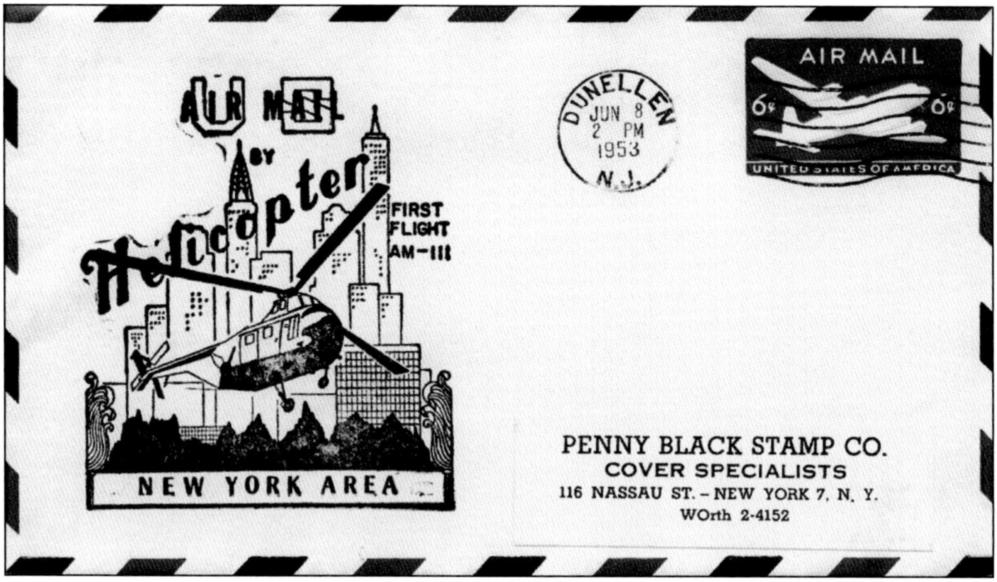


This postal first-day cover was issued for the first air mail by helicopter from Dunellen to New York City on June 8, 1953. The Dunellen Post Office was considered a Class A post office because of the tremendous mailings of the Art Color Printing Company, which printed about 11 million magazines per month. (Courtesy of John Triolo.)

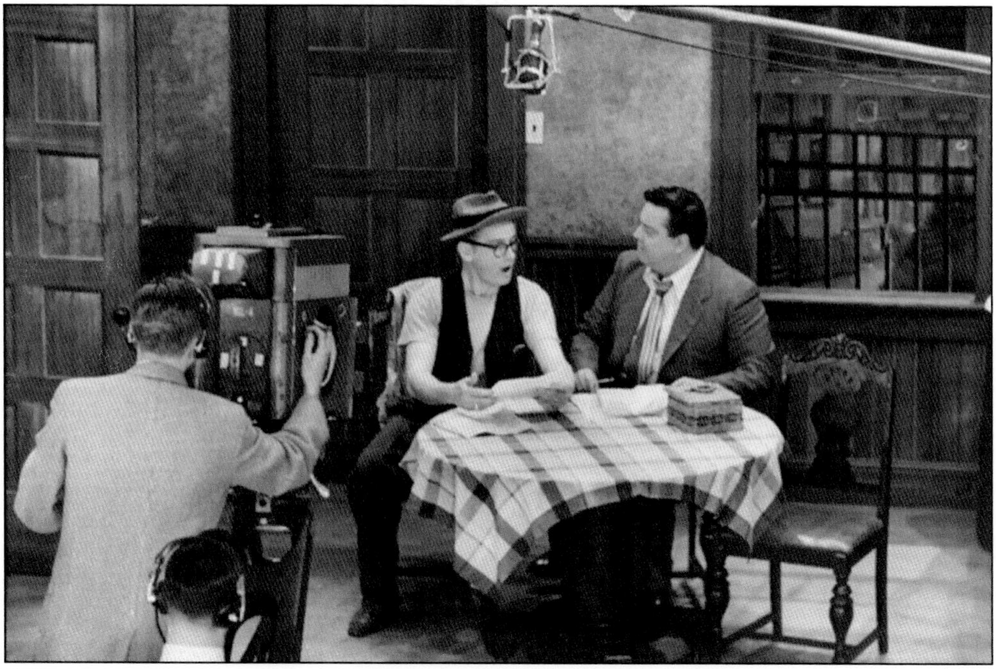

Walter Stone, chief writer for the *Honeymooners* television series, was born in Dunellen in 1920. His father had a store at 625 Dunellen Avenue. Walter wrote 111 episodes and five specials for Jackie Gleason. The March 3, 1957, episode entitled "The Curse of the Kramdens" had the *Honeymooners* cast visiting the village of Dunellen in Scotland. Stone contributed to the 1962 Dunellen Diamond Jubilee as the head of the radio and television committee.

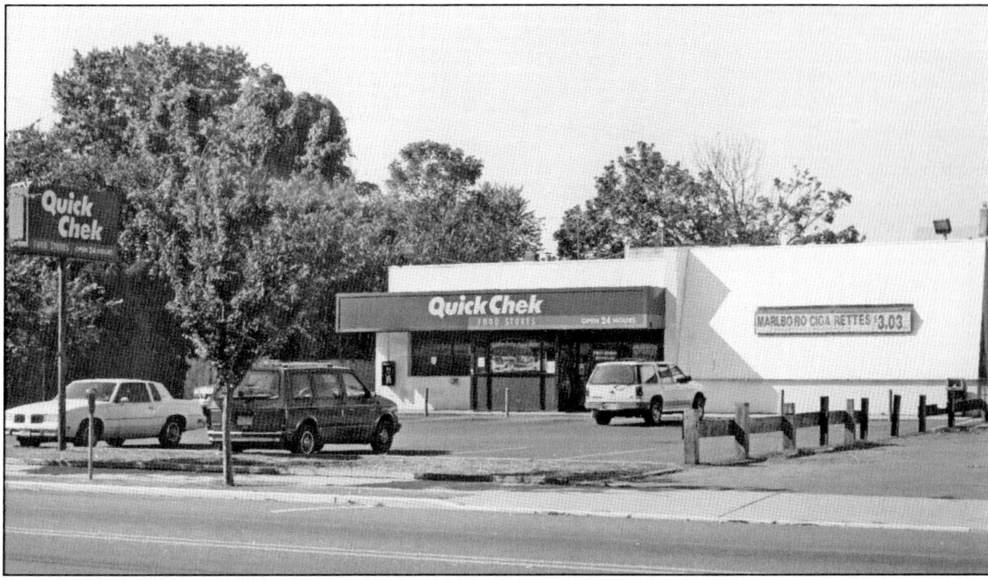


In 1967, Carlton Durling founded Quick Chek stores. The first store was opened in Dunellen in a new building at 419 North Avenue. It was much more than a typical convenience store. Since then, Quick Chek has grown to more than 120 stores throughout New Jersey and southern New York State and has more than 2,600 employees. The Dunellen store was later opened in an enlarged building directly across the street.

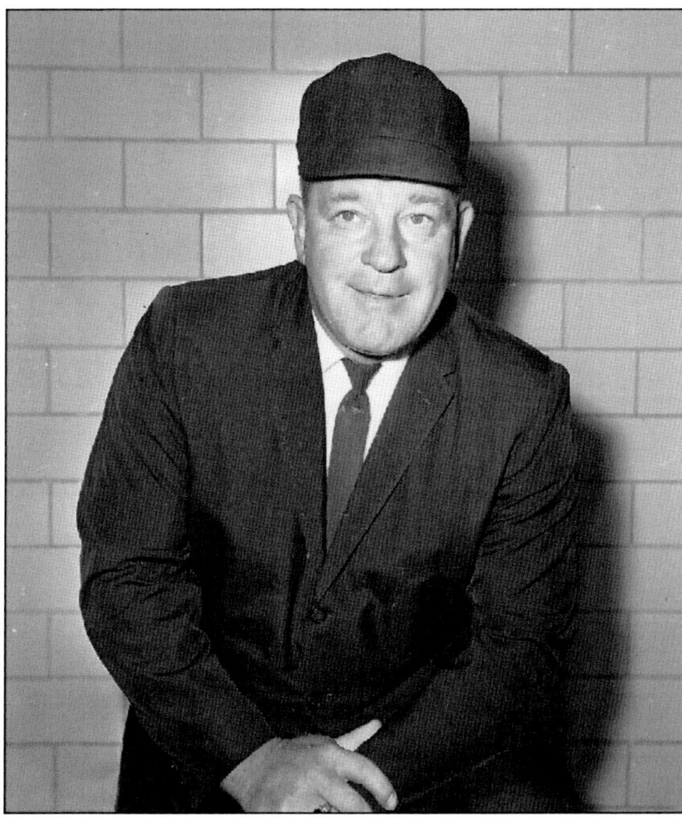

Dunellen resident Frank Umont worked in the American League from 1954 until retiring after the 1973 season. He umpired in four World Series, four all-star games, and a league championship series. During the latter part of his 20-year career, he became famous as the first Major League umpire to wear glasses. Frank gave back to the town by arranging appearances of famous Yankees at the Dunellen Little League banquet every year.

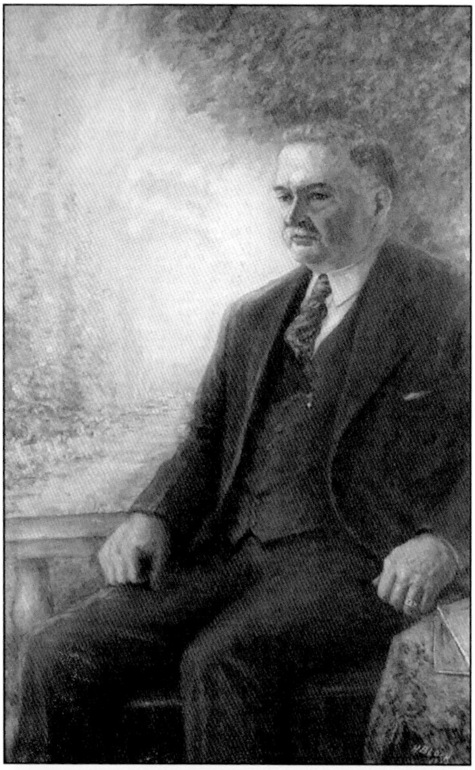

Shown here is Henry Block's painting of Arnold A. Schwartz, the Dunellen Public Library's namesake. Block was born in Lithuania, and after arriving in America, he settled in Dunellen at 200 Third Street. In Peter Falk's *Who Was Who in American Art*, Block is credited with being the first artist to engrave woodblock prints in full color. Some of his paintings hang in the New York Public Library, the Phillips Memorial Gallery in Washington, DC, the Art Institute of Chicago, and the Columbus Gallery of Fine Arts, and many are included in private collections. (Courtesy of Dunellen Public Library.)

It is now time to leave Dunellen with knowledge of its history, establishment, residents, and little-known facts. (Courtesy of John Triolo.)

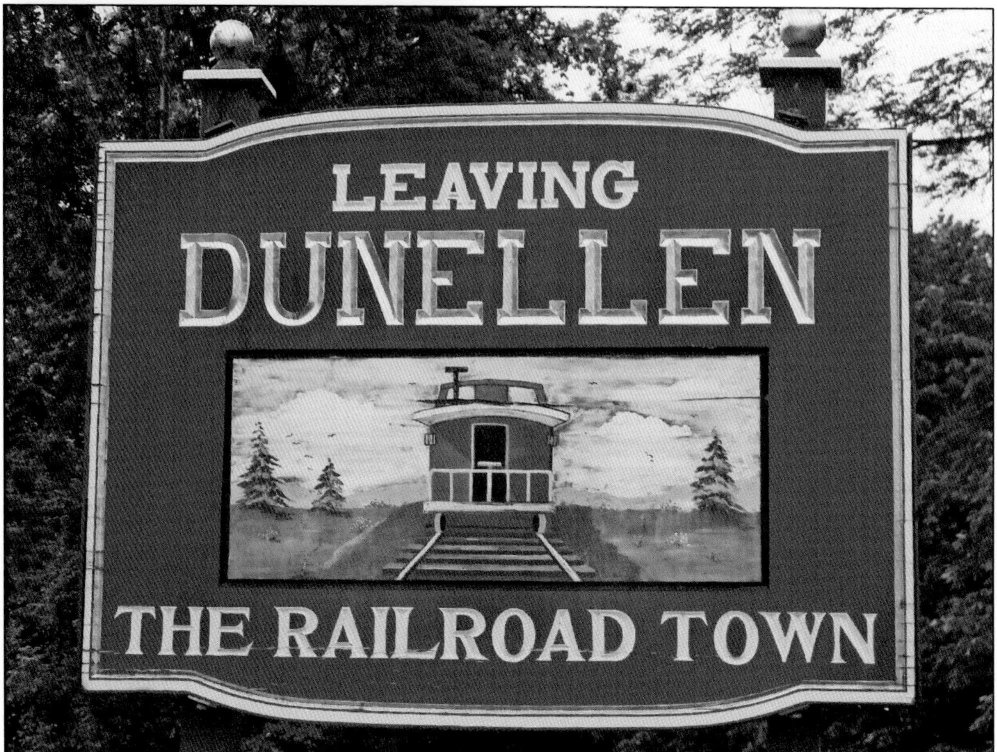

# BIBLIOGRAPHY


Bolen, Wilbur F. *History and Souvenir Program 1887–1962 Diamond Jubilee*. Dunellen, NJ: *Weekly Call*, 1962.

Brinckmann, John. *The Union Trolley Line*. Highlands, NJ: New Jersey Chapter, National Railway Historical Society, 1988.

Burnet, Gerard E. *Camelback Twilight*. Vol. 2, *The Hard Coal Carriers*. Flanders, NJ: RAE Publishing, 1995.

Cawley, James, and Margaret Cawley. *Along the Old York Road*. Rahway, NJ: Quinn & Boden, 1965.

*Dunellen Directory*. Trenton, NJ: MacCrellish & Quigley, 1881, 1885, and 1909.

Federal Writers Project, WPA. *The Story of Dunellen*. Dunellen, NJ: Art Color Printing Company, 1937.

Komelski, Peter. *26 Miles to Jersey City*. Flanders, NJ: Railroad Avenue Enterprises, 1983.

Laurie, Maxine, and March Mappen. *Encyclopedia of New Jersey*. New Brunswick, NJ: Rutgers University Press, 1999.

Miers, Earl Schenck. *Where the Raritan Flows*. Rahway, NJ: Quinn & Boden, 1964.

Ott, Wesley. *The History of Dunellen, New Jersey, 1887–1987: Centennial Edition*. Dunellen, NJ: Pentacle Communications, 1987.

*Polk's Plainfield City Directories*. New York City, NY: R.L. Polk & Company Publishers, 1912, 1924, and 1938.

Society of Colonial Wars in the State of New Jersey. *Historic Roadsides in New Jersey*. Philadelphia, PA: Press of Innes and Sons, 1928.

Spier, Leslie. *Geological Survey of New Jersey*. Union Hill, NJ: Dispatch Printing, 1915.

*St. John the Evangelist, Dunellen, New Jersey*. South Hackensack, NJ: Custom Books, 1980.

VanSickle, Emogene. *The Old York Road and Its Stage Coach Days*. Flemington, NJ: *Hunterdon County Democrat*, 1936.